Workbook/Laboratory Manual
to accompany

Yookoso!
An Invitation to Contemporary Japanese

Second Edition

Suzuko Hamasaki
University of California, Irvine

Hifumi Ito
University of California, San Diego

Hiroko Kataoka
California State University, Long Beach

Akemi Morioka
University of California, Irvine

Yasu-Hiko Tohsaku
University of California, San Diego

Boston Burr Ridge, IL Dubuque, IA Madison, WI New York San Francisco St. Louis
Bangkok Bogotá Caracas Lisbon London Madrid
Mexico City Milan New Delhi Seoul Singapore Sydney Taipei Toronto

McGraw-Hill Higher Education

*A Division of The **McGraw-Hill** Companies*

This is an  book.

Workbook/Laboratory Manual to accompany
***Yookoso!** An Invitation to Contemporary Japanese*

8 9 QPD/QPD 05

ISBN 0-07-072339-7

http://www.mhhe.com

Contents

To the Instructor

This Workbook/Laboratory Manual is designed to accompany *Yookoso! An Invitation to Contemporary Japanese, Second Edition.* It offers a variety of listening and writing exercises to reinforce the language functions, pronunciation, vocabulary, and structures that are presented in the main text. It also includes explanations, charts, and exercises for the newly introduced **hiragana, katakana,** and **kanji.**

The *Getting Started* chapter contains *Listening Comprehension Activities* and *Writing Activities,* which are all written in romanization because students have not yet learned all the **hiragana** and **katakana** at this point. *Getting Started* also provides students with sections called *Hiragana Practice* and *Katakana Practice,* which allow them to learn all of these Japanese characters before they begin working in Chapter One.

Each numbered chapter consists of three sections: *Listening Comprehension Activities, Kanji Practice and Exercises,* and *Writing Activities.* The *Listening Comprehension Activities* and *Writing Activities* for each chapter are divided into subsections corresponding to those in the main textbook. After completing a given subsection in the main textbook, the instructor can assign the appropriate exercises in the *Workbook/Laboratory Manual.* All the *Listening Comprehension Activities* and *Writing Activities* are written in **hiragana, katakana,** and **kanji.** Only those **kanji** previously presented for active mastery are used. We recommend that students finish the *Kanji Practice and Exercises* before doing the *Writing Activities.*

In the *Listening Comprehension Activities,* we have made every effort to provide students with authentic-sounding Japanese discourse, in both dialogues and monologues, but the questions and instructions are given in English so that the student can concentrate fully on the content of the recorded material without spending a lot of time decoding written Japanese. The activities in this section develop listening comprehension through dialogues, interviews, and narratives. All spoken material for the *Listening Comprehension Activities* is recorded in the audio program, and audio scripts are included in the *Instructor's Manual.*

The *Kanji Practice and Exercises* section in Chapters One through Seven consists of two parts. The first part is a chart of the active **kanji** presented in the chapter, including pronunciations, meanings, examples of use, and stroke order. This part also includes some interesting and useful notes about **kanji** and the writing systems of Japanese (for example, the radicals and the principles of stroke order). The second part consists of exercises for both reading and writing those **kanji.**

In the *Writing Activities* section, the exercises progress from controlled, mechanical exercises to those requiring dialogue completion or creative or personalized responses. Many activities are based on drawings, realia or authentic materials. Any of these exercises may be done as group or pair activities in class or individually at home. In addition to topic- or function-based exercises, some chapters include opportunities for practicing specific grammatical structures presented in the *Language Notes* of the main text.

The cast of characters from the main text also appears throughout the *Workbook/Laboratory Manual.* The answers to all the exercises are included in the *Instructor's Manual.*

The authors would like to express their sincere appreciation to Thalia Dorwick, Vice President and Editor in Chief at McGraw-Hill, for her guidance, suggestions, and insightful comments on the development of this *Workbook/Laboratory Manual.* We are also deeply indebted to Peggy Potter and Pat Murray for their superb editing. Finally, we must note the invaluable assistance of the capable production staff at McGraw-Hill.

Suzuko Hamasaki
Hifumi Ito
Hiroko Kataoka
Akemi Morioko
Yasu-Hiko Tohsaku

To the Student

The format of the *Workbook/Laboratory Manual* follows that of the main textbook. Each of the numbered chapters consists of four sections: *Listening Comprehension Activities, Kanji Practice and Exercises, Writing Activities,* and *Review Exercises. Getting Started* has *Hiragana/Katakana Practice and Exercises* instead of *Kanji Practice and Exercises.*

The *Listening Comprehension Activities* section contains questions and activities based on the dialogues and narratives recorded in the accompanying audio program. The recordings give you opportunities to listen to spoken Japanese in a variety of contexts and practice and test your listening skills outside the classroom.

The *Listening Comprehension Activities* include open-ended, multiple-choice, or true/false questions, and fill-in-the-blank exercises for you to work on while listening to the recordings. The written instructions explain the task, provide you with a general idea of the context, and identify the speakers of the dialogues or narratives. In some cases, further instructions tell you how many times you should listen to the recordings while answering the questions. All instructions and questions are in English so that you can practice listening to spoken Japanese without worrying about understanding written Japanese.

We suggest that you follow these steps when you do the *Listening Comprehension Activities.*

1. Read the instructions carefully so that you understand the topic and context of the recording and who the speakers are. If possible, guess what vocabulary might be used, and figure out how much of it you already know in Japanese.
2. Study any new vocabulary that is provided after the instructions.
3. Before reading the questions in the tasks, listen to the recording once. Think about whether or not you have understood the gist of the passage and how much specific information you have been able to comprehend.
4. Read through the questions. Figure out what information you need to answer them.
5. Listen to the recording again, concentrating on finding the information you need.
6. Unless otherwise specified in the instructions, listen to the recordings as many times as necessary. Do not, however, stop the recording in the middle of the dialogues or narratives. (In real-life situations, no one will stop talking for your convenience unless, perhaps, you are engaged in a personal conversation.) If necessary, review the vocabulary, expressions, and structures in the corresponding sections of the main textbook before repeating this process.

In most of the listening activities, you can answer the questions without understanding everything in the recording. Even when listening to spoken English in everyday life you can often get the gist of a conversation or the specific information you want without understanding every word. You will find that the same strategy works for Japanese.

One effective way to develop your listening skills is to listen to your Japanese recordings as much as possible. You can listen to them while exercising, doing household chores, riding public transportation, or just relaxing. Or you can listen to them in the car while driving around town or while stuck in traffic. At any rate, try to pay attention to the general content of the recordings. You will find that the more you listen to them, the more you will understand, and the better your listening skills will become.

You can also use the audio program for improving your pronunciation. After you are able to comprehend the gist of a recorded segment, pay attention to the speakers' intonation and rhythm. Try to repeat their words after them and mimic their delivery.

It is natural for beginning students to speak Japanese with the accent of their native language. Worrying too much about pronunciation can slow down your speech production or even make you too self-conscious to communicate effectively. Native speakers are more interested in the content of your speech than in your pronunciation. On the other hand, severe pronunciation problems can prevent people from understanding you or lead to embarrassing mistakes: you must work on any such problems that your instructor points out.

The sections called *Hiragana/Katakana Practice and Exercises* and *Kanji Practice and Exercises* are designed to provide you with practice in writing **hiragana, katakana** and the active **kanji** presented in the main chapters of the textbook. Each section consists of charts on the meanings, readings, and strokes order of each character, followed by the exercises. The **hiragana/katakana** charts are self-explanatory, and the **kanji** charts are organized in the following way:

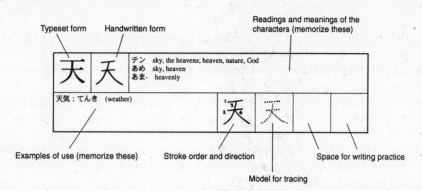

The Latin alphabet has no set stroke order, so many English-speaking students tend to ignore the rules for writing **kanji** and develop bad habits that result in misshapen characters. You must follow the set stroke order and direction. Your characters will look better, and practicing the correct way of writing will help imprint the shape of the character in your memory. These charts have only two spaces for practicing each character, so for additional practice use engineering graph paper. Better yet is the special "**kanji**-ruled" paper, called **genkooyooshi** in Japanese, that can often be found in Japanese and Chinese import stores.

It is always a good idea to learn a new **kanji** along with its most commonly occurring compounds or with its **okurigana** (**hiragana** endings) instead of as an isolated symbol. For this reason, we have provided exercises in which you either transcribe the pronunciation of a **kanji** or compound in **hiragana** or insert **kanji** into sentences. The more you see and write the new **kanji** in meaningful contexts, the better you will remember them.

The *Writing Activities* give you the opportunity to use the vocabulary, expressions, and structures presented in the main text in their written forms as you practice expressing your ideas and thoughts in Japanese. Like the *Listening Comprehension Activities*, the *Writing Activities* are divided into the same subsections as the main textbook, so refer to the relevant section if you have any questions. Only **kanji** presented before or in the current chapter are used in the *Writing Activities*. We recommend that you work with the *Kanji Practice and Exercises* first. Then the *Writing Activities* will provide extra reinforcement for the **kanji** you have just learned.

The cast of characters from the main text also appears throughout the *Workbook/Laboratory Manual*. These students use Japanese in their language class and as a means of communication with each other. As you hear and read about these characters and work through the exercises and activities in this manual, you will learn to talk and write about your own life and concerns as an English-speaking student of Japanese.

About the Authors

Suzuko Hamasaki has been a lecturer in Japanese at the Department of East Asian Languages and Literatures, University of California, Irvine, since 1991. For the past few years, she has been in charge of teaching and developing the advanced Japanese course. She holds an M.A. in linguistics from California State University, Fullerton.

Hifumi Ito has been a lecturer in Japanese at the Program in Japanese Studies, University of California, San Diego since 1989. Currently, she is coordinating the first-year Japanese language course and is in charge of Japanese TA supervision and training. She received her M.A. in Japanese from the University of Minnesota.

Hiroko C. Kataoka is associate professor in the Department of Asian and Asian-American Studies at California State University, Long Beach, and chief academic specialist at the Japan Foundation & Language Center in Los Angeles. In addition to the Japanese language, she has been teaching Japanese language pedagogy courses. She received her Ph.D. in education at the University of Illinois, Urbana-Champaign. She has written numerous books, articles, and conference reports on teaching Japanese. She has also given a number of workshops on language pedagogy.

Akemi Morioka has been academic coordinator of the Japanese program in the Department of East Asian Languages and Literatures at the University of California, Irvine, since 1989. She is an author of 日本について考えよう *Let's Think about Japan* (McGraw-Hill), a Japanese textbook for intermediate to advanced learners. She holds an M.A. in linguistics from California State University, Long Beach.

Yasu-Hiko Tohsaku is a full professor at the University of California, San Diego, where he is the director of the language program at the graduate school of International Relations and Pacific Studies and the coordinator of the undergraduate Japanese language program. He received his Ph.D. in linguistics from the University of California, San Diego. He is the author of numerous papers on second-language acquisition and Japanese language pedagogy. He is also the author of the main text of *Yookoso!*

PART ONE

Listening Comprehension Activities

Meeting Others and Introducing Yourself

Practice the dialogues in Part 1 of Getting Started and then carry on the following conversations with the persons indicated below. You will hear the person's voice on the tape; respond during the pause on the tape.

SIMPLE INTRODUCTIONS

You meet John Kawamura and Linda Brown for the first time at a party. Greet them.

With John Kawamura:

KAWAMURA: Hajimemashite.

YOU: *Hajimemashite*

KAWAMURA: Kawamura desu.

YOU: *McDonald desu*

KAWAMURA: Doozo yoroshiku.

YOU: *Doozo yoroshiku*

With Linda Brown:

YOU: *Hajimemashite*

BURAUN: Hajimemashite.

YOU: *McDonald desu*

BURAUN: Buraun desu.

YOU: *Doozo yoroshiku*

BURAUN: Doozo yoroshiku.

MEETING SOMEONE AND INTRODUCING YOURSELF: INQUIRING ABOUT SOMEONE'S NAME

You have to find Masao Hayashi in a crowd at party. You will hear a model conversation first. Then, it is your turn to go find him.

YOU: _____

STRANGER: Iie.

YOU: _____

STRANGER: Iie.

You walk around, looking for Mr. Hayashi.

YOU: _____

HAYASHI: Hai, soo desu.

YOU: _____. _____. _____.

HAYASHI: Hayashi desu. Hajimemashite. Doozo yoroshiku.

ASKING FOR SOMEONE'S NAME: INTRODUCTIONS USING NAME CARDS

You are at the Sony booth at Japan Expo, and need to talk to Mr. Takada, whom you have never met. You will hear a model conversation first. Then, it is your turn to ask his name and greet Mr. Takada at the booth, exchanging name cards.

YOU: _____. _____ka?

TAKADA: Hai, soo desu. Sonii no Takada desu. Onamae wa?

YOU: _____no _____. _____.

TAKADA: Hajimemashite. Kore, watashi no meeshi desu.

YOU: Doomo _____. _____.

TAKADA: Doomo arigatoo gozaimasu.

OVERALL REVIEW

A. Listen to the five short converstations between John Kawamura and Mei Lin Chin, and choose the appropriate answer from the choices in parentheses.

1. Kawamura and Chin meet for the first time and say to each other (hajimemashite / hai, soo desu).
2. Chin asks Kawamura if he is Mr. Kawamura or not and Kawamura answers (hajimemashite / hai, soo desu). Then, Chin greets Kawamura, saying (sumimasen / hajimemashite. doozo yoroshiku).

3. After Chin introduces herself, she asks Kawamura his name, saying (onamae wa? / Kawamura-san desu ka?)

4. Chin asks the wrong person if he is Kawamura and apologizes, saying (iie / shitsurei shimashita).

5. Kawamura says (sumimasen / hai, soo desu) before asking a question to identify Chin. Then Kawamura hands his name card to Chin, who says (watashi no meeshi desu. / arigatoo gozaimasu.) to thank him.

B. Listen as Kunio Sato looks for Mr. Smith from Bank of America among the people present at a party, and then complete the following summary, using the words or phrases listed below. Each item is used once.

Sato says _____ when he approaches a person for the first time and

_____ when he finds out it is not the right person. Smith says

_____ to affirm that he is indeed the person Sato is looking for. Sato and Smith

exchange _____ in order to introduce themselves. Sato and Smith greet each other

by saying _____ .

1. meeshi
2. shitsuree shimashita
3. hajimemashite
4. soo desu
5. sumimasen

EVERYDAY GREETINGS

A. Listen to the expressions on the tape and circle the appropriate meaning for each. Each expression will be repeated twice.

1. a. Good morning.   b. Good afternoon / Hello.   c. Good night.

2. a. How are you?   b. What is your name?   c. I am fine.

3. a. Good morning.   b. Good night.   c. Goodbye.

4. a. I am fine.   b. See you   c. Excuse me / I am sorry.

5. a. Thank you.   b. I am sorry.   c. It is nice to meet you.

6. a. Good afternoon.   b. Good night.   c. Goodbye.

7. a. How are you?   b. I haven't seen you for a long time.   c. How do you do?

8. a. How are you?   b. Thank you, I am fine.   c. See you again.

9. a. Good evening.   b. Excuse me.   c. See you later.

B. You are in the first day of an interpreters' training session. Let's warm up, putting the following English expressions into Japanese.

1. Good morning. _____

2. Good afternoon. _____

3. Good evening. _____

4. Good morning. It is fine weather, isn't it? _____

5. Good afternoon. How are you? _____

6. I haven't seen you for a long time. How are you? _____

7. Goodbye. _____

8. See you later _____

C. Listen to the following three dialogues and choose the words from the list below that describe the situations being portrayed. You may find more than one description appropriate for each situation, and some descriptions may be used more than once.

1. _____
2. _____
3. _____

   a. morning
   b. afternoon
   c. any time of the day
   d. saying goodbye
   e. meeting for the first time
   f. meeting after a long time

In the Classroom

A. Listen to the conversation between a student and a teacher on the tape and write the Japanese equivalent for each English word. Each conversation will be repeated twice.

1. door _____   4. chair _____

2. book _____   5. pen _____

3. desk _____

Now play the role of the student. Ask the teacher how to say each English word in Japanese, and then write the answer.

1. pencil _____   4. notebook _____

2. dictionary _____   5. window _____

3. paper _____

B. Listen to the teacher giving each student a command. Write the letter designating the command given to each student in the line following the student's name. You will hear each command twice.

1. Kawamura _____
2. Brown _____
3. Chin _____
4. Machida _____
5. Hayashi _____
6. Curtis _____
7. Gibson _____

a. Please listen.
b. Please write.
c. Please say it again.
d. Please look at the book.
e. Please say it in Japanese.
f. Please open your book.
g. Please close your book.

Writing Activities

Meeting Others and Introducing Yourself

A. Choose the best response from the right-hand column. Write the appropriate letter next to the number below.

1. _____ Hajimemashite.
2. _____ Doozo yoroshiku.
3. _____ Sumimasen, Kawamura-san desu ka.
4. _____ Buraun desu.

a. Chin desu.
b. Hai, soo desu.
c. Doozo yoroshiku.
d. Hajimemashite.

B. You are supposed to meet a Mr. Kawabe at the station. A Japanese man in a gray suit approaches you and starts a conversation. Fill in Kawabe's first line with your name and complete your part.

KAWABE: Sumimasen, _____-san desu ka.

YOU: _____

KAWABE: Kawabe desu. Hajimemashite. Doozo yoroshiku.

YOU: _____

_____

C. A stranger approaches you on the street, looking for someone he or she has never met. Write your half of the conversation. Be sure that what you write makes sense when taken together with what the stranger says.

STRANGER: Sumimasen, Kawamura-san desu ka.

YOU: _____

STRANGER: Shitsuree shimashita.

YOU: _____

D. You are looking for Mr. Hayashi, whom you have never met, in front of a station. Complete the following dialogue.

YOU: _____

STRANGER: Iie.

YOU: _____

STRANGER: Iie.

E. Choose the most appropriate response from the right-hand column.

1. _____ Sumimasen, Hayashi-san desu ka.
2. _____ Onamae wa?
3. _____ Hajimemashite.
4. _____ Doozo yoroshiku.

a. Chin desu.
b. Hajimemashite
c. Doozo yoroshiku
d. Iie

F. What would you say in the following situations? Choose your answers from the right-hand column.

1. _____ You are meeting someone for the first time.
2. _____ You want to know someone's name.
3. _____ You are introducing yourself and stating your professional affiliation.
4. _____ You are handing over your name card.
5. _____ Someone has given you his/her name card.
6. _____ You have finished introducing yourself.

a. Doozo yoroshiku.
b. Arigatoo gozaimasu.
c. Sonii no Kawamura desu.
d. Kore, watashi no meeshi desu.
e. Hajimemashite.
f. Onamae wa?

G. How do you think the following people would introduce themselves?

> EXAMPLE: Takada, who works for Sony.
> Sonii no Takada desu.

1. Yamashita, who works for Toyota.

   _____

2. Okuda, who teaches at Kyoto University.

   _____

3. Watanabe, who is a student at the University of Oregon.

   _____

4. Yoshida, who works for IBM.

   _____

5. You, who are a student at your university/college.

   _____

H. Write dialogues for the following situations, following the cues provided. Do not translate the cues. Just use them as general guidelines for the conversations.

1. Kawamura and Ms. Tanaka meet each other for the first time.

Kawamura meets Tanaka for the first time. He greets her.	K:	_____
Tanaka returns the greeting.	T:	_____
Kawamura says that he is Kawamura of the University of Tokyo.	K:	_____
Then he hands Tanaka his name card as he says, "Nice to meet you."	T:	_____
Tanaka thanks Kawamura and hands him her card as she says that she is Tanaka from Keio University and that she is glad to meet him.	·T:	_____
Kawamura thanks Tanaka.	K:	_____

2. Kawamura is supposed to meet Mr. Yamashita for the first time at a nearby train station.

Kawamura sees a man who is also looking K: _____
for someone, so he approaches him and
asks if he is Mr. Yamashita.

The man says he is not. M1: _____

Kawamura apologizes. K: _____

In the meantime, a different man M2: _____
approaches Kawamura and asks if he is
Kawamura.

Kawamura answers yes and asks the man K: _____
if he is Yamashita.

The man says he is Yamashita and greets Y: _____
Kawamura.

Kawamura returns the greeting and says, K: _____
"Nice to meet you."

Everyday Greetings

A. What would you say in the following situations? Write the letter of the most appropriate phrase in the blank next to the description of the situation.

1. _____ It's 8:00 A.M. Professor Yokoi comes into the classroom.

2. _____ You are about to go to bed, and you say good night to your family.

3. _____ You are saying goodbye to a friend whom you will see again soon.

4. _____ You run into Professor Yokoi on campus after lunch.

5. _____ Someone has asked about your health.

6. _____ You meet your friend, whom you have not seen for about a year.

7. _____ Someone remarks that it's nice weather.

8. _____ It's 7:00 P.M. You run into Professor Yokoi at a supermarket.

9. _____ It's the end of your Japanese class.

10. _____ Someone has just brought you the book you had asked to borrow.

a. Ja, mata.
b. Ohayoo gozaimasu.
c. Konban wa.
d. Arigatoo gozaimasu.
e. Shibaraku desu ne.
f. Okagesama de, genki desu.
g. Konnichi wa.
h. Oyasuminasai.
i. Soo desu ne.
j. Sayoonara.

B. Complete the dialogues according to the cues given. Be sure to fill in both your part and your neighbor's part.

1. You run into your Japanese neighbor at a grocery store in the afternoon. It's such a fine day. Greet her properly.

   YOU: _____

   NEIGHBOR: _____

   YOU: _____

   NEIGHBOR: _____

2. Your Japanese neighbor has just returned from a six-month overseas assignment. Greet him, then ask how he has been. Your neighbor will also ask you how you have been.

   YOU: _____

   NEIGHBOR: _____

   YOU: _____

   NEIGHBOR: _____

   YOU: _____

C. What might these people be saying to each other? Write a two-line dialogue for each of the following pictures.

1.

2.

3.

1. A: _____

    B: _____

2. A: _____

    B: _____

3. A: _____

    B: _____

4. A: _____

    B: _____

5. A: _____

    B: _____

Classroom Expressions

A. What would you say in the following situations in your Japanese class? Choose your answer from the options given, writing the appropriate letters in the blanks.

1. _____ You have a question.

2. _____ You don't know the answer to a question.

3. _____ You could not understand the question because your professor was speaking too fast.

4. _____ You understood what someone told you.

5. _____ You want to know how to say "Thank you" in Japanese.

6. _____ You need a little time to think about the answer.

a. Chotto matte kudasai.
b. Shitsumon ga arimasu.
c. Wakarimashita.
d. Wakarimasen.
e. Moo ichido, onegai shimasu.
f. *Thank you* wa Nihongo de nan to iimasu ka.

B. The following things can be found in a classroom. Divide the words first into: 1) things that students normally carry vs. things that are part of a classroom; then divide the same words into 2) things that are typically made of wood, paper, or other materials.

denki	tenjoo	kokuban	isu
kokuban-keshi	doa	chooku	tsukue
kami	jisho	hon	booru-pen
keshigomu	kaban	mado	kaaten
yuka	shaapu penshiru	enpitsu	teeburu
nooto	kabe	kyookasho	
mannenhitsu			

part of a classroom	students carry

made of wood	made of paper	made of other materials

C. Label as many things in the picture as you can.

D. Match each picture with the classroom command that it represents.

a.    b.    c.

d.    e.    f.

g.

1. _____ Hon o tojite kudasai.

2. _____ Hon o akete kudasai.

3. _____ Kiite kudasai.

4. _____ Mite kudasai.

5. _____ Itte kudasai.

6. _____ Nooto ni kaite kudasai.

7. _____ Te o agete kudasai.

PART TWO

Listening Comprehension Activities

Numbers Up to 20

A. Practice the numbers up to 20 by repeating after the tape.

0 1 2 3 4 5 6 7 8 9 10 11 12 13 14 15 16 17 18 19 20

B. Listen to the numbers on the tape and write them down.

1. _____   3. _____   5. _____   7. _____   9. _____

2. _____   4. _____   6. _____   8. _____   10. _____

C. Listen to Mr. Ezaki, the math teacher, giving you basic math questions. Write down the answers. You will hear each problem twice.

1. $1 + 2 =$ _____

2. $3 +$ _____ $=$ _____

3. _____ $+ 6 =$ _____

4. _____ $+$ _____ $=$ _____

5. $9 - 5 =$ _____

6. $8 -$ _____ $=$ _____

7. _____ $- 2$ _____ $=$ _____

8. _____ $-$ _____ $=$ _____

Asking and Giving Telephone Numbers

A. You will hear a series of statements about the phone number of each of the following people. Write down the number next to the person's name. You will hear each statement twice.

1. HENRY CURTIS: _____

2. MEI LIN CHIN: _____

3. JOHN KAWAMURA: _____

4. LINDA BROWN: _____

5. MASAO HAYASHI: _____

B. You will hear three dialogues in which a Japanese student who has just arrived at an American university asks another Japanese student for the phone numbers of various campus locations. Write the name of each building or office next to its phone number.

Useful Vocabulary

toshokan   *library*

PHONE NUMBERS   LOCATIONS

856-1293: _____

725-0601: _____

722-8740: _____

Asking and Telling Time

A. You want to call your friends in the following places, but you are not sure of the local time in each place. Ask a clerk at the service counter what time it is in each place and write down the time.

EXAMPLE: YOU: Rosanzerusu (L.A.) wa ima nan-ji desu ka?
            CLERK: Rosanzerusu wa ima gozen 11-ji desu.

EXAMPLE: Los Angeles 11:00 A.M.

1. Atlanta _____   4. Paris _____

2. Rio de Janeiro _____   5. Bangkok_____

3. Tokyo _____   6. Sydney _____

B. Listen to the tape and identify the times given in the following four statements, matching Column I with Column II. Each statement will be repeated twice.

Useful Vocabulary

~ kara   *from* ~

1. _____ Now   a. 6:30 p.m.
                              b. 8:00 p.m.
2. _____ Japanese class   c. 7:30 p.m.
                              d. 9:00 A.M.
3. _____ Supper

4. _____ Party

C. Listen to Professor Yokoi talk about her schedule for today, and fill in the blanks with the appropriate time.

Useful Vocabulary

kyoo   *today*
~kara ~made   *from~ until ~*
yasumi   *a break*

Professor Yokoi teaches Japanese at _____, _____, and

_____. She has a break between _____ and

_____, and has lunch between _____ and

_____. At _____, she has a meeting. She will go shopping

_____.

D. Answer the questions on the tape based on the following schedule. (You will hear two types of questions—yes/no questions and what questions, so be careful how you answer.)

EXAMPLE: (yes/no question) Jogingu wa 6-ji han desu ka? — **Hai,** soo desu./Hai, (jogingu wa) 6-ji han desu.
(What question) Jogingu wa nan-ji desu ka? — (Jogingu wa) **6-ji han** desu.

6:30	**Jogging**
7:00	Breakfast
9:00	Japanese Class
12:30	Lunch
3:00	Meeting
4:30	Shopping
6:00	Taking a walk
7:30	Dinner

EXAMPLE. Hai, soo desu.

1. _____   4. _____

2. _____   5. _____

3. _____   6. _____

Asking What Something Is

A. Listen as Professor Yokoi's students learn the names of classroom objects. Then circle the items found in the classroom.

table   chalk   textbook   door   ceiling   window   desk   chair

B. A Japanese traveling in the United States wants to try American cuisine. He visits a cafeteria with a friend who has lived in the States for several years and asks questions about the food. Answer the questions at the end of each of the four exchanges by circling either hai (yes) or iie (no). You will hear each conversation twice.

1. hai / iie   3. hai / iie

2. hai / iie   4. hai / iie

C. Pronunciation Practice

Read the Language Note on page 27 of your textbook. Then, listen to the words on the tape and circle the correct word pronounced. Each word will be said twice.

1. uchi / ushi   6. kekkoo /kekkon

2. hun / hon   7. chotto / choodo

3. kanji / sanji   8. juppun / juubun

4. kinen / kin'en   9. doomo / doomoo

5. tenki / genki   10. kyookasho / kyokashoo

Writing Activities

Numbers Up to 20

A. Complete each equation.

1. $2 + 5 = 7$ ni tasu _____ wa nana

2. $4 + 9 = 13$ _____ tasu _____ wa juu-san

3. $3 + 1 = 4$ _____ yon

4. $8 - 6 = 2$ _____ hiku _____ ni

5. $15 - 10 = 5$ juu-go _____

6. $4 \times 4 = 16$ _____ kakeru _____ wa _____

7. $2 \times 7 = 14$ ni _____ nana wa _____

8. $20 \div 4 = 5$ _____ waru yon _____

9. $14 \div 7 = 2$ juu-yon _____

10. $18 \div 9 = 2$ _____

B. What number(s) between 0 and 20 do you associate with the items in the left hand column? Match with the numbers in the right hand column.

1. _____ a carton of eggs
2. _____ a short stack of pancakes
3. _____ spider's legs
4. _____ a litter of puppies
5. _____ soccer
6. _____ compulsory education
7. _____ original colonies of the U.S.
8. _____ fingers and toes
9. _____ telephone push buttons
10. _____ driver's license

a. hachi
b. juu-go
c. juu-ku
d. roku
e. san
f. juu
g. juu-ni
h. yon
i. nana
j. juu-roku
k. juu-ichi
l. kyuu
m. go
n juu-san
o. ni
p. juu-shichi
q. ni-juu
r. ichi
s. juu-hachi
t. juu-shi

Asking and Giving Telephone Numbers

A. Find a partner and read the following telephone numbers aloud to each other. Then write down the reading for each in romanized Japanese.

Note: When telephone numbers are spoken, *two* and *five* are always pronounced as **nii** and **goo**, rather than **ni** and **go.**

1. 541-375-6859 _____
2. 206-443-0568 _____
3. 391-668-5521 _____
4. 800-555-1212 _____
5. 06-628-5352 _____
6. 075-283-5004 _____
7. 0424-69-1052 _____
8. 0727-61-2798 _____

B. Complete the dialogue, using the following information about Machida's and Brown's telephone numbers.

  MACHIDA: 492-6592
  BROWN: 672-0185

  BURAUN: Machida-san no denwa bangoo wa?

  MACHIDA: _____ kyuu _____ no roku _____ kyuu nii desu.

  BURAUN: Yon kyuu nii no roku goo kyuu nii desu ka.

  MACHIDA: Hai, soo desu. Buraun-san no _____ wa?

  BURAUN: Roku _____ nii _____ zero ichi hachi goo desu.

  MACHIDA: Roku nana nii no zero ichi hachi goo desu ka.

  BURAUN: Hai, _____.

  MACHIDA: Wakarimashita.

C. You want to find out what Ms. Tazawa's phone number is, so you ask Mr. Brown. When Mr. Brown gives you her phone number, you should confirm it. Write in your lines to complete the dialogue.

  YOU: _____

  BROWN: Goo hachi nana no san yon nana nana desu.

  YOU: _____

  BROWN: Hai, soo desu.

Asking and Telling Time

A. Ima nan-ji desu ka? Which is the clock that this person is looking at? Match each clock with the statements about the time of day.

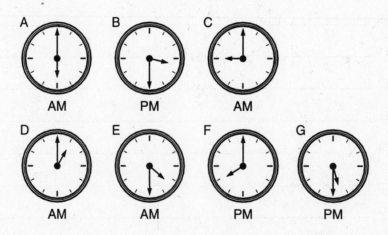

1. _____ Ima gozen roku-ji desu. Asa desu.

2. _____ Ima gozen ku-ji desu. Asa desu.

3. _____ Ima gogo hachi-ji desu. Yoru desu.

4. _____ Ima gogo san-ji han desu. Hiru desu.

5. _____ Ima gozen ichi-ji desu. Yoru desu.

6. _____ Ima gozen yo-ji han desu. Asa desu.

7. _____ Ima gogo go-ji han desu. Yuugata desu.

B. The following diagram indicates a day. Fill in each box with the appropriate word from the list below.

asa   hiru   yuugata   yoru   gozen   gogo

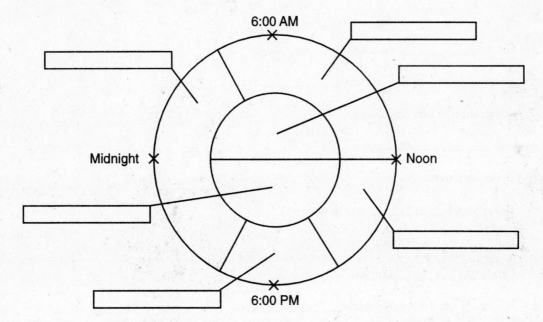

C. Complete the following dialogues, using the information in the table below.

	AM												PM												
Tokyo	12	1	2	3	4	5	6	7	8	9	10	11	12	1	2	3	4	5	6	7	8	9	10	11

					PM													AM						
Los Angeles	7	8	9	10	11	12	1	2	3	4	5	6	7	8	9	10	11	12	1	2	3	4	5	6

								AM												PM			
Paris	4	5	6	7	8	9	10	11	12	1	2	3	4	5	6	7	8	9	10	11	12	1	2	3

1. (A conversation in Japan)

    A: Ima nan-ji desu ka.

    B: Gogo roku-ji desu.

    A: Huransu wa _____ nan-ji desu ka.

    B: Eeto, _____ desu.

    A: Gozen _____ desu ka.

    B: Hai, soo desu. Huransu wa ima _____ desu.

2. (A conversation in Los Angeles)

    A: Ima _____ desu ka.

    B: Gogo yo-ji desu.

    A: Tookyoo wa _____ nan-ji desu ka.

    B: Eeto, _____ desu.

    A: Gozen _____ desu ka.

    B: Hai, soo desu. Tookyoo wa ima _____ desu.

3. (A conversation in Paris)

    A: (asks what time it is)

    _____

    B: (answers that it's 3:00 P.M.)

    _____

    A: (asks what time it is in Tokyo)

    _____

B: (answers after a little hesitation)

_____

A: (asks if it's P.M.)

_____

B: (answers in the affirmative, then says it's night in Japan.)

_____

D. Do you usually do the following in the A.M., the P.M., or both? Write each word in the time category you select for that activity.

asagohan	miitingu	undoo
hirugohan	deeto	benkyoo
bangohan	sanpo	paatii
Nihongo no kurasu	kaimono/shoppingu	eega

Gozen: _____

Gogo: _____

Gozen & Gogo: _____

E. Complete the dialogues, using the information on the following schedule.

6:30	Exercise
7:30	Breakfast
9:00	Japanese class
1:00	Lunch
4:00	Meeting
5:30	Taking a walk
7:00	Dinner
7:30	Date

1. A: Nihongo no kurasu wa nan-ji desu ka.

   B. _____ desu.

2. A. Asagohan wa nan-ji desu ka.

   B. _____ desu.

3. A: Undoo wa nan-ji desu ka.

   B. _____ desu.

4. A: Deeto wa nan-ji desu ka.

   B. _____ desu.

5. A: _____

   B. Shichi-ji desu.

6. A: _____

   B. Go-ji han desu.

7. A: _____

   B. Yo-ji desu.

8. A: _____

   B. Ichi-ji desu.

F. Please answer the following questions. (Be sure to add A.M. and P.M. when stating times.)

1. Anata no denwa bangoo wa. _____

2. Ima nan-ji desu ka. _____

3. Shikago wa ima nan-ji desu ka. _____

4. Sanhuranshisuko wa. _____

5. Jaa, Nyuu Yooku wa. _____

6. Nihongo no kurasu wa nan-ji desu ka. _____

G. Write up your own schedule for tomorrow, listing five to eight activities, and trade schedules with a classmate. Limiting yourself to questions you have learned in Japanese, write five questions about your classmate's schedule in his or her workbook in the blanks below labeled "classmate." Then take your own workbook back and answer your classmate's questions in the blanks labeled "you."

    EXAMPLE: breakfast   7:00 A.M.
              CLASSMATE: Asagohan wa nan-ji desu ka.
              YOU: Shichi-ji desu.

1. CLASSMATE: _____

   YOU: _____

2. CLASSMATE: _____

   YOU: _____

3. CLASSMATE: _____

   YOU: _____

4. CLASSMATE: _____

   YOU: _____

5. CLASSMATE: _____

   YOU: _____

Asking What Something Is

A. Suppose that someone asked you the following questions about food. How would you answer?

1. A: Teriyaki wa Nihon ryoori desu ka.

   B: Hai, _____

2. A: Biiru wa o-sake desu ka.

   B: Hai, _____

3. A: Banana wa yasai desu ka.

   B: Iie, _____

4. A: Tomato wa kudamono desu ka.

   B: _____

5. A: Sukiyaki wa Mekishiko ryoori desu ka.

   B: _____

B. How would you ask questions in the following situations in Japanese?

1. You want to know what that thing over there is.

   _____

2. You want to know if something is Japanese food.

   _____

Getting Started: Part Two   **25**

3. You want to know if that thing over there is sushi.

   _____

4. You want to know what this thing (that you are holding) is.

   _____

5. You want to know if that thing (that the listener is holding) is an American dish.

   _____

C. Practice Dialogue 6 and its variation, following the directions for each situation below.

   1. You are at a multi-national Asian restaurant.

      YOU: (get the waiter's attention, then ask what that [food] over there is)

      _____ .

      WAITER: (says it's green curry ("guriin karee"))

      _____

      YOU: (ask if it's Japanese food)

      _____

      WAITER: (answers that it's not; it's Thai food)

      _____

      YOU: (order green curry)

      _____

   2. You are at a 'sunakku' (a combination coffee shop and casual bar) in Japan. You see someone with an interesting-looking bright green drink with what looks like ice cream or whipped cream on top, so you ask what it is. You find out that it is 'kuriimu sooda.' You now want to know if it's an alcoholic beverage. The waiter says no, so you order it.

      YOU: _____

      WAITER: _____

      YOU: _____

      WAITER: _____

      YOU: _____

D. You are a tourist in Japan. You have encountered some unfamiliar foods and beverages, which are depicted in the drawings. Complete the dialogues in which you find out what each item is called and what category of food or drink it belongs to. Be sure that your lines make sense when taken together with what the Japanese person says.

1.   YOU: _____

    JAPANESE: Udon (noodles) desu.

    YOU: _____

    JAPANESE: Ee, soo desu.

2.   YOU: _____

    JAPANESE: Momo (*peach*) desu.

    YOU: _____

    JAPANESE: Ee, soo desu.

3.   YOU: _____

    JAPANESE: Mugicha (barley tea) desu.

    YOU: _____

    JAPANESE: Iie, chigaimasu.

Hiragana Practice

Practice hiragana あ〜お.

	hira-gana	stroke order	trace	practice							
a	あ	あ	あ								
i	い	い	い								
u	う	う	う								
e	え	え	え								
o	お	お	お								

Transcribe the following romanized words into hiragana.

1. ai (love)

_____

2. ie (house)

_____

3. ou (to chase)

_____

4. au (to meet)

_____

5. aoi (blue)

_____

6. ue (up, top)

_____

7. oi (nephew)

_____

Copy these words and read them out loud.

1. いえ (house)
2. おい (nephew)
3. おう (to chase)
4. あおい (blue)
5. うえ (up, top)
6. あい (love)
7. いう (to say)

Practice hiragana か〜こ.

	hira-gana	stroke order	trace	practice					
ka	か	が	か						
ki	き	き	き						
ku	く	ぐ	く						
ke	け	け	け						
ko	こ	こ	こ						

Transcribe the following romanized words into hiragana.

1. akai (red)

   _____

2. kiku (to listen)

   _____

3. kaku (to write)

   _____

4. koke (moss)

   _____

5. kakoi (enclosure)

   _____

6. kuki (stem)

   _____

7. koi (karp)

   _____

Copy these words and read them out loud.

1. かき (persimmon)
2. くき (stem)
3. あかい (red)
4. かこい (enclosure)
5. こい (carp)
6. こけ (moss)
7. おく (to put)
8. あき (autumn)
9. えき (train station)
10. こえ (voice)
11. かお (face)
12. いけ (pond)

Practice hiragana さ～そ.

	hira-gana	stroke order	trace	practice						
sa	さ	さ	さ							
shi	し	し	し							
su	す	す	す							
se	せ	せ	せ							
so	そ	そ	そ							

Transcribe the following romanized words into hiragana.

1. shio (salt)

_____

2. sekai (world)

_____

3. kasa (umbrella)

_____

4. suika (watermelon)

_____

5. shika (deer)

_____

6. soko (bottom)

_____

7. sukoshi (little, few)

_____

Copy these words and read them out loud.

1. しあい (athletic contest)
2. かさ (umbrella)
3. さけ (rice wine)
4. すし (sushi)
5. せかい (world)
6. そこ (bottom)
7. せき (seat)
8. さか (slope)
9. あせ (sweat)
10. きそ (base)
11. うし (cow)
12. えさ (animal food)

Practice hiragana た〜と.

	hira-gana	stroke order	trace	practice							
ta	た	た	た								
chi	ち	ち	ち								
tsu	つ	つ	つ								
te	て	て	て								
to	と	と	と								

Transcribe the following romanized words into hiragana.

1. takai (high)

    _____

2. tsuki (moon)

    _____

3. chikai (near)

    _____

4. tokasu (to melt)

    _____

5. tsukau (to use)

    _____

6. teki (enemy)

    _____

7. chikatetsu (subway)

    _____

Copy these words and read them out loud.

1. ちかい (near)
2. つきあう (to associate with)
3. たかい (high)
4. てき (enemy)
5. とき (time)
6. つち (earth, ground)
7. いた (board)
8. あつい (hot)
9. こと (Japanese zither)
10. たすけて！(Help!)
11. ちたい (zone)
12. きつい (tight)

Practice hiragana な〜の.

	hira-gana	stroke order	trace	practice							
na	な	な	な								
ni	に	に	に								
nu	ぬ	ぬ	ぬ								
ne	ね	ね	ね								
no	の	の	の								

Transcribe the following romanized words into hiragana.

1. neko (cat)

_____

2. inu (dog)

_____

3. kani (crab)

_____

4. kane (money)

_____

5. natsu (summer)

_____

6. nanika (something)

_____

7. nuno (cloth)

_____

Copy these words and read them out loud.

1. なく (to cry)
2. にく (meat)
3. かね (money)
4. ぬの (cloth)
5. ぬし (master)
6. さかな (fish)
7. のきした (under the eaves)
8. とね (name of a river)
9. なし (pear)
10. なす (eggplant)
11. にし (west)
12. しぬ (to die)
13. ぬか (rice bran)
14. たね (seed)
15. たぬき (badger)

Practice hiragana は〜ほ.

	hira-gana	stroke order	trace	practice					
ha	は	は	は						
hi	ひ	ひ	ひ						
hu	ふ	ふ	ふ						
he	へ	へ	へ						
ho	ほ	ほ	ほ						

Transcribe the following romanized words into hiragana.

1. hune (boat)

   _____

2. hashi (bridge)

   _____

3. hi (fire)

   _____

4. hoshi (star)

   _____

5. hue (flute)

   _____

6. heta (unskilled)

   _____

7. hikoku (defendant)

   _____

Copy these words and read them out loud.

1. ひと (person)
2. ほね (bone)
3. ふし (joint)
4. はこ (box)
5. ふね (boat)
6. へた (unskilled)
7. ほか (other)
8. へそ (navel)
9. へきち (remote area)
10. ふとい (thick in circumference)
11. ほそい (thin, fine)
12. はた (loom)
13. はたけ (non-rice field)
14. そふ ([my] grandfather)
15. ひふ (skin)

Practice hiragana ま〜も.

	hira-gana	stroke order	trace	practice							
ma	ま	ま	ま								
mi	み	み	み								
mu	む	む	む								
me	め	め	め								
mo	も	も	も								

Transcribe the following romanized words into hiragana.

1. musume (daughter)

   _____

2. mame (bean)

   _____

3. kumo (cloud)

   _____

4. mimi (ear)

   _____

5. mukashi (olden days)

   _____

6. makoto (sincerity)

   _____

7. michishio (high tide)

   _____

Copy these words and read them out loud.

1. また (again)
2. みけねこ (calico cat)
3. むし (insect)
4. めし (meal)
5. かも (wild duck)
6. むすめ (daughter)
7. もも (peach)
8. みみ (ear)
9. かめ (tortoise)
10. まつ (pine)
11. はちみつ (honey)
12. もしもし (hello [on the phone])
13. あたま (head)
14. みこ (shrine maiden)
15. さめ (shark)

Practice hiragana や〜よ.

	hira-gana	stroke order	trace	practice						
ya	や	や	や							
yu	ゆ	ゆ	ゆ							
yo	よ	よ	よ							

Transcribe the following romanized words into hiragana.

1. yasai (vegetable)

_____

2. yuka (floor)

_____

3. yotsuyu (night dew)

_____

4. yuki (snow)

_____

5. yosoku (estimate)

_____

6. yume (dream)

_____

7. yoyaku (reservation)

_____

8. yakimochi (jealousy)

_____

Copy these words and read them out loud.

1. やく (to bake, roast)
2. きやく (convenant)
3. ゆか (floor)
4. にえゆ (boiling water)
5. よなか (midnight)
6. かよう (to commute)
7. やきもの (pottery)
8. よそく (estimate)

9. あゆ (a kind of fish)
10. まゆ (eyebrow)
11. ふゆ (winter)
12. やたい (vendor's stall)
13. よむ (to read)
14. やま (mountain)
15. よつや (an area of Tokyo)

Practice hiragana ら～ろ.

	hira-gana	stroke order	trace	practice							
ra	ら	ら	ら								
ri	り	り	り								
ru	る	る	る								
re	れ	れ	れ								
ro	ろ	ろ	ろ								

Transcribe the following romanized words into hiragana.

1. rikai (understanding)

_____

2. raku (comfortable)

_____

3. roku (six)

_____

4. raretsu (enumeration)

_____

5. rusu (not at home)

_____

6. rokuro (lathe)

_____

7. ruiseki (accumulation)

_____

Copy these words and read them out loud.

1. りし (interest on money)
2. かりる (to borrow)
3. るいすい (analogy)
4. からい (spicy)
5. しろい (white)
6. ひろい (wide, spacious)
7. るり (lapis lazuli)
8. れきし (history)
9. かるい (lightweight)
10. おさらい (run-through)
11. いろ (color)
12. ころす (to kill)
13. とろり (like a thick liquid)
14. てら (Buddhist temple)
15. つり (fishing)

Practice hiragana わ, を*, and ん.

	hira-gana	stroke order	trace	practice							
wa	わ	わ	わ								
o	を	を	を								
n	ん	ん	ん								

Transcribe the following romanized words into hiragana.

1. watashi (I, me)
2. wakai (young)
3. kawa (river)
4. hon (book)
5. kin (gold)
6. henka (change)
7. kinen (commemoration)
8. kin'en** (no smoking)

Copy these words and read them out loud.

1. しにん (dead person)
2. わすれる (to forget)
3. わかる (to understand)
4. きんし (forbidden)
5. おわん (bowl)
6. こわい (frightening)
7. らいねん (next year)
8. にんにく (garlic)
9. たんい (unit)
10. ほんや (bookstore)
11. かわり (substitute)
12. みかん (mandarin orange)
13. ふたん (burden)
14. わし (handmade paper)
15. あわ (foam)

*This を is used to indicate the direct object of a verb.

**The ' (apostrophe) is used to indicate that "n" and "e" are separate syllables. It should not be transcribed.

Your instructor will read out one of the following pairs. Circle the one that is read.

1. はし (bridge) ／ ほし (star)

2. さる (monkey) ／ きる (to wear)

3. いえ (house) ／ こえ (voice)

4. あす (tomorrow) ／ めす (female animal)

5. まつ (to wait) ／ もつ (to have)

6. おれ (I, me) ／ あれ (that one over there)

7. へさき (head of boat) ／ くさき (trees and plants)

8. きわ (edge) ／ きれ (cloth)

9. かえる (frog) ／ かえろ (short word for "Let's go home")

10. つめ (nail) ／ しぬ (to die)

11. むすめ (daughter) ／ ぬすむ (to steal)

12. たにん (others) ／ にたえ (picture that resembles)

Fill in each blank with one hiragana that will make the word the same if read from either the right or left, as shown in the examples. Then read them out loud.

EXAMPLES:　み_____ → みみ (ear)
こね_____ → こねこ (kitten)

1. も_____ (peach)

2. つ_____ (pipe)

3. は_____ (mother)

4. ち_____ (father)

5. こ_____ (this place)

6. す_____ (soot)

7. さ_____ (bamboo grass)

8. ふう_____ (married couple)

9. きて_____ (steam whistle)

10. さか_____ (upside down)

11. みな_____ (south)

12. やお_____ (vegetable store)

13. しる _____ (mark)

14. きつ _____ _____ (woodpecker)

15. かいと _____ _____ (shells and squids)

16. にわの _____ _____ (alligator in the yard)

17. うまく _____ _____ (to dance well)

18. たしかに _____ _____ _____ (I surely lent it.)

19. るすにな _____ _____ _____ (What will you do while you are alone at home.)

20. わたしまけ _____ _____ _____ _____ (I was defeated.)

Practice hiragana が〜ご.

	hira-gana	practice								
ga	が									
gi	ぎ									
gu	ぐ									
ge	げ									
go	ご									

Transcribe the following romanized words into hiragana.

1. gin (silver)

    _____

2. gengo (language)

    _____

3. guai (condition)

    _____

4. gogo (P.M.)

    _____

5. giron (argument)

    _____

6. sagasu (to look for)

    _____

7. hiragana

    _____

Copy these words and read them out loud.

1. がまん (putting up with)
2. はぎしり (grinding one's teeth)
3. にほんご (Japanese language)
4. かげ (shadow)
5. ぐんたい (the military)
6. ごみ (trash)
7. らいげつ (next month)
8. おんがく (music)

9. かぐ (furniture)
10. が (moth)
11. あご (chin)
12. えんげき (acting)
13. がまぐち (coin purse)
14. すぎ (cedar)
15. げた (Japanese clogs)

Practice hiragana ざ～ぞ.

	hira-gana	practice								
za	ざ									
ji	じ									
zu	ず									
ze	ぜ									
zo	ぞ									

Transcribe the following romanized words into hiragana.

1. kazu (number)

   _____

2. zaru (basket)

   _____

3. zatsuji (routine duties)

   _____

4. jikan (hour)

   _____

5. jiken (incident)

   _____

6. zokugo (slang)

   _____

7. zentai (whole)

   _____

Copy these words and read them out loud.

1. ずるい (sneaky)
2. じんけん (human rights)
3. ひざ (knee)
4. じこく (time, hour)
5. かぜ (wind)
6. かぞく (family)
7. ぎんざ (an area in Tokyo)
8. おじ (uncle)
9. ずきん (hood)
10. ぜんぜん (not at all)
11. ざんねん (regrettable)
12. なぞ (riddle)
13. ざくろ (pomegranate)
14. はじめ (beginning)
15. ずれ (lag)

Practice hiragana だ〜ど. (ぢ and づ are used less extensively than じ and ず.)

	hira-gana	practice									
da	だ										
ji	ぢ										
zu	づ										
de	で										
do	ど										

Transcribe the following romanized words into hiragana.

1. dame (no good)

   _____

2. hanaji (nosebleed)

   _____

3. doku (poison)

   _____

4. kizuku (to notice)

   _____

5. dekiru (be able to)

   _____

6. denwa (telephone)

   _____

7. daidokoro (kitchen)

   _____

Copy these words and read them out loud.

1. かだん (flower bed)
2. たどん (briquet)
3. わかづま (young wife)
4. みぢか (close at hand)
5. しんでん (sanctuary)
6. だます (to deceive)
7. どれ (which one)
8. めだつ (to be noticeable)
9. だけ (only)
10. どこ (where)
11. できごと (event)
12. つづく (to continue)
13. こづつみ (parcel)
14. ただ (free)
15. ちぢむ (to shrink)
16. どだい (foundation)

Practice hiragana ば〜ぼ.

	hira-gana	practice								
ba	ば									
bi	び									
bu	ぶ									
be	べ									
bo	ぼ									

Transcribe the following romanized words into hiragana.

1. kaban (bag)

_____

2. benri (convenient)

_____

3. kabi (mold)

_____

4. bonchi (basin)

_____

5. bitoku (virtue)

_____

6. haba (width)

_____

7. bunka (culture)

_____

Copy these words and read them out loud.

1. かば (hippopotamus)
2. びじん (beautiful woman)
3. ぶし (warrior)
4. べんかい (excuse)
5. ぼくとつ (simplicity)
6. ぶんべん (childbirth)
7. びぶん (differential)
8. かびん (vase)
9. おぼん (the Bon festival)
10. ばか (fool)
11. くべつ (distinction)
12. ぼこくご (native language)
13. はんぶん (half)
14. ふべん (inconvenience)
15. へび (snake)
16. ぶんぼ (denominator)

Practice hiragana ぱ〜ぽ.

	hira-gana	practice										
pa	ぱ											
pi	ぴ											
pu	ぷ											
pe	ぺ											
po	ぽ											

Transcribe the following romanized words into hiragana.

1. yutanpo (hot-water bottle)

   _____

2. pakutsuku (to bite at)

   _____

3. petenshi (impostor)

   _____

4. pinhane (kickback)

   _____

5. kanpai (cheers)

   _____

6. sanpo (taking a walk)

   _____

7. kinpen (neighborhood)

   _____

Copy these words and read them out loud.

1. かんぱん (deck)
2. えんぴつ (pencil)
3. さんぷん (three minutes)
4. きんぺん (neighborhood)
5. さんぽ (taking a walk)
6. ざんぱん (leftovers)
7. ぽつぽつ (in drops)
8. あんぴ (well-being)
9. おんぱ (sound wave)
10. なんぱ (shipwreck)
11. こんぽん (source)
12. しんぷ (Catholic priest)
13. さんぽ (stroll)
14. ぴんはね (kickback)
15. たんぽ (mortgage)
16. しんぱい (worry)

Your instructor will read out one of the following pairs. Circle the one that is read.

1. かんばん (sign) ／ かんぱん (deck)

2. ぶんか (culture) ／ ふんか (eruption)

3. かがく (science) ／ ががく (court music and dance)

4. じごく (hell) ／ じこく (time, hour)

5. げんかく (strict) ／ けんがく (study by observation)

6. だんたい (group) ／ たんだい (junior college)

7. かげ (shadow) ／ がけ (cliff)

8. たんぽ (mortgage) ／ たんぼ (rice field)

9. ぜんたい (whole) ／ せんだい (predecessor)

10. きんぺん (vicinity) ／ きんべん (diligence)

11. してん (municipal streetcar) ／ じてん (dictionary)

12. かざん (volcano) ／ かさん (addition)

Find the following romanized words in the array of syllables and circle them. They may be written top to bottom, bottom to top, left to right, right to left, or diagonally starting from either top or bottom.

abunai (dangerous), aoi (blue), atama (head), bushi (warrior), chigai (difference), chikai (near), danro (fireplace), gairaigo (loan words), hebi (snake), hekichi (remote area), henka (change), hiza (knee), hon (book), ibiki (snore), ika (squid), itai (painful), kakoi (enclosure), kanpai (Cheers!), kazan (volcano), kaze (wind), kazoku (family), kon'ya (tonight), kushi (comb), mainichi (everyday), nanpa (shipwreck), nigatsu (February), Nihongo (Japanese language), ongaku (music), raigetsu (next month), rekishi (history), ruisui (analogy), sakana (fish), sekai (world), shichi (seven), shinpu (Catholic priest), tebukuro (glove), tsutsu (pipe), tsuzuku (to be continued), wadai (topic), wasureru (to forget), yonaka (midnight), zakuro (pomegranate), zure (lag)

つつんきよぷやでか

しがげほざなまんびん

ちにいまさかなこしへ

がたらたまこぜいきん

いなぶあおいびちれぱ

らしんごんきかんぱい

いくんぱがいつせろる

ごほかぞくすづざくろ

にかいおずいくひぶん

いだわすれるへうてだ

PART THREE

Listening Comprehension Activities

Talking About Daily Activities

A. Listen to the tape and circle the time you hear. You will hear each time twice.

1.	2:05	2:15	4.	6:19	9:19
2.	4:06	5:06	5.	3:01	3:08
3.	1:07	7:07	6.	8:12	1:12

B. Listen to Masao Hayashi and Linda Brown talking, and fill in the blanks.

Linda Brown gets up at _____ o'clock in the morning and goes

_____ . After that, she _____ and leaves home at

_____ o'clock. Hayashi, however, does not go to _____ in

the morning and doesn't get up until _____ o'clock.

C. Listen to Heather Gibson talk about her daily activities and fill in the chart below with appropriate time or activities.

EXAMPLE: <u>6:00</u> get up

1. 7:00   _____

2. _____   go to Japanese class

3. _____   have lunch

4. afternoon   _____

5. _____   go home

6. 7:00   _____

7. from _____ to _____   study Japanese

8. 11:30   _____

D. Listen to Masao Hayashi and Linda Brown's conversation, and fill in the blanks.

    Useful Vocabulary

    shookai shimasu   *to introduce*

Brown is on her way to _____ to see her friend, Yukiko, who is

_____. Brown and Yukiko talk on

_____ very often. The language they use for communication is

_____. Brown invited Hayashi to come with her, because she wants

to _____ him to Yukiko. Hayashi

_____ the offer.

E. The student council is surveying college students about their daily lives. Listen and answer the questions based on your daily life.

1. _____

2. _____

3. _____

4. _____

5. _____

6. _____

7. _____

Talking About Future Activities and Events

A. The actress Himiko has a week off next week. Listen to Masaru Honda interviewing her about plans for that week and choose the activities Himiko will do over the following days.

    Useful Vocabulary

    oyasumi   *day off, holiday, vacation*
    rirakkusu   *relax*

1.	tomorrow:	a. go shopping	b. read	c. relax at home
2.	the day after tomorrow:	a. meet friends	b. clean the house	c. watch TV
3.	weekend:	a. go shopping	b. watch a movie	c. go to a party with friends
4.	the week after next:	a. shoot a movie	b. talk on TV	c. travel

B. Hitomi Machida and John Kawamura are talking about their weekend activities. Fill in the blanks in the following passage.

Kawamura usually _____ until noon on weekends. Then he watches

_____. Machida is inviting Kawamura to go to

_____ together. Kawamura thought Machida was

_____. Machida replied that

_____ and said that she would go with

_____.

C. Hitomi Machida left a message on your answering machine inviting you to go to a movie and a restaurant with her. Unfortunately. you can't accept her invitation because your friend is coming from San Francisco, and you are going to Disneyland together. Listen to Hitomi Machida's message and complete the following e-mail message in reply to her.

E-mail to Machida-san:

Machida-san, _____ arigatoo. Watashi mo eega wa

_____ desu. Demo, konshuu no

_____ , tomodachi ga S.F. kara kimasu. Sorede, tomodachi to

Disneyland e _____ masu. Demo, raishuu wa hima desu. Issho ni

eega e iki _____. Soshite, bangohan o

_____ mashoo.

Talking About Likes and Dislikes

A. Listen to the tape and write the words in English. They are English words pronounced in accordance with Japanese pronunciation. You will hear each word twice.

1. _____   4. _____

2. _____   5. _____

3. _____   6. _____

B. Listen to the description of Hitomi Machida and John Kawamura's likes and dislikes. Then mark each statement below with M if it is true of Machida and K if it is true of Kawamura.

1. _____ loves Japanese food.

2. _____ doesn't like fish.

3. _____ doesn't like fruit.

4. _____ likes sake.

5. _____ doesn't drink Coke.

6. _____ goes to see movies.

7. _____ likes rock'n'roll.

8. _____ doesn't like sports.

9. _____ watches soccer on TV.

10. _____ hates studying.

C. Listen as Masaru Honda, a reporter, interviews Himiko, a popular Japanese actress. After hearing the conversation, circle the things Himiko likes and cross out the things she doesn't like.

tennis   golf   studying   music   cooking   Italian cuisine   Japanese food   wine   beer

Writing Activities

Talking About Daily Activities

A. Here are eight statements about John Kawamura's typical day. Mark each one as either true (T) or false (F), basing your answers on Kawamura's schedule as given in Activity 1, p.33, of the main textbook.

1. _____ Gozen juuni-ji ni nemasu.

2. _____ Gogo san-ji ni koohii o nomimasu.

3. _____ Gogo shichi-ji ni bangohan o tabemasu.

4. _____ Gogo ichi-ji ni hirugohan o tabemasu.

5. _____ Gozen ku-ji ni gakkoo e ikimasu.

6. _____ Gozen roku-ji ni okimasu.

7. _____ Gozen roku-ji ni jogingu o shimasu.

8. _____ Gogo san-ji ni toshokan e ikimasu.

B. Categorize the following words related to daily activities (most of them appear on p.34 of the main textbook) according to when, how often, how long, and with whom you do them. Place each in appropriate box below.

a. okimasu	i. koohii o nomimasu	q. shinbun o yomimasu
b. asagohan o tabemasu	j. ocha o nomimasu	r. zasshi o yomimasu
c. hirugohan o tabemasu	k. biiru o nomimasu	s. ongaku o kikimasu
d. bangohan o tabemasu	l. uchi e kaerimasu	t. Nihongo o benkyoo
e. gakkoo e ikimasu	m. undoo o shimasu	shimasu
f. kurasu e ikimasu	n. jogingu o shimasu	u. nemasu
g. toshokan e ikimasu	o. terebi o mimasu	
h. shigoto ni ikimasu	p. hon o yomimasu	

1. Whether you do them or not

do	do not do

2. When you do them

in the A.M.	in the P.M.

3. How frequently you do them

only once a day	more than once a day

4. How long you spend doing them

more than 30 minutes per day	less than 30 minutes per day

5. Who you do them with

alone	with others

C. Complete the following dialogues, basing your answers on Kawamura's schedule in Activity 1, page 33, of the main textbook.

1. A: Kawamura-san wa nan-ji ni asagohan o tabemasu ka.

   B: _____ ni tabemasu.

2. A: Kawamura-san wa mainichi hon _____ yomimasu ka.

   B: Hai, yomimasu.

   A: Nan-ji ni _____ ka.

   B: _____ ni yomimasu.

3. A: Kawamura-san wa _____ ni koohii o nomimasu ka.

   B: _____ ni nomimasu.

4. A: Kawamura-san wa gogo san-ji goro doko e ikimasu ka.

   B: _____ e ikimasu.

5. A: Kawamura-san wa gogo hachi-ji _____ nani o shimasu ka.

B: Terebi o _____.

A: Gozen hachi-ji _____ nani o shimasu ka.

B: _____.

D. Match each clock with the time expression it represents.

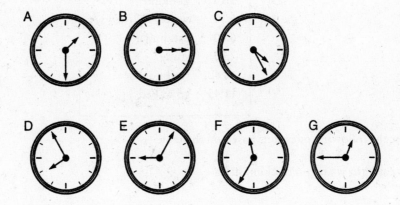

A   B   C

D   E   F   G

1. _____ san-ji juugo-hun

2. _____ yo-ji nijuugo-hun

3. _____ ku-ji go-hun

4. _____ shichi-ji gojuugo-hun

5. _____ juuni-ji yonjuugo-hun

6. _____ juuichi-ji sanjuugo-hun

7. _____ ichi-ji han

E. The table below is Ms. Suzuki's typical weekday schedule.

7:00	get up
7:20	eat breakfast
7:50	go to school
8:00	go to class
10:30	drink coffee
3:30	go to the library
5:15	go home
5:30	watch TV (news)
6:40	eat dinner
7:30	study
10:40	read books
11:45	go to bed

1.   Answer the following questions based on the table.

   a.   Suzuki-san wa nan-ji ni okimasu ka.

   _____

   b.   Asagohan o tabemasu ka.

   _____

   c.   Nan-ji ni terebi o mimasu ka. Dorama o mimasu ka.

   _____

   d.   Hirugohan o tabemasu ka.

   _____

   e.   Nan-ji ni nemasu ka.

   _____

2.   Make five questions concerning Suzuki-san's daily activities. If you are working with a partner, ask her/him your questions.

   a.   _____

   b.   _____

   c.   _____

   d.   _____

   e.   _____

F. Categorize the following words (they appear on pp.35 and 39 of the main textbook) according to when and how often you do them. Write in appropriate boxes.

a. tegami o kakimasu	h. shigoto ni ikimasu	m. undoo o shimasu
b. deeto o shimasu	i. tomodachi to	n. jogingu o shimasu
c. kaimono ni ikimasu	hanashimasu	o. terebi o mimasu
d. ichinichi-juu nemasu	j. Nihongo o renshuu	p. hon o yomimasu
e. tomodachi ni aimasu	shimasu	q. ongaku o kikimasu
f. kurasu e ikimasu	k. biiru o nomimasu	
g. toshokan e ikimasu	l. denwa o shimasu	

1. Whether you do them or not

do	do not do

2. When you do them

weekends	weekdays

3. How often you do them

very often	seldom do

G. Based on Dialogue 2 on page 37 of the main textbook, decide whether each of the following statement is true or not.

1. T F   Gibuson-san wa amari eega ni ikimasen.

2. T F   Hayashi-san wa yoku eega ni ikimasu.

3. T F   Gibson-san wa terebi o yoku mimasu.

4. T F   Hayashi-san wa terebi o amari mimasen.

H. Answer each of the following questions by telling if and how often you do the activities asked about.

Useful Vocabulary

mainichi *everyday*
yoku *frequently*
tokidoki *sometimes*
amari ⁓masen *not often*
zenzen ⁓masen *not at all*

1. Asagohan o tabemasu ka.

    _____

2. Gakkoo e ikimasu ka.

    _____

3. Kurasu ni demasu ka.

    _____

4. Hirugohan o tabemasu ka.

    _____

5. Kaimono ni ikimasu ka.

    _____

6. Koohii o nomimasu ka.

    _____

7. Toshokan e ikimasu ka.

    _____

8. Terebi o mimasu ka.

    _____

9. Ongaku o kikimasu ka.

_____

10. Benkyoo shimasu ka.

_____

11. Tegami o kakimasu ka.

_____

12. Deeto shimasu ka.

_____

13. Kaimono ni ikimasu ka.

_____

14. Tomodachi ni aimasu ka.

_____

15. Nihongo o renshuu shimasu ka.

_____

I. Answer the following questions regarding your own daily schedule.

1. Maiasa nan-ji ni okimasu ka.

_____

2. Maiasa jogingu o shimasu ka.

_____

3. Maiasa asagohan o tabemasu ka.

_____

4. Nan-ji ni gakkoo e ikimasu ka.

_____

5. Mainichi hirugohan o tabemasu ka.

_____

6. Mainichi kurasu ni demasu ka.

_____

7. Mainichi juusu o nomimasu ka.

_____

8. Mainichi toshokan e ikimasu ka.

_____

9. Mainichi terebi o mimasu ka.

_____

10. Mainichi undoo o shimasu ka.

_____

11. Mainichi hon o yomimasu ka.

_____

12. Nan-ji ni benkyoo shimasu ka.

_____

13. Doko de benkyoo shimasu ka.

_____

14. Mainichi nan-ji ni nemasu ka.

_____

J. Write up your own daily schedule in Japanese. If it's not the same every day, choose one day of the week. Write at least seven sentences.

1. _____

2. _____

3. _____

4. _____

5. _____

6. _____

7. _____

Talking About Future Activities

A. Suppose the following is a calendar for this month and today is the 7th. Connect the words below with the day(s) they represent.

Su	M	Tu	W	Th	F	Sa
		1	2	3	4	5
6	7	8	9	10	11	12
13	14	15	16	17	18	19
20	21	22	23	24	25	26
27	28	29	30	31		

saraishuu   kyoo   konshuu   ashita   asatte   raishuu

B. The following statements indicate what some people are going to do this weekend. Fill in the blanks with appropriate particles to make complete sentences. If you do not need any particle, write X.

1. Ooyama-san wa tegami _____ kakimasu.

2. Hayashi-san wa deeto _____ shimasu.

3. Hujii-san wa kaimono _____ ikimasu.

4. Kusakabe-san wa toshokan _____ ikimasu.

5. Watanabe-san wa ichinichijuu _____ nemasu.

6. Iwakawa-san wa tomodachi _____ aimasu.

7. Makita-san wa hon _____ yomimasu.

8. Ninomiya-san wa terebi _____ mimasu.

9. Nakadate-san wa eega _____ ikimasu.

C. Practice Dialogue 3 on page 39 of the main textbook by substituting different conversation partners and words. The last line by Machida may be omitted when the content is inappropriate.

1. YOSHIMURA: Tanabe-san wa _____

    shimasu ka.

    TANABE: (go on a date with Yamashita)

    _____

    _____ Yoshimura-san wa?

    YOSHIMURA: (sleep all day)

    _____

2. GOTOO: _____

    _____

    YOKOTA: (meet a friend)

    _____

    GOTOO: (practice Japanese)

    _____

    YOKOTA: ('You sure are diligent!')

    _____

3. TANIMURA: _____

    _____

    HOSHINO: (write letters)

    _____

    TANIMURA: (make phone calls)

    _____

4. (Make up your own dialogue)

    YOUR FRIEND: _____

    _____

    YOU: _____

    _____

    YOUR FRIEND: _____

D. What are you planning to do at the following times? Write a short sentence for each. If you do not have any plans, make some up, or, if you absolutely cannot think of anything, say, 'Mada wakarimasen (I don't know yet.).'

1. ashita

   _____

2. asatte

   _____

3. konshuu no shuumatsu

   _____

4. raishuu no shuumatsu

   _____

5. saraishuu no shuumatsu

   _____

Talking about Likes and Dislikes

A. Classify the following words into the categories below.

Nihon ryoori	aisutii	tenisu	juusu
biiru	wain	sanpo	suiee
huttobooru	sukii	kurashikku	paatii
bokushingu	rokku	Maikeru Jakuson	rappu
yasai	Itaria ryoori	burokkorii	Tom Kuruuzu
koohii	Juria Robaatsu	Huransu ryoori	aisu kuriimu
eega	sakkaa	Madonna	Mekishiko ryoori
jazu	sakana	benkyoo	koora
niku	kakuteru	piza	

Food items	
Alcoholic drinks	e.g. uisukii
Non-alcoholic drinks	
National cuisines	
Sports	
Music	
Celebrities	
Other	

B. Complete the following conversations by answering the questions, expressing your likes and dislikes. If the prescribed part of the answer does not match your personal taste, pretend that it does.

    EXAMPLE: A: Aisu kuriimu ga suki desu ka.
               B: Ee, toku ni chokoreeto aisu kuriimu ga suki desu.

1. A: Eega ga suki desu ka.

    B: Ee, toku ni _____ ga suki desu.

2. A: Undoo ga suki desu ka.

    B: Ee, toku ni _____ ga suki desu.

3. A: Yasai ga suki desu ka.

    B: Iie, kirai desu. Toku ni _____ ga kirai desu.

4. A: Benkyoo ga suki desu ka.

   B: Iie, kirai desu. Toku ni _____ ga kirai desu.

5. A: Nihon ryoori ga _____ desu ka.

   B: Ee, toku ni _____ ga suki desu.

6. A: Supootsu ga suki desu ka.

   B: Ee, toku ni _____ ga suki desu.

C. Trade workbooks with a classmate. Write questions in which you ask your classmate whether he or she likes a certain thing in each category given. Then take back your own workbook and answer the questions your classmate has written. Add things you especially like or dislike to your answer.

EXAMPLE: (music)
        Q: Kurashikku ga suki desu ka.
        A: Iie, kirai desu.
   or A: Hai, suki desu. Toku ni opera ga suki desu.

1. (sports)

   Q: _____

   A: _____

2. (Japanese food)

   Q: _____

   A: _____

3. (drink)

   Q: _____

   A: _____

4. (television program)

   Q: _____

   A: _____

5. (national cuisine)

   Q: _____

   A: _____

6. (celebrity)

   Q: _____

   A: _____

D. Work in pairs.

Step 1. List three items that you like for each category.

sports: _____ _____ _____

musicians (in English): _____ _____ _____

drinks: _____ _____ _____

Step 2. Ask your partner if s/he likes the items that you listed. Circle each item for which s/he says "yes."

Step 3. How many items did you circle? _____

Hiragana Practice

Practice the following hiragana.

	hiragana		practice							
kya	き	や*								
kyu	き	ゅ								
kyo	き	ょ								
sha	し	ゃ								
shu	し	ゅ								
sho	し	ょ								
cha	ち	ゃ								
chu	ち	ゅ								
cho	ち	ょ								

* Place these small characters in the lower left corner of the box when writing horizontally.

	hiragana		practice							
nya	に	ゃ								
nyu	に	ゅ								
nyo	に	ょ								
hya	ひ	ゃ								
hyu	ひ	ゅ								
hyo	ひ	ょ								
mya	み	ゃ								
myu	み	ゅ								
myo	み	ょ								
rya	り	ゃ								
ryu	り	ゅ								
ryo	り	ょ								
gya	ぎ	ゃ								
gyu	ぎ	ゅ								
gyo	ぎ	ょ								

	hiragana		practice								
ja	じ	ゃ									
ju	じ	ゅ									
jo	じ	ょ									
bya	び	ゃ									
byu	び	ゅ									
byo	び	ょ									
pya	ぴ	ゃ									
pyu	ぴ	ゅ									
pyo	ぴ	ょ									

Transcribe the following romanized words into hiragana.

1. kyaku (guest)

   _____

2. shuhu (housewife)

   _____

3. jisho (dictionary)

   _____

4. chokusetsu (direct)

   _____

5. hyaku (hundred)

6. shain (company employee)

   _____

7. kyoka (permission)

   _____

8. myaku (pulse)

   _____

9. ryokan (inn)

   _____

10. ryakusu (to abbreviate)

    _____

11. gyomin (fisherman)

    _____

12. gyaku (reverse)

    _____

13. kanja (patient)

14. joshi (particle)

    _____

Copy these words and read them out loud.

1. きゃくしゃ (passenger train)
2. じしょ (dictionary)
3. しゃくや (rented house)
4. しょり (management)
5. しゅみ (hobby)
6. きんぎょ (goldfish)
7. ひゃくにん (one hundred people)
8. しょみん (commoner)
9. ひしょ (secretary)
10. りょかん (inn)
11. じゅり (acceptance)
12. じゅけん (taking a test)
13. こんにゃく (a kind of vegetable)
14. さんびゃく (three hundred)
15. りゃくだつ (plunder)

The following romanized words all contain double vowels. Transcribe them into hiragana.

1. kooshoo (negotiation)

   _____

2. kyuuryoo (salary)

   _____

3. bangoo (number)

   _____

4. Eego (English)

   _____

5. Chuugoku (China)

   _____

6. bunpoo (grammar)

   _____

7. getsuyoobi (Monday)

   _____

8. tooi (far)*

   _____

9. kuuki (air)

   _____

10. heewa (peace)

    _____

11. ookii (big)*

    _____

12. huutoo (envelope)

    _____

13. kakee (family finance)

    _____

14. kyuuka (vacation)

    _____

15. okaasan (mother)

    _____

16. ojiisan (grandfather)

    _____

17. reezooko (refrigerator)

    _____

18. sensee (teacher)

    _____

19. utsukushii (beautiful)

    _____

20. gyuunyuu (cow's milk)

    _____

21. shuujin (prisoner)

    _____

22. meeshi (name card)

    _____

23. Tookyoo (Tokyo)

    _____

24. Oosaka (Osaka)*

    _____

25. suugaku (mathematics)

    _____

26. jinkoo (population)

    _____

27. hontoo (really)

    _____

28. doroboo (thief)

    _____

29. chiisai (small)

    _____

30. huuhu (married couple)

    _____

---

* In hiragana, these words are written with "oo" instead of the more common "ou."

Copy these words and read them out loud.

1. そうこ (warehouse)
2. こおり (ice)
3. こきょう (home town)
4. しょうにん (witness)
5. ぎゅうにく (beef)
6. おにいさん (older brother)
7. かいてい (revision)
8. くうき (air)

9. おねえさん (big sister)
10. まあまあ (so-so)
11. へいわ (peace)
12. ゆうそう (sending by mail)
13. くつう (pain)
14. ぜいせい (tax system)
15. かどう (flower arranging)

The following romanized words all contain double consonants. Transcribe them into hiragana.

1. hakkiri (clearly)

_____

2. tassha (healthy)

_____

3. sotto (softly)

_____

4. happyaku (eight hundred)

_____

5. kokki (national flag)

_____

6. shippai (failure)

_____

7. kitto (surely)

_____

8. kitte (stamp)

_____

9. kesshi (desperate)

_____

10. hossa (heart attack)

_____

11. sekkachi (impatient person)

_____

12. shakkin (debt)

_____

NOTE: The double *n* is not represented by the small つ. In this case, the first *n* is represented by ん.

shinnen (new year) → しんねん

hannin (criminal) → はんにん

konnyaku (devil's tongue, a kind of vegetable) → こんにゃく

kanna (carpenter's plane) → かんな

The following romanized words all contain double consonants. Transcribe them into hiragana.

1. sennin (one thousand people)

   _____

2. onna (woman)

   _____

3. sannen (three years)

   _____

4. tannoo (gall bladder)

   _____

5. mannen' yuki (perpetual snow)

   _____

6. kinniku (muscle)

   _____

7. sennuki (bottle opener)

   _____

8. donna (what kind)

   _____

Copy these words and read them out loud.

1. きって (stamp)
2. けっし (desperate)
3. いっち (concurrence)
4. すっかり (entirely)
5. はっぷん (eight minutes)
6. しゃっくり (hiccough)
7. ひょっとこ (jester)
8. ひっぱる (to pull)
9. かっこ (parentheses)
10. じっこう (implementation)
11. はっぱ (leaf)
12. けってい (decision)
13. さっか (writer)
14. やっと (at last)
15. とっきょ (patent)
16. せんにゅう (sneaking into)
17. たんに (merely)
18. ばんねんに (in one's late years)

Your instructor will read out one of the following pairs. Circle the one that is read.

1. おばさん (aunt)／おばあさん (grandmother)

2. おじさん (uncle)／おじいさん (grandfather)

3. しゅじん (master)／しゅうじん (prisoner)

4. せかい (world)／せいかい (correct answer)

5. こうこ (pickles)／こうこう (high school)

6. いっしょ (together)／いっしょう (lifetime)

7. りょうしゃ (both of them)／りょうしゃ (user)

8. じゅうか (gunfire)／じゆうか (liberalization)

9. しゅっちょう (business trip)／しゅちょう (claim)

10. きいた (I heard.)／きった (I cut it.)

Mind Stretchers

You want to buy a Japanese toy (*omocha*) for your friend's child in your home country. There are two stores, with signs reading おもちゃ and おもちや respectively, standing next to each other. Which store do you go in to buy the toy?

_____

When you got home, you found a message written by your younger host sister, who is six years old. It says "おかあさんといっしょにかどのびょういんにいきます." Which place at the corner did she go with her mother, hospital (*byooin*) or beauty parlor (*biyooin*)?

_____

There is a sign that says "どうぞごじゆうにおとりください" in front of candy samples at the candy shop. It means "Please feel free to take (one)." However, you saw one passer-by taking as many as fifty-two of them. Why do you think that this person did so?

_____

Tongue Twisters (はやくちことば)

Try to say the following as fast as you can!

1. なまむぎ、なまごめ、なまたまご
   (raw barley, uncooked rice, raw egg)
2. きゅうこう、とっきゅう、ちょうとっきゅう
   (express train, special express train, super-express train)
3. とうきょうとっきょきょかきょくきょくちょう
   (a bureau chief of the Tokyo Patent Office)
4. ぼうずがびょうぶにじょうずにぼうずのえをかいた
   (A priest drew a picture of a priest skillfully on the screen.)
5. かえるぴょこぴょこみぴょこぴょこあわせてぴょこぴょこむぴょこぴょこ
   (A frog hops and hops; three hops; he hops and hops; six hops altogether)
6. となりのきゃくは* よくかきくうきゃくだ
   (*This は should be read as *wa*. See the main textbook p.45 [Getting Started, Part 3.])
   (The guest next door is a guest who eats a lot of persimmons.)

Hiragana Derivations

Hiragana were originally derived from simplified, cursive forms of kanji.

		k	s	t	n	h	m	y	r	w	n
a	あ 安	か 加	さ 左	た 太	な 奈	は 波	ま 末	や 也	ら 良	わ 和	ん 尤
i	い 以	き 幾	し 之	ち 知	に 仁	ひ 比	み 美		り 利		
u	う 宇	く 久	す 寸	つ 川	ぬ 奴	ふ 不	む 武	ゆ 由	る 留		
e	え 衣	け 計	せ 世	て 天	ね 祢	へ 部	め 女		れ 礼		
o	お 於	こ 己	そ 曽	と 止	の 乃	ほ 保	も 毛	よ 与	ろ 呂	を 遠	

PART FOUR

Listening Comprehension Activities

Talking About Activities and Events in the Past

A. You are at a doctor's office because you have not been feeling well since last night. The doctor asks you several questions about what you did yesterday, so answer his questions.

1. _____

2. _____

3. _____

4. _____

5. _____

6. _____

7. _____

B. Listen to the conversation between Takeshi Mimura and Masao Hayashi as they talk about what they have done. Then complete each sentence by writing the initials of the person it refers to.

_____ went to school

_____ did not go to school

_____ went to see a movie yesterday

_____ saw a movie last week

_____ went to Japanese class at 9 o'clock

_____ studied at the library for three hours

C. Henry Curtis came home late last night. His girlfriend, Ms. Chen, is angry and asks him what he was doing yesterday. (Their common language is Japanese.) Listen to their conversation and fill in the blanks in the following passage.

> **Useful Vocabulary**
>
> uso   *a lie*
> yasumi   *closed*

Curtis claims that he was home at _____, but Chen knew it was

_____, because she called him at _____. Curtis says that he

was at the _____ until _____ to do

_____. Curtis tells her another lie, saying that he ate dinner at

_____ which was not open yesterday. Chen was upset and said

_____ to Curtis.

Inviting Someone to Do Something

A. A friend wants to do some things together with you. First, listen to his invitation and then accept or reject it, using the most appropriate expressions. You will hear the invitation twice.

> when you accept: Ee, ii desu ne.
> when you decline: Sumimasen ga, chotto--. *Or,* chotto....

1. _____

2. _____

3. _____

4. _____

5. _____

6. _____

7. _____

B. Listen to Masao Hayashi inviting Linda Brown to do some things with him. Then read the following statements and mark each one either true (T) or false (F).

1. _____ They had not seen each other for a while.

2. _____ Hayashi wants to have lunch with Brown tomorrow afternoon.

3. _____ Brown will be studying in the library today.

4. _____ They are going to drink coffee together tomorrow.

5. _____ Hayashi wants to go to a restaurant with Brown on Friday evening.

6. _____ It seems that Brown doesn't want to go out with Hayashi.

C. Suppose your favorite movie star is asking you to go out tonight. What would you answer to his or her questions? Write your answers, stating more than simply yes/no.

Useful Vocabulary

hima   *free time*
ato   *after*
ryoori   *dishes, food, cooking*

1. _____

2. _____

3. _____

4. _____

5. _____

6. _____

Talking About Weekly Schedules

A. Listen and number the days according to the order they are said on the tape.

1. Sun. _____, Mon. _____, Tues. _____, Wed. _____, Thu. _____, Fri. _____, Sat. _____

2. Sun. _____, Mon. _____, Tues. _____, Wed. _____, Thu. _____, Fri. _____, Sat. _____

3. Sun. _____, Mon. _____, Tues. _____, Wed. _____, Thu. _____, Fri. _____, Sat. _____

B. Masao Hayashi is inviting Mei Lin Chin to a party. Fill in the blanks in the following passage.

1. What kind of party is Hayashi going to have? _____

2. When is the party scheduled? _____

3. Who is coming to the party? _____

4. Can Chin go to the party? If not, why? _____

5. Does Chin like sukiyaki? _____

6. What is Hayashi going to ask Machida and the others about? _____

C. Fumiko Mori likes to take lessons. Listen to her talking about her schedule and fill in the chart.

Useful Vocabulary

narau   *to learn*
ocha   *tea ceremony*
ohana   *flower arranging*

Lessons

Sunday: _____

Monday: _____

Tuesday: _____

Wednesday: _____

Thursday: _____

Friday: _____

Saturday: _____

From next month: _____

Talking About the Weather

A. Henry Curtis is in Hokkaido, Japan. He is talking on the phone with his friend, Hitomi Machida, who is now in Okinawa, Japan. Fill in the blanks in the following passage.

In Okinawa, the weather today is very _____ and warm. But, it is

_____ in Hokkaido and is expected to _____ this afternoon.

Curtis doesn't mind _____, but Machida doesn't like it. Curtis says he spends rainy

days _____ing, etc.

B. Listen to the brief weather forecasts for the following four cities in Japan, and choose the appropriate forecast for each city.

1. Tokyo _____
2. Osaka _____
3. Sapporo _____
4. Fukuoka _____

a. fine/sunny
b. cloudy
c. rainy
d. snowy

Writing Activities

Talking about Activities and Events in the Past

A. Suppose the following is a calendar for this month and today is the 16th. Connect the words below with the day(s) they represent.

Su	M	Tu	W	Th	F	Sa
29	30	1	2	3	4	5
6	7	8	9	10	11	12
13	14	15	16	17	18	19
20	21	22	23	24	25	26
27	28	29	30	31	1	2

kyoo   kinoo   ashita   asatte   ototoi
saraishuu   konshuu   sensenshuu   raishuu   senshuu

B. Decide whether Mr. Kawamura did each of the following in the past (P), will do it in the future (F), or habitually does it (H).

EXAMPLE: __H__ Mainichi shichi-ji ni okimasu.

1. _____ Kinoo eega ni ikimashita.

2. _____ Ashita toshokan e ikimasu.

3. _____ Tokidoki gogo ni-ji ni hirugohan o tabemasu.

4. _____ Go-ji ni asagohan o tabemashita.

5. _____ Raishuu deeto o shimasu.

6. _____ Sensenshuu tegami o kakimashita.

7. _____ Asagohan wa zenzen tabemasen.

8. _____ Yoku terebi o mimasu.

9. _____ Asatte denwa o shimasu.

10. _____ Ongaku wa amari kikimasen.

C. Here are ten statements about Linda Brown's schedule for yesterday. Mark each one as either true (T) or false (F), basing your answers on Brown's schedule as given in Activity 1, p.51, of the main textbook.

1. _____ Gozen go-ji ni okimashita.

2. _____ Gozen hachi-ji ni koohii o nomimashita.

3. _____ Gogo go-ji han ni uchi ni kaerimashita.

4. _____ Gogo hachi-ji ni bangohan o tabemashita.

5. _____ Gozen juuichi-ji gojuppun ni hirugohan o tabemashita.

6. _____ Gozen hachi-ji ni gakkoo e ikimashita.

7. _____ Gozen roku-ji nijuugo-hun ni sanpo o shimashita.

8. _____ Gogo ku-ji yonjuppun ni hon o yomimashita.

9. _____ Gogo juuichi-ji sanjuppun ni nemashita.

10. _____ Gogo hachi-ji ni terebi o mimashita.

D. You are asking a friend several questions about what he or she did yesterday and last week. Which question word do you think you should use? Choose the best one for each blank from the box below. You may use the same word more than once.

nani/nan	nan-ji	itsu	dare	donna	doko

1. A: _____ ni okimashita ka.

   B: Ku-ji ni okimashita.

2. A: Kinoo no gogo _____ e ikimashita ka.

   B: Toshokan e ikimashita.

3. A: _____ eega ni ikimashita ka.

   B: Senshuu ikimashita.

4. A: _____ to eega o mimashita ka.

   B: Tanaka-san to mimashita.

5. A: _____ eega o mimashita ka.

   B: Komedii o mimashita.

6. A: Kinoo _____ ni bangohan o tabemashita ka.

   B: Roku-ji han ni tabemashita.

   A: _____ de tabemashita ka.

   B: Makudonarudo de tabemashita.

   A: _____ o tabemashita ka.

   B: Biggu makku o tabemashita.

E. Suppose you, instead of Hayashi as in Dialogue 1, p. 50 in the main textbook, are going to Dr. Miyai because of some problem with your stomach. Answer the doctor's questions truthfully. (If you do not know what the food you ate is called in Japanese, use English words.)

1. MIYAI: Kinoo no yoru nani o tabemashita ka.

   YOU: Eeto, _____ ka.

   _____ o tabemashita.

   MIYAI: Hoka ni wa?

   YOU: Eeto, _____ o tabemashita.

2. MIYAI: Ototoi no yoru nani o tabemashita ka.

   YOU: _____

   _____

   MIYAI: Hoka ni wa?

   YOU: _____

   _____

F. The table below depicts what Ms. Takahashi did yesterday.

7:10	got up
7:30	ate breakfast
7:50	wrote a letter
9:10	went shopping
10:30	drank coffee
12:00	came home
12:30	ate lunch
1:25	went to the library and studied Japanese
5:25	came home
5:30	watched TV (news)
6:30	went on a date
7:00	ate dinner
9:00	went to a movie
11:30	came home
12:10	went to bed

1. Answer the following questions based on the table.

   a. Takahashi-san wa asagohan o tabemashita ka. Nan-ji ni tabemashita ka.

   _____

   b. Gogo nani o shimashita ka. (list two things)

   _____

   c. Nan-ji kara nan-ji made, doko de Nihongo o benkyoo shimashita ka.

   _____

   d. Nan-ji kara nan-ji made deeto shimashita ka. Nani o shimashita ka.

   _____

   e. Gogo ichi-ji ni tegami o kakimashita ka. Nan-ji ni kakimashita ka.

   _____

   f. Gogo ku-ji kara nani o shimashita ka.

   _____

2. Make five questions concerning Takahashi-san's activities yesterday. If you are working with a partner, ask her or him to answer your questions.

    a. _____

    b. _____

    c. _____

    d. _____

    e. _____

G. Truthfully answer the following questions regarding your own daily schedule.

1. Kinoo nan-ji ni okimashita ka.

    _____

2. Kinoo asagohan o tabemashita ka.

    _____

3. Kinoo terebi o mimashita ka. (If yes: Nan-ji kara nani o mimashita ka.)

    _____

4. Kinoo wa gakkoo e ikimashita ka. (If yes: Nan-ji ni ikimashita ka.)

    _____

5. Kinoo tomodachi to hanashimashita ka. (If yes: Doko de hanashimashita ka.)

    _____

6. Kinoo Nihongo o benkyoo shimashita ka. (If yes: Nan-ji kara nan-ji made shimashita ka.)

    _____

7. Kinoo hon o yomimashita ka. (If yes: nani o yomimashita ka.)

    _____

8. Kinoo bangohan o tabemashita ka. (If yes: Doko de, dare to, nani o tabemashita ka.)

    _____

H. Write up your own schedule for yesterday. Then present the schedule in Japanese. Write *at least* seven sentences.

1. _____
2. _____
3. _____
4. _____
5. _____
6. _____
7. _____

Inviting Someone to Do Something

A. You'd like to invite several people to do something with you. How would you invite them? You'd like to invite:

1. Mr. Watanabe, to eat lunch with you.

   _____

2. Mr. Okada, to see a movie with you.

   _____

3. Mr. Ishii, to go shopping with you.

   _____

4. Mr. Garcia, to study Japanese with you.

   _____

5. Mr. Lee, to play tennis with you.

   _____

B. Suppose today is the 14th. In the blanks, write the date of the days listed below, referring to the calendar below.

1. konshuu no kin'yoobi _____

2. senshuu no mokuyoobi _____

3. raishuu no getsuyoobi _____

4. saraishuu no suiyoobi _____

5. sensenshuu no doyoobi _____

6. raishuu no nichiyoobi _____

7. konshuu no mokuyoobi _____

8. senshuu no suiyoobi _____

Su	M	Tu	W	Th	F	Sa
29	30	1	2	3	4	5
6	7	8	9	10	11	12
13	14	15	16	17	18	19
20	21	22	23	24	25	26
27	28	29	30	31	1	2

C. Suppose each of the following people has invited you to do something with him or her this weekend. How would you respond? You may accept or decline the invitation as long as you are polite.

1. (Ms. Igarashi, a classmate) Ashita, issho ni toshokan de benkyoo shimasen ka.

   _____

2. (Mr. Sato, a next-door neighbor) Ii otenki desu nee. Issho ni tenisu o shimasen ka.

   _____

3. (Ms. Koishi, Your Japanese teacher, to all the students in class) Doyoobi ni paatii o shimasen ka.

   _____

4. (Ms/r. Yamaji, a roommate, tired of cooking) Kyoo wa resutoran de bangohan o tabemasen ka.

   _____

5. (Ms. Wada, a friend) Nichiyoobi, issho ni kaimono ni ikimasen ka.

   _____

D. Pretend that you are going to ask someone out for a date. Think of a few things you'd like to do, and invite him or her to do these activities with you. You can make suggestions using, "sorekara" (*and then*) between two sentences.

_____

_____

_____

_____

Talking about Weekly Schedules

A. The following is your schedule for this week and the next. (Today is the 26th.) Answer the questions below based on this schedule.

The week of 24–30		
	A.M.	P.M.
24 Sun.	laundry	grocery shopping, tennis w/ Gwen
25 Mon.	class	lunch w/ Matt
26 Tu.	class	dinner w/ Taka
27 Wed.	class	project
28 Thu.	class	
29 Fri.	class	lunch w/ Taka, dinner w/ Sumiko
30 Sat.	project	tennis w/ Gwen

The week of 1–7		
	A.M.	P.M.
1 Sun.	laundry	grocery shopping, dinner w/ Gwen
2 Mon.	class	lunch w/ Matt
3 Tu.	bkft. with Matt	class
4 Wed.	class	
5 Thu.		lunch w/ Sumiko, class
6 Fri.	class	
7 Sat.		dinner & karaoke w/ Jose

1. Nan'yoobi ni tenisu o shimasu ka. Dare to shimasu ka.

    _____

2. Itsu Matto-san to hirugohan o tabemasu ka. Asagohan wa?

    _____

3. Raishuu wa nan'yoobi ni kaimono ni ikimasu ka. Konshuu wa?

   _____

4. Raishuu wa nan'yoobi ni karaoke ni ikimasu ka. Kin'yoobi wa?

   _____

5. Kayoobi wa itsu kurasu ni ikimasu ka. Suiyoobi wa?

   _____

6. Konshuu no kin'yoobi wa dare to bangohan o tabemasu ka. Hirugohan wa?

   _____

B. You've been invited to do some things. You can accept some, but you have to decline the other invitations because of other obligations. Complete the dialogues by studying your schedule above and following the example of Dialogue 4, p.55 in the main textbook. If you have to turn down the invitation, be sure to suggest an alternative day that is convenient for you.

1. YOSHIDA: Konshuu no kin'yoobi, issho ni yuugohan o tabemasen ka.

   YOU: Eeto, _____

   YOSHIDA: Sore wa zannen desu ne.

   YOU: Demo, _____

2. PARK: Konshuu no mokuyoobi no gogo, issho ni Nihongo o benkyoo shimasen ka.

   YOU: _____

   PARK: Soo desu ka. Zannen desu ne.

   YOU: _____

3. TOKUDA: Raishuu no kin'yoobi no gogo, issho ni tenisu o shimasen ka.

   YOU: _____

   TOKUDA: Jaa, mata kin'yoobi ni!

4. KAWAMOTO: Raishuu no getsuyoobi, issho ni hirugohan o tabemasen ka.

   YOU: _____

   PARK: Sore wa zannen desu ne.

   YOU: _____

Talking about Weather

A. The four adjectives used to describe temperature, **atsui**, **samui**, **atatakai**, and **suzushii**, are not exactly the same as, or as simple as, their dictionary translations, namely, *hot, cold, warm,* and *cool.* First of all, **atsui** and **samui** tend to have negative connotations, indicating discomfort from the heat or cold. On the other hand, **atatakai** and **suzushii** imply comfort, indicating that the temperature is either warmer (in winter) or cooler (in summer) than expected at that time of the year. Therefore, you do not say **atatakai** to describe a lower-than-usual and comfortable temperature in the summer, or **suzushii** to describe rather chilly, but not completely cold, weather in winter. **Atatakai** is also associated with spring, when it is no longer cold and uncomfortable. Once the temperature gets uncomfortably warm in spring, **atsui** should be used instead. Likewise, **suzushii** is associated with autumn, when it is no longer hot. When the temperature gets much lower, it becomes **samui**, and on certain days when it is warmer than expected, we can again use **atatakai** to indicate comfort.

Keeping the above in mind, decide which adjective one should use on the following days in Tokyo where there are four distinct seasons. Choose the most appropriate one and write it in the blanks.

1. _____ It's August and the temperature is 95F.

2. _____ It's January and it's snowing outside.

3. _____ It's September and the temperature is 75F.

4. _____ It's April and it's 75F.

5. _____ It's May but it's rainy out and it's only about 55F.

6. _____ It's February but it's about 65F today.

7. _____ It's July today but the temperature is only about 75F.

8. _____ It's May but it's 85F today.

9. _____ It's October but it's 35F today.

a. Kyoo wa atsui desu nee.
b. Kyoo wa samui desu nee.
c. Kyoo wa atatakai desu nee.
d. Kyoo wa suzushii desu nee.

B. How would you greet someone when the weather is:

1. very nice. _____

2. rather crummy. _____

3. raining cats and dogs. _____

4. snowing hard. _____

5. raining hard and windy, almost like a storm. _____

C. Write up a dialogue for the situation in each of the pictures. The two people in the pictures are encountering each other for the first time that day.

a.

_____

_____

_____

_____

b.

_____

_____

_____

_____

c.

_____

_____

_____

_____

d.

_____

_____

_____

_____

Katakana Practice

Practice katakana ア〜ノ.

	kata-kana	stroke order	trace	practice							
a	ア	ア	ア								
i	イ	イ	イ								
u	ウ	ウ	ウ								
e	エ	エ	エ								
o	オ	オ	オ								
ka	カ	カ	カ								
ki	キ	キ	キ								
ku	ク	ク	ク								
ke	ケ	ケ	ケ								
ko	コ	コ	コ								
sa	サ	サ	サ								
shi	シ	シ	シ								
su	ス	ス	ス								
se	セ	セ	セ								
so	ソ	ソ	ソ								

	kata-kana	stroke order	trace	practice							
ta	タ	タ	タ								
chi	チ	チ	チ								
tsu	ツ	ツ	ツ								
te	テ	テ	テ								
to	ト	ト	ト								
na	ナ	ナ	ナ								
ni	ニ	ニ	ニ								
nu	ヌ	ヌ	ヌ								
ne	ネ	ネ	ネ								
no	ノ	ノ	ノ								

Transcribe the following romanized words into katakana. Not all of them are in common use in Japan; some are found only in compound words or phrases.

1. aisu (ice)

2. ekisaito (excite)

3. kakao (cacao)

4. kiui (kiwi)

5. kisu (kiss)

6. Kenia (Kenya)

7. kokoa (cocoa)

8. sauna (sauna)

9. shinia (senior)

10. sukai (sky)

11. sonata (sonata)

12. tsuisuto (twist)

13. naito (night)

14. tekisuto (textbook)

15. Tai (Thailand)

16. Suisu (Switzerland)

17. oashisu (oasis)

18. saiki (psyche)

19. sukuea (square)

20. naisu (nice)

21. taitsu (tights)

22. tsuna (tuna)

23. katsu (cutlet)

24. sutoa (store)

Connect the hiragana and katakana that have the same pronunciation as shown in the example. Write the katakana equivalents for the remaining hiragana.

EXAMPLE:

あ お さ ち ね と て つ く い こ に た す え の ぬ し

ア ク ネ ス ヌ サ ト イ ツ シ コ エ

Practice katakana ハ〜ン.

	kata-kana	stroke order	trace	practice						
ha	ハ	ハ	ハ							
hi	ヒ	ヒ	ヒ							
hu	フ	フ	フ							
he	ヘ	ヘ	ヘ							
ho	ホ	ホ	ホ							
ma	マ	マ	マ							
mi	ミ	ミ	ミ							
mu	ム	ム	ム							
me	メ	メ	メ							
mo	モ	モ	モ							
ya	ヤ	ヤ	ヤ							
yu	ユ	ユ	ユ							
yo	ヨ	ヨ	ヨ							

	kata-kana	stroke order	trace	practice						
ra	ラ	ラ	ラ							
ri	リ	リ	リ							
ru	ル	ル	ル							
re	レ	レ	レ							
ro	ロ	ロ	ロ							
wa	ワ	ウ	ワ							
o	ヲ	ヲ	ヲ							
n	ン	ン	ン							

Transcribe the following romanized words into katakana.

1. Haichi (Haiti)

   _____

2. Huransu (France)

   _____

3. remon (lemon)

   _____

4. warutsu (waltz)

   _____

5. waihu (wife)

   _____

6. Kurisumasu (Christmas)

   _____

7. Washinton (Washington)

   _____

8. airon (iron)

   _____

9. Hawai (Hawaii)

   _____

10. Mekishiko (Mexico)

    _____

11. Sanhuranshisuko (San Francisco)

    _____

12. Irinoi (Illinois)

    _____

13. Mosukuwa (Moscow)

    _____

14. Shiatoru (Seattle)

    _____

Connect the hiragana and katakana that have the same pronunciation as shown in the example. Write the katakana equivalents for the remaining hiragana.

EXAMPLE:

は　る　ろ　ま　ふ　わ　す　む　ら　よ　れ　め　ぬ　ほ　み　ゆ　ん　え

ハ　メ　ワ　ラ　フ　ル　レ　ム　マ　ユ　ン　ホ

Practice katakana ガ～ボ.

	kata-kana	practice									
ga	ガ										
gi	ギ										
gu	グ										
ge	ゲ										
go	ゴ										
za	ザ										
ji	ジ										
zu	ズ										
ze	ゼ										
zo	ゾ										
da	ダ										
ji	ヂ										
zu	ヅ										
de	デ										
do	ド										

	kata-kana	practice								
ba	バ									
bi	ビ									
bu	ブ									
be	ベ									
bo	ボ									
pa	パ									
pi	ピ									
pu	プ									
pe	ペ									
po	ポ									

Transcribe the following romanized words into katakana.

1. gesuto (guest)

   _____

2. baiorin (violin)

   _____

3. posuto (mailbox)

   _____

4. daibingu (diving)

   _____

5. doraibu (drive)

   _____

6. Pepushi (Pepsi)

   _____

7. Supein (Spain)

   _____

8. parasoru (parasol)

   _____

9. bikini (bikini)

   _____

10. Guamu (Guam)

    _____

11. pinpon (ping-pong)

    _____

12. Bikutoria (Victoria)

    _____

Practice the following katakana.

	katakana		practice							
kya	キ	ャ*								
kyu	キ	ュ								
kyo	キ	ョ								
sha	シ	ャ								
shu	シ	ュ								
sho	シ	ョ								

* Place these small characters in the lower left corner when writing horizontally.

	katakana		practice							
cha	チ	ャ								
chu	チ	ュ								
cho	チ	ョ								
nya	ニ	ャ								
nyu	ニ	ュ								
nyo	ニ	ョ								
hya	ヒ	ャ								
hyu	ヒ	ュ								
hyo	ヒ	ョ								
mya	ミ	ャ								
myu	ミ	ュ								
myo	ミ	ョ								
rya	リ	ャ								
ryu	リ	ュ								
ryo	リ	ョ								
gya	ギ	ャ								
gyu	ギ	ュ								
gyo	ギ	ョ								

	katakana		practice								
ja	ジ	ャ									
ju	ジ	ュ									
jo	ジ	ョ									
bya	ビ	ャ									
byu	ビ	ュ									
byo	ビ	ョ									
pya	ピ	ャ									
pyu	ピ	ュ									
pyo	ピ	ョ									

Transcribe the following romanized words into katakana.

1. kyabetsu (cabbage)

   _____

2. Jakaruta (Jakarta)

   _____

3. gyanburu (gamble)

   _____

4. jointo (joint)

   _____

5. jogingu (jogging)

   _____

6. jazu (jazz)

   _____

7. shaberu (shovel)

   _____

8. chansu (chance)

   _____

9. Chunijia (Tunisia)

   _____

10. Ainshutain (Einstein)

   _____

11. amachua (amateur)

   _____

12. nyuansu (nuance)

   _____

The following romanized words all contain double vowels. Transcribe them into katakana. Remember that double vowels are indicated by writing a " — " after the vowel to be lengthened.

1. koohii (coffee)

    _____

2. hurawaa (flower)

    _____

3. meetoru (meter)

    _____

4. biiru (beer)

    _____

5. juusaa (juicer)

    _____

6. chaamingu (charming)

    _____

7. tawaa (tower)

    _____

8. shiitsu (sheet)

    _____

9. roodoshoo (road show)

    _____

10. nyuusu (news)

    _____

11. chiizu (cheese)

    _____

12. oobaakooto (overcoat)

    _____

13. konpyuuta (computer)

    _____

14. sukeeto (skate)

    _____

15. bareebooru (volleyball)

    _____

16. huriizaa (freezer)

    _____

The following romanized words all contain double consonants. Transcribe them into katakana. Remember that double consonants are indicated by writing a small " ッ " before the consonant to be doubled.

1. kukkii (cookie)

    _____

2. kyatto huudo* (cat food)

    _____

3. piinattsu (peanut)

    _____

4. torakku (track)

    _____

5. jaketto (jacket)

    _____

6. kicchin (kitchen)

    _____

7. middonaito shoo* (midnight show)

    _____

8. burudoggu (bulldog)

    _____

9. burijji (bridge)

    _____

10. happii (happy)

    _____

_____

* A midpoint (·) may be used between the first word and the second word. See the main textbook (Getting Started, p.73, Part 5).

What do the following katakana words mean?

1. チョコレート

   _____

2. オーストラリア

   _____

3. ドリーム

   _____

4. ミュージック

   _____

5. カセットテープ

   _____

6. レストラン

   _____

7. シャワー

   _____

8. チーズバーガー

   _____

9. セーター

   _____

10. バレーボール

    _____

11. ショッピング

    _____

12. アメリカ

    _____

13. デパート

    _____

14. カー・ステレオ

    _____

15. シャツ

    _____

16. ビジネス

    _____

17. クレジット・カード

    _____

18. テスト

    _____

19. インターネット

    _____

20. ポップ・アーチスト

    _____

21. プラットホーム

    _____

Name _____ Date _____ Class _____

Geography Test! What are these cities? Write the English name of each one.

アカプルコ	_____	ニューヨーク	_____
アテネ	_____	バンクーバー	_____
アトランタ	_____	バンコク	_____
カイロ	_____	パリ	_____
さっぽろ	_____	ヒューストン	_____
シアトル	_____	ペキン	_____
シカゴ	_____	ホノルル	_____
シドニー	_____	マドリード	_____
シンガポール	_____	モスクワ	_____
ストックホルム	_____	リオデジャネイロ	_____
ソウル	_____	ローマ	_____
とうきょう	_____	ロサンゼルス	_____
トロント	_____	ロンドン	_____

Look at the picture on page 9 in your textbook. Write each word in either hiragana or katakana, whichever is appropriate.

Read the following sentences out loud. Watch for particles!

1. こんにちは。
2. こんばんは。
3. としょかんへいきます。
4. きのうわたしはテレビでニュースをみました。
5. ブラウンさんといっしょににほんごをべんきょうしましたか。
6. オーストラリアはいまなんじですか。

Transcribe the following romanized sentences using hiragana and katakana as appropriate. Remember that particles 'e', 'o', and 'wa' are written with special hiragana (see main text, p. 45).

1. Doozo yoroshiku.

   _____

2. Shitsuree shimashita.

   _____

3. Buraun-san no denwa bangoo wa nan-ban desu ka.

   _____

4. Senshuu Nyuu Yooku e ikimashita.

   _____

5. Hayashi-san wa kinoo resutoran de Nihon ryoori o tabemashita.

   _____

6. Watashi wa aisu kuriimu to chokoreeto ga daisuki desu.

   _____

PART FIVE

Listening Comprehension Activities

Asking Location

A. Listen as customers ask for directions at the information counter in a department store, and find out where certain things are located. Then indicate each location by writing its number in the appropriate place on the drawing.

7階	
6階	
5階	
4階	
3階	restrooms
2階	shoe department
1階	book department

B. Hitomi Machida is showing John Kawamura the campus. Listen to their dialogue. Then read the statements and mark each one either true (T) or false (F).

1. _____ Professor Yokoi's office is on the third floor.

2. _____ The library is near Professor Yokoi's office.

3. _____ Kawamura is going to the library right now.

4. _____ The cafeteria is some distance from where they are.

5. _____ Kawamura thinks it is convenient having a coffee-stand near by.

Numbers from 21 to 10,000

A. Listen to the numbers on the tape and write them down. You will hear each number twice.

1. _____   6. _____

2. _____   7. _____

3. _____   8. _____

4. _____   9. _____

5. _____   10. _____

B. Here is Mr. Ezaki, the math teacher, again. This time he is going to give you more difficult math problems. Listen to him carefully and write down the answers. You will hear each problem twice.

1. $20 + 30 =$ _____

2. $55 +$ _____ $=$ _____

3. _____ $+ 6000 =$ _____

4. _____ $+$ _____ $=$ _____

5. _____ $-$ _____ $= 160$

6. $10000 -$ _____ $=$ _____

7. _____ $-$ _____ $=$ _____

8. _____ $-$ _____ $=$ _____

Asking About Existence

A. The following scene takes place at a busy kiosk in Tokyo Station. Listen to the conversation between the attendant and a series of four customers, and circle the items the kiosk has.

Coke   Yomiuri (Newspaper)   Mainichi (Newspaper)   umbrella

pantyhose   Lark (cigarette)   Hope (cigarette)

B. Listen as Henry Curtis and Hitomi Machida order lunch at a fast food restaurant near their university in Tokyo. Then read the statements below and mark them either true (T) or false (F).

Useful Vocabulary

oniku   *beef*

zenbu de   *in total*

1. _____ Curtis will have a fish sandwich for lunch.

2. _____ The restaurant does not have a chicken burger.

3. _____ Curtis will pay 420 yen in total.

4. _____ Pepperoni pizza costs 320 yen.

5. _____ Machida will pay 800 yen.

Asking About Price

A. Hitomi Machida is at a shop looking for a birthday present for her mother. Listen to the dialogue between Machida and the shop clerk, and write down the price for each item.

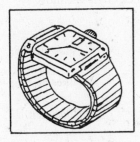 

B. Listen as Masao Hayashi and Linda Brown order lunch at a restaurant near their university in Tokyo. Then write the receipt for their order.

RECEIPT	
Order	**Price**
Gyuudon (Beef and noodle soup)	_____ yen
Ramen & _____	570 yen
Coffee	_____ yen
_____	150 yen
Total:	_____ yen
Tax (5%)	75 yen
Grand Total	1,565 yen

C. Listen to the questions or request on the tape and choose the most appropriate response from a–e. You will hear each question twice.

1. _____
2. _____
3. _____
4. _____
5. _____

a. 580-en desu.
b. Hotto o onegai shimasu.
c. Hai, arimasu.
d. Iie, kekkoo desu.
e. Hai, arigatoo gozaimasu.

Talking More About Likes and Dislikes

A. Listen as Linda Brown asks about some of her classmates' likes and dislikes. Then circle the most appropriate answer for each classmate.

1. a. prefers tennis   b. prefers soccer   c. likes both   d. likes neither

2. a. prefers rock'n' roll   b. prefers jazz   c. likes both   d. likes neither

3. a. prefers beer   b. prefers wine   c. likes both   d. likes neither

4. a. prefers video tapes   b. prefers movies   c. likes both   d. likes neither

5. a. likes both   b. likes neither   c. too hard to answer   d. doesn't like the question

B. Ms. Sato is looking for a date. Listen to her talk about her likes and dislikes, and answer true (T) or false (F) for each statement.

1. _____ Sato is an undergraduate student.

2. _____ She likes both study and sports.

3. _____ She prefers tennis to dance.

4. _____ She watched a movie with her roommate last weekend.

5. _____ She doesn't like either movies or TV dramas.

6. _____ She can fix both sukiyaki and sushi well.

Writing Activities

Asking Location

A. Complete the following dialogues between a customer and information clerk at Tobu Department Store. Refer to the store directory below, which tells the floor on which each item can be found.

8	hon
7	teeburu
6	seetaa
5	tokee/mannenhitsu
4	doresu
3	kasa
2	shatsu/sokkusu
1	kutsu/tebukuro
B1	aisu kuriimu

1. A: Sumimasen. Hon wa doko desu ka.

   B: Hai, hon wa _____ desu.

   A: A, soo desu ka. Arigatoo gozaimasu.

2. A: Sumimasen. Shatsu wa _____ desu ka.

   B: Hai, shatsu wa _____ desu.

   A: A, soo desu ka. _____ .

3. A: _____ . Teeburu wa

   _____ ka.

   B: Hai, _____ wa _____

   desu.

   A: A, _____ . Arigatoo gozaimasu.

4. A: _____ wa doko desu ka.

   B: _____ wa ik-kai desu.

   A: A, _____ .

5. A: _____ . Seetaa _____ .

   B: _____ .

B. Fill in the blanks to complete each dialogue based on the information in the diagram below. Measure distances from the university.

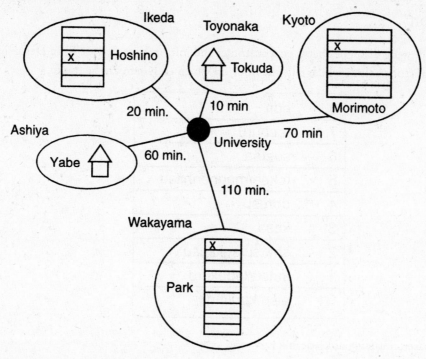

1. A: Paaku-san no uchi wa doko desu ka.

    B: _____ desu.

    A: _____ tooi desu ne.

    B: Ee.

    A: Apaato/manshon desu ka.

    B: Hai, _____ -kai desu.

2. A: Yabe-san no _____.

    B: _____ desu.

    A: _____ desu ne.

    B: _____.

    A: Apaato desu ka.

    B: _____.

3. A: Hoshino-san _____.

    B: _____.

    A: _____ desu ne.

B: Ee.

A: _____.

B: Ee, _____-kai desu.

4. A: Tokuda-san _____.

B: _____ desu.

A: _____ desu ne.

B: _____.

A: _____.

B: _____.

5. A: Morimoto-san _____.

B: _____.

A: _____.

B: _____.

A: _____.

B: _____.

C. Here is a diagram of Yasuda International's office. Answer the questions based on the diagram.

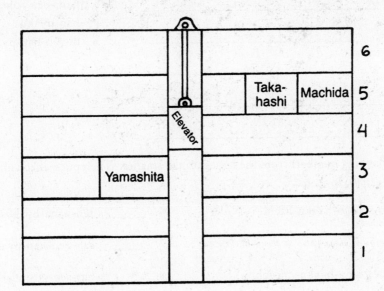

1. Machida-san no ofisu wa doko desu ka.

_____

2. Machida-san no ofisu wa Takahashi-san no ofisu ni chikai desu ka.

_____

3. Machida-san no ofisu wa Yamashita-san no ofisu ni chikai desu ka.

_____

4. Jaa, Yamashita-san no ofisu wa doko desu ka.

_____

5. Yamashita-san no ofisu wa erebeetaa kara tooi desu ka.

_____

Numbers from 21 to 10,000

A. Match each arithmetical expression with its correct answer.

1. 8300 + 382 = _____

2. 400 ÷ 50 = _____

3. 65 + 200 = _____

4. 40 × 70 = _____

5. 5000 − 3500 = _____

6. 9999 ÷ 3 = _____

7. 7700 − 10 = _____

8. 8 × 100 = _____

a. ni-hyaku-roku-juu-go
b. san-zen-san-byaku-san-juu-san
c. sen-go-hyaku
d. hachi
e. has-sen-rop-pyaku-hachi-juu-ni
f. nana-sen-rop-pyaku-kyuu-juu
g. hap-pyaku
h. ni-sen-hap-pyaku

B. Rank-order the following numbers from the largest to the smallest. Then put a check mark on any numbers that have a zero (0) in them.

1. _____ kyuu-sen-go-hyaku-hachi

2. _____ rop-pyaku-san-juu

3. _____ san-zen-yon-hyaku-juu-ichi

4. _____ kyuu-sen-go-juu-kyuu

5. _____ ni-hyaku-roku-juu-ichi

6. _____ sen-nana-hyaku-roku-juu-go

7. _____ san-zen-hap-pyaku-ichi

8. _____ has-sen-go-juu-roku

9. _____ go-sen-san-byaku-ni-juu

10. _____ hap-pyaku-san-juu-hachi

Asking About Existence/Asking About Price

A. Complete the following dialogues, basing your answers on the menu below.

```
                        Menyuu

        supagetti    750-en       koohii    380-en

        piza         500-en       juusu     400-en

        suupu        450-en       koora     750-en

        suteeki      890-en

        teriyaki     790-en

        sarada       370-en
```

1. A: Sumimasen. Supagetti wa arimasu ka.

    B: Hai, arimasu.

    A: Ja, supagetti o _____.

    B: Hai, _____-en desu.

2. A: Sumimasen. Piza wa _____ ka.

    B: Hai, _____.

    A: Ja, _____.

    B: Hai, _____ desu.

3. A: _____. Tenpura _____.

    A: Sumimasen ga, chotto…

    A: Ja, teriyaki wa _____ ka.

    B: Hai, _____.

    A: Ja, teriyaki _____.

    B: Hai, _____.

4   A: _____. Aisu kuriimu

        _____ arimasu ka.

     B: Sumimasen ga, _____...

     A: Ja, koohii _____ arimasu ka.

     B: Hai, arimasu.

     A: Ja, koohii _____ onegai shimasu.

     B: Hai, 380-_____ desu.

5.   A: _____. Hanbaagaa

        _____.

     B: _____.

     A: _____, suteeki wa arimasu ka.

     B: Hai, arimasu.

     A: _____.

     B: Hai, _____.

6.   A: Sumimasen. Piza wa arimasu ka.

     B: Hai, _____.

     A: Ikura desu ka.

     B: _____-en desu.

     A: Ja, piza to koohii o kudasai.

     B: Arigatoo gozaimasu. _____-en desu.

7.   A: Sumimasen. Suteeki _____.

     B: Hai, arimasu.

     A: _____ desu ka.

     B: _____-en desu.

     A: Ja, suteeki to sarada o _____.

     B: Arigatoo gozaimasu. _____ desu.

8. A: _____. Supagetti _____.

   B: Hai, _____.

   A: _____ ka.

   B: _____ desu.

   A: Ja, _____ suupu o kudasai.

   B: _____ desu

B. Choose the most appropriate response from the second column.

1. _____ Fisshubaagaa wa arimasu ka.   a. 350-en desu.
                                            b. Hai, arimasu.
2. _____ Ikura desu ka.   c. Kekkoo desu.
                                            c. Arigatoo gozaimasu. 350-en desu.
3. _____ Chiizubaagaa o onegai shimasu.

4. _____ Onion ringu wa ikaga desu ka.

C. In the first column are some statements and courtesy phrases, each of which could be the response to a question or courtesy phrase in the second column. Match them.

1. _____ 560-en desu.   a. Hon wa doko desu ka.
                                            b. Koora to keeki o onegai shimasu.
2. _____ Sumimasen ga chotto...   c. Tokee wa arimasu ka.
                                            d. Kono seetaa wa ikura desu ka.
3. _____ Arigatoo gozaimasu.   e. Daigaku ni chikai desu ka.
                                            f. Chin-san no uchi wa doko desu ka.
4. _____ Kekkoo desu.   g. Hurenchi hurai wa ikaga desu ka.

5. _____ Hai, hon wa yon-kai desu.

6. _____ Majiro desu.

7. _____ Iie, chotto tooi desu.

D. How would you ask or respond with the following to the waiter or waitress at a cafeteria.

1. If they have hamburgers

   _____

2. How much the hamburger is

   _____

3. To give you a hamburger and a coke

   _____

4. No, thank you.

   _____

E. Large department stores in Japan usually have a restaurant floor, sometimes containing several different restaurants. Window displays featuring realistic plastic models of the food allow shoppers to see what each restaurant offers. In some, after choosing what they want to eat, customers buy tickets for the food from the cashier, sit down at a table, and wait for the waiter or waitress to take their tickets and bring the meal.

Using this list as a menu, make up a conversation between yourself and the cashier. You may want to review Dialogues 3–5 in your main text before doing this exercise.

Situation: You're at a department store, and you want to have something to eat and something to drink. You go to the cashier at a restaurant and order food and a beverage. You find that the food item you want is sold out, so you choose something else. Then you order a drink and pay the correct amount.

Menyuu

karee raisu	580
sandoicchi	600
supagetti	550
oyako donburi	600
yakiniku teeshoku	900
okosama ranchi	450
sushi moriawase	800
raamen	500
tempura soba	750
koohii	300
koora	300
juusu	300
biiru	500
sooda	300

YOU: _____ 1

CASHIER: _____ 2

YOU: _____ 3

CASHIER: _____ 4

YOU: _____ 5

CASHIER: _____ 6

YOU: _____ 7

CASHIER: _____ 8

Talking More About Likes and Dislikes

A. You are working as a waiter or waitress at an inn which is known for its restaurant. Tonight's menu is written below. A Japanese couple is staying tonight, so you are going to try out your Japanese. Write up the questions you have to ask them, so you can practice before facing them.

Today's Menu

Appetizer (zensai)	Shrimp Cocktail or Smoked Salmon (shurinpu kakuteru) (sumooku saamon)
Soup	Home-made Onion Soup or Asparagus Soup (onion) (asuparagasu)
Salad	Garden Salad with French or Ranch Dressing (gaaden) (hurenchi) (ranchi) or Caesar Salad (shiizaa)
Entree (mein)	Teriyaki Steak or Roast Duck with Orange or Cherry Sauce (roosuto dakku) (cherii) (soosu)
Dessert (dezaato)	Chocolate Mousse or Strawberry Chiffon Pie (muusu) (sutoroberii shifon pai)
Coffee or Tea	

EXAMPLE: (appetizer)   Zensai wa shurinpu kakuteru to sumooku saamon to dochira ga ii desu ka
(which would you prefer).

1. (soup or salad, including a choice of soup or a choice of salad with a choice of dressing)

_____

_____

_____

2. (entree, including a choice of sauce if duck)

_____

_____

3. (dessert)

_____

4. (coffee or tea)

_____

B. How would you ask questions in each of the following situations? Choose the best question word from the box below and make up questions.

doko	nani/nan	nan-ji	ikura	dochira	dare

1. A customer wants to know how much a hamburger is.

_____

2. A new student on campus wants to know where the library is.

_____

3. A traveller who just arrived in Japan wants to know what time it is now in Tokyo.

_____

4. The waitress wants to know whether you want coffee or tea.

_____

5. An American student wants to know how ("what") you say "good morning" in Japanese.

_____

C. A computerized dating service owned by some Japanese university students sends a questionnaire to prospective clients in order to build up its data base. You come across the first page of such a questionnaire. Try filling it out just for fun!

Namae: _____

Denwa bangoo: _____

Please check the best answer for you. If you do not like either, please write in what you like instead.

1. Nihon ryoori to Amerika ryoori to dochira ga suki desu ka.
   _____ Nihon ryoori ga suki desu.
   _____ Amerika ryoori ga suki desu.
   _____ Dochira mo suki desu.
   _____ Dochira mo kirai desu.
   _____ Wakarimasen.

2. Jazu to rokku to dochira ga suki desu ka.
   _____ Jazu ga suki desu.
   _____ Rokku ga suki desu.
   _____ Dochira mo suki desu.
   _____ Dochira mo kirai desu.
   _____ Wakarimasen.

3. Supootsu to ongaku to dochira ga suki desu ka.
   _____ Supootsu ga suki desu.
   _____ Ongaku ga suki desu.
   _____ Dochira mo suki desu.
   _____ Dochira mo kirai desu.
   _____ Wakarimasen.

4. Terebi to eega to dochira ga suki desu ka.
   _____ Terebi ga suki desu.
   _____ Eega ga suki desu.
   _____ Dochira mo suki desu.
   _____ Dochira mo kirai desu.
   _____ Wakarimasen.

5. Ryoo to apaato to dochira ga suki desu ka.
   _____ Ryoo ga suki desu.
   _____ Apaato ga suki desu.
   _____ Dochira mo suki desu.
   _____ Dochira mo kirai desu.
   _____ Wakarimasen.

D. If you were to register for this service, what other likes and dislikes would you be interested in finding out from a prospective date? Make up three questions that you would like to see in the questionnaire. Then call up a classmate and ask those questions to see if your questions work, and write down his/her answers.

1. Q: _____

   A: _____

2. Q: _____

   A: _____

3. Q: _____

   A: _____

Katakana Practice

Practice the following katakana.

	katakana		practice							
ye	イ	エ*								
wi	ウ	ィ								
we	ウ	エ								
wo	ウ	ォ								
kye	キ	エ								
gye	ギ	エ								

---

* Place these small characters in the lower left corner when writing horizontally.

	katakana		practice								
kwa	ク	ァ									
kwi	ク	ィ									
kwe	ク	ェ									
kwo	ク	ォ									
she	シ	ェ									
che	チ	ェ									
tsa	ツ	ァ									
tse	ツ	ェ									
tso	ツ	ォ									
ti	テ	ィ									
di	デ	ィ									
dyu	デ	ュ									
tu	ト	ゥ									
du	ド	ゥ									
hye	ヒ	ェ									

	katakana		practice								
fa	フ	ァ									
fi	フ	ィ									
fyu	フ	ュ									
fe	フ	エ									
fo	フ	オ									
va	ヴ	ァ									
vi	ヴ	ィ									
vu	ヴ										
ve	ヴ	エ									
vo	ヴ	オ									

Transcribe the following romanized words into katakana.

1. faamu (farm)

   _____

2. chero (cello)

   _____

3. aamuchea (arm chair)

   _____

4. paatii (party)

   _____

5. faibu (five)

   _____

6. dyuo (duo)

   _____

7. sheebaa (shaver)

   _____

8. weeto (weight)

   _____

9. Fiijii (Fiji)

   _____

10. fensu (fence)

    _____

11. woo (war)

    _____

12. janbo (jumbo)

    _____

13. chekku (check)

    _____

14. jesuchaa (gesture)

    _____

15. sheekaa (shaker)

    _____

16. fooku (fork)

    _____

17. dyuetto (duet)

    _____

18. birudingu (building)

    _____

19. wokka (vodka)

    _____

20. Viinasu (Venus)

    _____

A friend from your home country is visiting you in Japan. You both get hungry and now are at a coffee shop called Yookoo for lunch. Since your friend does not know Japanese, you have to help him or her with the menu. Look at the menu on page 69 of your textbook and, using English, answer the following questions.

1. Your friend said that he/she is very hungry and can eat a lot. What would you suggest for him or her? Why?

   _____

   _____

2. You remember that your friend liked something that contained cinnamon when you were out together in your home country. What drink would you suggest?

   _____

3. You are going to have some dessert. Do they have cakes on the menu?

   _____

4. You may want to try something cold. Do they have ice cream?

   _____

5. What other food and drink will you order for yourself? Why?

   _____

   _____

6. Today is the first anniversary of the coffee shop "Yookoo" and they are giving a glass of juice (from the menu) to each customer free of charge. What kind would you like?

   _____

Katakana Derivations

The Katakana were created from parts of kanji.

		k	s	t	n	h	m	y	r	w	n
a	ア 阿	カ 加	サ 散	タ 多	ナ 奈	ハ 八	マ 末	ヤ 也	ラ 良	ワ 和	ン 尓
i	イ 伊	キ 幾	シ 之	チ 千	ニ 仁	ヒ 比	ミ 三		リ 利		
u	ウ 宇	ク 久	ス 須	ツ 川	ヌ 奴	フ 不	ム 牟	ユ 由	ル 流		
e	エ 江	ケ 介	セ 世	テ 天	ネ 祢	ヘ 部	メ 女		レ 礼		
o	オ 於	コ 己	ソ 曽	ト 止	ノ 乃	ホ 保	モ 毛	ヨ 興	ロ 呂	ヲ 乎	

Japanese Writing Systems

Now that you've learned hiragana and katakana, you can practice writing complete sentences. Transcribe the following sentences into hiragana. Particles you have to watch for are underlined.

1. Kyoo <u>wa</u> kin'yoobi desu ka. (Is today Friday?)

   _____

2. Juu-ji ni gakkoo <u>e</u> kimashita. (I came to school at ten.)

   _____

3. Nihongo <u>o</u> benkyoo shimashita. (I studied Japanese.)

   _____

4. Kore <u>wa</u> kyookasho desu. (This is a textbook.)

_____

5. Watashi <u>wa</u> Yamada-san to issho ni Sano-san no uchi <u>e</u> ikimashita. (I went to Mr. Sano's house with Mr. Yamada.)

_____

6. Yuugohan ni niku <u>o</u> tabemashita. (I ate meat for dinner.)

_____

Now watch out for katakana words, too!

7. Kinoo Rosanzerusu <u>e</u> ikimashita. (I went to Los Angeles yesterday.)

_____

8. Terebi de myuujikku shoo <u>o</u> mimashita. (I watched a musical show on TV.)

_____

9. Senshuu Chappurin no eega <u>o</u> mimashita. (I saw a [Charlie] Chaplin movie last week.)

_____

10. Satoo-san <u>wa</u> kafeteria <u>e</u> itte, remoneedo <u>o</u> nomimashita. (Mr. Sato went to the cafeteria and drank lemonade.)

_____

11. Supagetti <u>wa</u> arimasu ka. (Do you have spaghetti?)

_____

12. Buraun-san <u>wa</u> fisshubaagaa <u>o</u> tabemashita. (Mr. Brown ate a fish burger.)

_____

13. Depaato de aoi shatsu <u>o</u> kaimashita. (I bought a blue shirt at the department store.)

_____

14. Kyoo <u>wa</u> basu de gakkoo <u>e</u> kimashita. (I came to school by bus today.)

_____

15. Kawamura-san <u>wa</u> mainichi imooto-san to jogingu <u>o</u> shimasu. (Mr. Kawamura jogs with his sister every day.)

_____

CHAPTER **1**

CLASSMATES

クラスメート

Listening Comprehension Activities

Vocabulary and Grammar 1A: Nationalities and Languages

A. Using the following chart, answer the questions orally. You will then hear the correct answer. Then stop the tape and write the answer.

PERSON	COUNTRY	LANGUAGE
Mei Lin Chin	Taiwan	Chinese
Linda Brown	America	English
John Kim	Korea	Korean
Diana King	England	English
Antonio Coronado	Mexico	Spanish

1. _____

2. _____

3. _____

4. _____

5. _____

6. _____

7. _____

8. _____

9. _____

B. Listen as James White tells Hitomi Machida about his roommate and friend who appears in a photo. Then complete the Japanese summary by filling in the blanks.

コロナドさんは、ホワイトさんの ＿＿＿＿＿＿＿＿ です。アメリカ人

＿＿＿＿＿＿＿＿。コロナドさんは ＿＿＿＿＿＿＿＿ 人です。メキシコ人は

＿＿＿＿＿＿＿＿ を話します。モレノさんは、ホワイトさんの

＿＿＿＿＿＿＿＿ です。お国は ＿＿＿＿＿＿＿＿ です。フィリピン人は

＿＿＿＿＿＿＿＿ を話します。

C. Listen to the passage about Maria Nakajima, and find out what languages each member of her family speaks. Then complete the following sentences by filling in the names of the appropriate languages.

Useful Vocabulary: それで *therefore*, さらに *furthermore*, おとうさん *father*, そして *and*, おかあさん *mother*, でも *but*, ～語で *in the ～ language*

1. Maria speaks ＿＿＿＿＿＿＿＿＿＿＿＿＿＿＿＿＿＿＿＿＿＿＿＿＿＿＿＿.

2. Maria's mother speaks ＿＿＿＿＿＿＿＿＿＿＿＿＿＿＿＿＿＿＿＿＿＿＿＿＿.

3. Maria's father speaks ＿＿＿＿＿＿＿＿＿＿＿＿＿＿＿＿＿＿＿＿＿＿＿＿＿.

4. Maria speaks in ＿＿＿＿＿＿＿＿＿＿＿＿＿＿＿＿＿＿＿＿＿ with her father.

5. The three of them speak in ＿＿＿＿＿＿＿＿＿＿＿＿＿＿＿＿＿＿＿ together.

Vocabulary and Grammar 1B: Personal Information

A. Listen to the tape and circle the appropriate meaning of each word.

1. name   academic year   address

2. hometown   telephone number   address

3. living place   academic year   country

4. address   university   hometown

5. living place   graduate school   professor

B. The interviewer is asking three different students, Yu, Tanaka, and Kim, for information about their personal lives. You will hear each question twice. Write the letter of the best answer in the blank corresponding to the question.

ユー

1. _____
2. _____
3. _____

YU

a. 224-5679 です。
b. ユーです。
c. ちゅうごくです。
d. 日本語です。

たなか

1. _____
2. _____
3. _____

TANAKA

a. めいじ大学です。
b. とうきょうです。
c. 学生です。
d. 二年生です。

キム

1. _____
2. _____
3. _____

KIM

a. キムです。
b. かんこく語と日本語です。
c. かんこくです。
d. 大学いん生です。

C. Listen as four students introduce themselves. Then complete each of the following sentences by writing in the initials of the person best described by the statement.

(LJ: Louis Johnson, PY: Peggy Yu, SL: Susanna Lopez, JW: Julie Wilson)

EXAMPLE: LJ is from New York.

1. _____ is from Hong Kong.
2. _____ lives in Los Angeles.
3. _____ lives in San Francisco.
4. _____ is from Spain.
5. _____ is a sophomore.
6. _____ is a senior.
7. _____ is a graduate student.
8. _____ 's phone number is 849-3215.
9. _____ studies Chinese.

D. Listen to the conversation between Andy Lin and Maria Nakajima at a party. Then determine whether each of the following statements is true (T) or false (F).

Useful Vocabulary: 本とう <ruby>ほん</ruby> *true*

1. _____ Nakajima and Lin have met each other before.

2. _____ They are from San Jose.

3. _____ They are both students.

4. _____ They go to the same school.

5. _____ They take Japanese class at the same time.

E. Mr. Yamada and Ms. Yamaguchi are having a blind date. Listen to their conversation and choose the most appropriate answer from a, b, and c.

Useful Vocabulary: かいしゃ *company*, うた *song*

1. What does Yamada do for Toyota?
   a. marketing   b. car designing   c. test driving

2. Why does Yamada say "thank you" to Yamaguchi?
   a. because she has a Toyota
   b. because her car is designed by Yamada
   c. because she praised Yamada's work

3. What is he working on now?
   a. designing a new car   b. test driving   c. car sales

4. How long does he work each day?
   a. from morning till noon
   b. from noon till night
   c. from morning till night

5. What does he like to do on weekends?
   a. work
   b. drink with his co-corkers
   c. go singing with his co-workers

6. What kind of music do you think Yamada likes?
   a. classical   b. American popular   c. jazz

F. Professor Yokoi has too many students in her 12:00 class, and is trying to move some of them to her 9:00 class. Now she is looking at the class roster. Listen to her, and write what classes each person is taking at 9:00.

Kawamura: _____   Curtis: _____

Brown: _____   Mimura: _____

Chin: _____

G. Listen to Hitomi Machida and John Kawamura talk about the classes they are going to take next quarter. Then, in the list below, find the classes each of them is going to take.

      Useful Vocabulary: むずかしい *hard,* がんばります *I'll do my best*

      List of the classes: Japanese, mathematics, linguistics, Spanish, physical education, sociology, music, engineering

Machida: _____

Kawamura: _____

H. Your friend from Japan, who just arrived in the U.S. yesterday, needs to fill out the application form for English as a Second Language class. Since she knows very little English, she needs your help. Fill out the form for her, based on the conversation on the tape.

      Useful Vocabulary: じゅうしょ *address*

Application for ESL

Name: _____

Date of Birth: _____ Age: _____

Address: _____

_____

Tel. number: _____

Name of school in Japan: _____

Major: _____

How well can you speak English? ☐ not at all ☐ a little ☐ well ☐ very well

---

Vocabulary and Grammar 1C: Around Campus

A. Hitomi Machida is working at the information booth at her college. Listen as she answers questions, and circle the places that are mentioned which can be found on campus.

library, bookstore, cafeteria, dormitory, bank, ATM, laboratory, teacher's office

B. Linda Brown is giving a campus tour to a Japanese student. Listen to their conversation and identify the buildings that are on her college campus.

Useful Vocabulary: みえません *can't be seen*

1. The big building is _____.

2. The white building is _____.

3. A building that can't be seen from here is _____.

4. The beautiful blue building is _____.

5. The building beyond the student center is _____.

C. After the Japanese class, Hitomi Machida is asking her classmates where they are going so that she can find someone who can return her book to the library. Identify where each person is going after listening to their conversation.

Useful Vocabulary: かりたい *want to borrow*, かえしてくれませんか *Will you return it for me?*

1. _____ Curtis
2. _____ Hayashi
3. _____ Kawamura
4. _____ Mimura
5. _____ Gibson
6. _____ Machida

    a. language lab
    b. work
    c. library
    d. class
    e. teacher's office
    f. gym
    g. home
    h. friend's house

D. A lot of things have accumulated in the East Asian Language Department's lost-and-found collection, and Professor Yokoi is trying to find the owners. Listen as she asks her students about the various objects, and then match each object with its owner.

Useful Vocabulary: 日本せい *made in Japan,* キーホルダー *key chain,* わすれもの *things left behind,* わすれものをしないでください *Please do not forget to take your belongings with you.*

1. _____ umbrella

2. _____ key chain

3. _____ dictionary

4. _____ mechanical pencil

5. _____ magazine

6. _____ textbook

a. Kawamura
b. Curtis
c. Kim
d. Chin
e. Gibson
f. Brown

E. Listen to Mei Lin Chin's monologue, and rank the days of the week from her favorite to the day she likes least.

Favorite day of the week

#1 _____

#2 _____

#3 _____

#4 _____

#5 _____

#6 _____

Day of the week she likes least: _____

F. Listen to the tape and fill out the class schedule of Hitomi Machida, Mei Lin Chin, and Henry Curtis in English.

	MACHIDA	CHIN	CURTIS
Monday			
Tuesday			
Wednesday			
Thursday			
Friday			

G. Mei Lin Chin is trying to choose a language class. Listen to the conversation between Chin and Curtis. Then fill in the blanks by choosing the most appropriate words.

Useful Vocabulary: こうこう *high school*

1. Curtis is taking a _____ class.
   a. French   b. German   c. Chinese

2. The first-year French class meets _____ days a week.
   a. 2   b. 3   c. 5

3. Chin doesn't want to take French class because _____.
   a. she doesn't like the language
   b. of the homework assignments
   c. the class meets every day

4. Chin studied German _____.
   a. two years ago   b. at high school   c. her sophomore year

5. Curtis recommends that Chin take a second-year German class because _____.
   a. it is more interesting than French
   b. Chin is already fluent in German
   c. the class doesn't meet every day

Kanji Practice and Exercises

1	日	日	ニチ、ニ-、ニッ-　day; sun; Sunday; (as prefix or suffix) Japan ジツ、ひ、-び、-ぴ　sun; day -か　day			
	日本：にほん／にっぽん　(Japan) 日よう日：にちようび　(Sunday)			日		
2	本	本	ホン、-ボン　book; this; main; origin ホン、-ポン、-ボン　(counter for long objects) もと　origin			
	日本：にほん／にっぽん　(Japan) 本：ほん　(book)			本		
3	学	学	ガク、ガッ-　learning, study; science; (as suffix) -ology まな-ぶ　to learn, to study 学生：がくせい　(student)			
	学年：がくねん　(academic year) 学こう：がっこう　(school)			学		
4	生	生	セイ　birth; life; (as suffix) student ショウ　birth; life　う-まれる　to be born い-きる　to live なま　raw			
	なま　raw 学生：がくせい　(student) 一年生：いちねんせい　(1st year student) ～生まれ：～うまれ　(one who was born in ～)			生		
5	名	名	メイ、ミョウ、な　name; reputation; fame			
	名し：めいし　(name card) 名まえ：なまえ　(name)			名		

6	年 年	ネン、とし　year; age				
	学年：がくねん　(academic year) 一年生：いちねんせい　(1st year student) 二年生：にねんせい　(2nd year student) 年：とし　(age)		年	年		
7	何 何	カ、なに、なん　what				
	何：なに　(what) 何ご：なにご　(what language) 何ですか：なんですか　(What is it?) 何年生：なんねんせい　(what year student)		何	何		
8	月 月	ゲツ、ゲッ-　moon; month; Monday ガツ、ガッ-　month つき　moon; month				
	月よう日：げつようび　(Monday) 何月生まれ：なんがつうまれ　(What month were 　you born in?) 一月：いちがつ　(January)		月	月		
9	人 人	ジン、ニン、ひと、-びと　man; person; human being				
	日本人：にほんじん　(a Japanese) アメリカ人：あめりかじん　(an American) この人：このひと　(this person)		人	人		
10	一 一	イチ、イツ、イッ-、ひと-つ、ひと-　one; a				
	一月：いちがつ　(January) 一年生：いちねんせい　(1st year student) 一さい：いっさい　(one year old) 一つ：ひとつ　(one year old/one item)		一	一		
11	二 二	ニ、ふた-つ、ふた-　two				
	二月：にがつ　(February) 二年生：にねんせい　(2nd year student) 二つ：ふたつ　(two years old / two items)		二	二		

12	三	三	サン、みっ-つ、み-、み-つ　three

三月：さんがつ　(March)
三年生：さんねんせい　(3rd year student)
三つ：みっつ　(three years old / three items)

13	四	四	シ、よっ-つ、よ-、よ-つ　four

四月：しがつ　(April)
四年生：よねんせい　(4th year student)
四さい：よんさい　(four years old)
四つ：よっつ　(four years old / four items)

14	五	五	ゴ、いつ-つ、いつ-　five

五月：ごがつ　(May)
五さい：ごさい　(five years old)
五つ：いつつ　(five years old / five items)

15	六	六	ロク、ロッ-、リク、むっ-つ、む、む-つ、むい-　six

六月：ろくがつ　(June)
六さい：ろくさい　(six years old)
六つ：むっつ　(six years old / six items)
六かい：ろっかい　(sixth floor)

16	七	七	シチ、なな-つ、なな、なの-　seven

七月：しちがつ　(July)
七さい：ななさい　(seven years old)
七つ：ななつ　(seven years old / seven items)

17	八	八	ハチ、ハッ-、やっ-つ、や、や-つ、よう-　eight

八月：はちがつ　(August)
八さい：はっさい　(eight years old)
八つ：やっつ　(eight years old / eight items)
八かい：はっかい　(eighth floor)

18	九	九	ク、キュウ、ここの-つ、ここの- nine			
	九月：くがつ　(September) 九さい：きゅうさい　(nine years old) 九つ：ここのつ　(nine years old / nine items) 九じ：くじ　(nine o'clock)			九	九	
19	十	十	ジュウ、ジッ、ジュッ、とお、と- ten			
	十月：じゅうがつ　(October) 十さい：じゅっさい／じっさい　(ten years old) 十：とお／じゅう　(ten years old / ten items) 十かい：じゅっかい／じっかい　(tenth floor)			十	十	
20	百	百	ヒャク、ヒャッ-、-ビャク、-ピャク　hundred; many			
	百さい：ひゃくさい　(100 years old) 三百：さんびゃく　(three hundred) 六百：ろっぴゃく　(six hundred) 八百：はっぴゃく　(eight hundred)			百	百	
21	先	先	セン、さき　earlier; ahead; priority; future; destination; the tip ま-ず　first			
	先生：せんせい　(teacher)			先	先	
22	話	話	ワ、はなし　conversation, story はな-す　speak			
	話します：はなします　((will) speak)			話	話	
23	語	語	ゴ　word, term; language かた-る　talk, relate かた-らう　converse			
	日本語：にほんご　(Japanese language) えい語：えいご　(English language) スペイン語：すぺいんご　(Spanish language) 何語：なにご　(what language)			語	語	

24	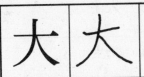	ダイ　big, large, great; (short for 大学, university); (as suffix) the size of... タイ、おお-きい、おお-　big, large, great おお-いに　very much, greatly

| 大学：だいがく　(university)
大学生：だいがくせい　(university student)
大すきです：だいすきです　(I like it very much)
大きい：おおきい　(big) | 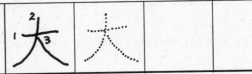 | | |

Kanji Exercises

A. Match each kanji or kanji compound with the letter of its closest English equivalent.

1. 日本 ＿＿＿

2. 何 ＿＿＿

3. 五十九 ＿＿＿

4. 学生 ＿＿＿

5. 名 ＿＿＿

6. 四月生まれ ＿＿＿

7. 人 ＿＿＿

8. 百 ＿＿＿

9. 一年生 ＿＿＿

10. 学年 ＿＿＿

11. 本 ＿＿＿

12. 月よう日 ＿＿＿

13. 七さい ＿＿＿

14. 十八 ＿＿＿

15. 日本人 ＿＿＿

16. 日本語 ＿＿＿

17. 話 ＿＿＿

18. 大 ＿＿＿

a. freshman/first year student　b. seven years old　c. person　d. hundred　e. book
f. Japanese person　g. fifty-nine　h. name　i. academic year　j. what　k. Monday　l. Sunday
m. sixteen　n. eighteen　o. eighty　p. Japan　q. to speak　r. student　s. Japanese language
t. one who was born in April　u. big

B. Write hurigana for each kanji or kanji compound. Pay special attention to the changes in pronunciation that may occur when kanji are compounded.

1. 何月生まれ
   _____

2. 名まえ
   _____

3. 九月
   _____

4. 日本人
   _____

5. 八さい
   _____

6. 学生
   _____

7. 月よう日
   _____

8. 百さい
   _____

9. 大きい
   _____

10. 四月
    _____

11. 一年生
    _____

12. 日よう日
    _____

13. 四さい
    _____

14. 六月
    _____

15. 一さい
    _____

16. 三つ
    _____

17. 五つ
    _____

18. 十二月
    _____

19. 九さい

_____

21. 何語

_____

23. 大学

_____

20. 話します

_____

22. 四年生

_____

24. 先生

_____

C. Fill in the blank with the kanji for the word or phrase that is spelled out in hiragana under the line.

1. わたしは＿＿＿＿＿＿＿＿＿＿ではありません。
   にほんじん

2. ＿＿＿＿＿＿＿＿＿＿ですか。
   なんねんせい

3. お＿＿＿＿＿＿＿＿＿＿まえは＿＿＿＿＿＿＿＿＿＿ですか。
   な　　　　　　　　　　　　　なん

4. わたしは＿＿＿＿＿＿＿＿＿＿ ＿＿＿＿＿＿＿＿＿＿まれです。
   ごがつ　　　　　　　　　　う

5. カワムラさんは＿＿＿＿＿＿＿＿＿＿です。
   がくせい

   たなかさんは＿＿＿＿＿＿＿＿＿＿です。
   せんせい

6. これはだれの＿＿＿＿＿＿＿＿＿＿ですか。
   ほん

7. コンピュータのクラスは＿＿＿＿＿＿＿＿＿＿よう＿＿＿＿＿＿＿＿＿＿です。
   げつ　　　　　　　　　　び

8. チンさんは＿＿＿＿＿＿＿＿＿＿を＿＿＿＿＿＿＿＿＿＿しますか。
   なにご　　　　　　　　　　はな

D. Write the kanji for the numbers one to ten and for the number one hundred in order.

1 ＿＿＿ 　　　4 ＿＿＿ 　　　7 ＿＿＿ 　　　10 ＿＿＿

2 ＿＿＿ 　　　5 ＿＿＿ 　　　8 ＿＿＿ 　　　100 ＿＿＿

3 ＿＿＿ 　　　6 ＿＿＿ 　　　9 ＿＿＿

Kanji in Everyday Life

1. You are getting hungry while strolling around in a tourist town in Japan. Then you see a sign 日本一うまいそば at a *soba* (buckwheat noodle) shop. Would you like to try to eat that *soba*? Why or why not?

_____

2. You enter the above *soba* shop and are ready to order a bowl of *zaru soba* (served on a bamboo plate). But you notice that there are two kinds of *zaru-soba*: ざるそば and ざるそば大盛. When you are very hungry, which would you like to order? Why?

   _____

3. Your host father, who is a company employee, took you out to a movie that you wanted to see. Now he is at the ticket window, where the prices are written vertically as follows:

   大人 二〇〇〇円
   大学生 一五〇〇円
   小中高生 一〇〇〇円

   He bought two tickets for you and himself. How much did he pay? What does 大人 mean?

   _____

4. You received a new year's card from your Japanese friend. It says 本年もどうぞよろしく. What does 本年 mean?

   _____

5. Yamato is the old name of Japan and it is often written this way 大和. What do you think 和語 means?

   _____

6. You went to an English conversation school in Japan to apply for a part-time teaching position and you were given a form to fill in. There is a column 生年月日 in the form. What do you need to write in that column?

   _____

Writing Activities

Vocabulary and Grammar 1A: Nationalities and Languages

A. Fill in the blanks with the name of the language or languages spoken by each group of people. If you don't know, look up the information in an encyclopedia or world almanac.

　　EXAMPLE: 日本人は_____を話します。→ 日本人は日本語を話します。

1. アメリカ人は_____を話します。

2. メキシコ人は_____を話します。

3. カナダ人は＿＿＿＿＿＿＿＿を話します。

4. イギリス人は＿＿＿＿＿＿＿＿を話します。

5. ちゅうごく人は＿＿＿＿＿＿＿＿を話します。

6. ブラジル人は＿＿＿＿＿＿＿＿を話します。

7. アルゼンチン人は＿＿＿＿＿＿＿＿を話します。

B. Read the five self-introductions below and try to figure out which country each person comes from. If you aren't sure, check a world almanac or atlas to see if you have guessed correctly. Then write in the names of the countries in the blanks below.

a. わたしはホセ・ガルシアです。しゅっしんはアカプルコです。スペイン語を話します。

b. わたしはパウロ・イソベです。みなみアメリカのしゅっしんです。ポルトガル語を話します。日本語もちょっと話します。

c. わたしはキャシー・マイヤーです。フランス語もえい語も話します。しゅっしんはケベックです。

d. わたしはポーン・サナサフォーンです。タイ語とフランス語を話します。しゅっしんはチェンマイです。

e. わたしはジャミラ・サイードです。フランス語とアラビア語を話します。しゅっしんはアフリカです。

Answers:　　a. ＿＿＿＿＿＿＿＿＿＿　c. ＿＿＿＿＿＿＿＿＿＿　e. ＿＿＿＿＿＿＿＿＿＿

　　　　　　b. ＿＿＿＿＿＿＿＿＿＿　d. ＿＿＿＿＿＿＿＿＿＿

C. John Kawamura was very busy yesterday. Choose one word from each column to form a meaningful activity that he might have done, and fill in the blanks to make sentences.

COLUMN A	COLUMN B
~~Japanese language~~	cassette tape
university	library
TV	~~homework~~
friend	letter
Japanese	ice cream
Baskin Robbins	news

EXAMPLE: <u>日本語の</u> <u>しゅくだいを</u> しました。

1. _____ _____ よみました。

2. _____ _____ みました。

3. _____ _____ ききました。

4. _____ _____ いきました。

5. _____ _____ たべました。

Vocabulary and Grammar 1B: Personal Information

A. The lefthand column is a list of academic subjects. The righthand column is a list of words or expressions associated with these subjects. Match the items by writing the appropriate letter in the blank.

1. _____ すう学
2. _____ けいざい学
3. _____ おんがく
4. _____ か学
5. _____ ぶん学
6. _____ がいこく語

a. クラシック
b. スペイン語
c. ヘミングウェイ
d. $x2 - 4\sqrt{3}x + 12 \leqq 0$
e. マルクス
f. H_2O, CO_2

B. Match each question in the left-hand column with the most appropriate response in the right-hand column.

1. _____ お名まえは何ですか。
2. _____ ごしゅっしんはどこですか。
3. _____ おすまいはどこですか。
4. _____ おいくつですか。
5. _____ おでん話ばんごうは何ばんですか。
6. _____ 何月生まれですか。
7. _____ せんこうは何ですか。
8. _____ 何年生ですか。

a. アメリカです。
b. たなかひろしです。
c. 12月生まれです。
d. 1年生です。
e. 大学のりょうです。
f. 21 さいです。
g. コンピュータ・サイエンスです。
h. 03-456-9872 です。

C. Here is a list of five of John Kawamura's friends from his Japanese class. Write a brief paragraph about each of them, using all the personal information in the chart.

NAME	HOMETOWN	YEAR	AGE	BIRTH MO.	MAJOR	LANGUAGES
1. Kim (キム)	Seoul, Korea (ソウル)	soph.	20	May	economics	Korean
2. Vogel (フォーゲル)	Geneva, Switzerland (ジュネーブ、スイス)	jr.	22	April	engineering	German French
3. Lim (リム)	Kota Bharu, Malaysia (コタバル、マレーシア)	jr.	23	July	sociology	English Chinese Malay (マレー語)
4. Perez (ペレス)	Dallas, Texas (ダラス、テキサス)	fresh.	18	October	math	English Spanish
5. Cohen (コーエン)	Des Moines, Iowa (デモイン、アイオワ)	grad.	28	Sept.	history	English

1. _____
_____
_____

2. _____
_____
_____

3. _____
_____

4. _____
_____
_____

5. _____
_____
_____

D. Now write paragraphs about two of your own friends, following the same format as exercise C.

1. _____

_____

_____

2. _____

_____

_____

Vocabulary and Grammar 1C: Around Campus

A. Complete the following conversations, using the information in this directory for a campus building.

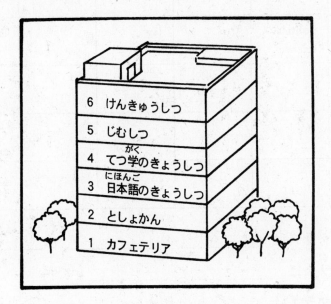

1. A: すみません。としょかんはどこですか。

   B: あのビルの _____ かいです。

2. A: すみません。日本語のきょうしつはどこですか。

   B: あのビルの _____ かいです。

3. A: _____。じむしつはどこですか。

   B: あのビルの _____。

4. A: すみません。＿＿＿＿＿＿＿＿ はどこですか。

   B: あのビルの 1 かいです。

5. A: ＿＿＿＿＿＿＿＿。＿＿＿＿＿＿＿＿ はどこですか。

   B: ＿＿＿＿＿＿＿＿ 6 かいです。

B. Look over this student's weekly schedule. Then fill in the blanks in the Japanese statements with the appropriate days of the week.

	SUN	MON	TUE	WED	THURS	FRI	SAT
9:00		French		French		French	
10:00			history		history		
11:00		political science		law		economics	
12:00							
1:00							
2:00							

1. フランス語のクラスは ＿＿＿＿＿＿ と ＿＿＿＿＿＿ と ＿＿＿＿＿＿ です。

2. れきし学のクラスは ＿＿＿＿＿＿ と ＿＿＿＿＿＿ です。

3. けいざい学のクラスは ＿＿＿＿＿＿ です。

4. せいじ学のクラスは ＿＿＿＿＿＿ です。

5. ほう学のクラスは ＿＿＿＿＿＿ です。

C. This was Linda Brown's weekly class schedule the semester before she came to Japan. Read over the schedule and answer the questions below in Japanese.

Linda Brown's Schedule

TIME	MON	TUE	WED	THURS	FRI
8:00		Japanese history		Japanese history	
9:00					
10:00	Japanese	Japanese	Japanese	Japanese	Japanese
11:00					
12:00	Chinese history		Chinese history		Chinese history
1:00	Japanese literature	Japanese	Japanese literature	Japanese	
2:00					
3:00	Korean history		Korean history		Korean history

1. ブラウンさんの日本のれきしのクラスは何よう日の何じですか。

_____

2. ちゅうごくのれきしのクラスはかよう日ともくよう日ですか。

_____

3. 日本語のクラスは11じですか。何よう日ですか。

_____

4. ほかに (other than that)、ブラウンさんは何をべんきょうしています (is studying) か。

_____

5. それは何よう日の何じですか。

_____

6. ブラウンさんのせんこうは何ですか。 (Take a guess.)

_____

D. Fill in the blanks with the appropriate particle and complete the conversation.

A: これは、だれ＿＿＿＿¹ しゃしんですか。

B: それ＿＿＿＿²、わたし＿＿＿＿³ しゃしんです。

A: この人＿＿＿＿⁴、だれですか。

B: その人＿＿＿＿⁵、まちださんです。

A: まちださん＿＿＿＿⁶ 日本人です＿＿＿＿⁷。

B: はい、日本人です。

A: まちださん＿＿＿＿⁸、大学＿＿＿＿⁹ 先生です＿＿＿＿¹⁰。

B: いいえ、先生＿＿＿＿¹¹ ありません。学生です。

A: まちださん＿＿＿＿¹² せんこう＿＿＿＿¹³ 何ですか。

B: 日本ぶん学です。

A: そうですか。わたし＿＿＿＿¹⁴ せんこう＿＿＿＿¹⁵ 日本ぶん学です。

B: そうですか。

E. Using these question words, make up questions that would yield the following answers, and write them in the blanks marked "A."

何　だれ／どなた　いつ　どこ／どちら　何さい　いくら

1. A: ＿＿

   B: これはコンピュータです。

2. A: ＿＿

   B: あのビルのです。

3. A: ＿＿

   B: 大の先生です。

4. A: ＿＿

   B: 日よう日にテニスをします。

5. A: ＿＿

   B: 2,000 えんです。

6. A: ＿＿

   B: 30 さいです。

7. A: _____

    B: とうきょうのごしゅっしんです。

8. A: _____

    B: それはブラウンさんのテレビです。

9. A: _____

    B: わたしのせんこうはしゃかい学です。

10. A: _____

    B: それはか学の本です。

Chapter 1 Review

A. You have just arrived at the Japanese university where you will be studying for a year. The international students' office has introduced you to a Japanese student, so you can ask whatever questions you have concerning the university. Now both of you are standing at the entrance to the campus. Try asking the Japanese student the following questions. Then, if you have other questions of your own, ask them, too.

1. You'd like to know what that building is. _____

    _____

2. Point to a statue and find out who it is. _____

    _____

3. Ask who your Japanese teacher is. _____

    _____

4. Find out how old your Japanese teacher is. _____

    _____

5. You'd like to know where students eat lunch. _____

    _____

6. Find out how much lunch at the cafeteria costs. _____

    _____

7. You'd like to know what time classes start in the morning. _____

    _____

8. Ask in which building Japanese classes are held. _____

_____

9. Ask in which direction the library is._____

_____

10. Find out what students do on Saturday afternoons._____

_____

11. Your own questions: _____

_____

B. You would like to find a Japanese pen pal, so you write up an advertisement to send to a popular Japanese magazine. Include the following information:

1. Your name.
2. Your age
3. The name of your school and where it is located.
4. What year you are in school.
5. Your major.
6. Where you are from.
7. What languages you speak.
8. Your likes and dislikes.
9. What kind of person you would like to write to.

   Useful Vocabulary: …をさがしています *I am looking for...*

Begin your advertisement in the following way:

ペンパルをさがしています。 _____

_____

_____

_____

_____

_____

_____

CHAPTER **2**

MY TOWN

わたしの町

Listening Comprehension Activities

Vocabulary and Grammar 2A: Commuting

A. Listen to the statements on the tape and fill in the blanks with the words stated. Then write the meaning of the word in English in the blanks at the end of each sentence.

1. わたしのうちは学こうに_____ です。 _____

2. スーパーはうちから_____ です。 _____

3. うちから学こうまで_____ でいきます。 _____

4. りょうから大学まで_____ いきます。 _____

5. _____ はとてもべんりです。 _____

   うちから大学まで_____ です。 _____

6. うちから学こうまで_____ で１０分、そして、バスで

   _____ です。 _____ _____

B. Listen to the description of residence and commuting conditions of three people, and fill in the blanks in the following chart.

NAME/TYPE OF RESIDENCE	PLACE	PROXIMITY TO SCHOOL	TRANSPORTATION METHOD	TIME REQUIRED
Kawamura's apartment	Shinjuku	( )	subway	( )
Hayashi's apartment	( )	( )	( )	10 minutes
Prof. Yokoi's house	Yokohama	( )	( ) and ( )	( ) and ( )

C. John Kawamura is considering moving to a new apartment, so he goes to look at several apartments now available. Listen to the conversation he has with the manager of one apartment building. Then complete the English summary by filling in the blanks.

Useful Vocabulary: いろいろな *various*, みせ *store*

Kawamura wonders whether the apartment is _____. The manager tells him

that it is _____ minutes by _____ and _____ minutes on foot. The next thing Kawamura asks is

whether there is a _____ nearby. There is, and it is only _____ minutes away on foot. The

_____, which is only _____ minutes away, is even closer. The manager tells Kawamura that the

apartment is really very convenient, because it is also very close to a _____ and a

_____.

D. Listen to the questions about your living environment, teachers, and friends on the tape and circle the most appropriate adjective(s).

1. (大きい　　小さい)

2. (あたらしい　ふるい)

3. (きれい　　きたない)

4. (しずか　　うるさい)

5. (有名　　しずか　　にぎやか　　あたらしい　　ふるい)

6. (おもしろい　つまらない)

7. (やさしい　　おもしろい　　しずか　　うるさい)

8. (やさしい　　おもしろい　　しずか　　うるさい)

E. You will hear descriptions of the cities of Kyoto and Sapporo. Choose the words that describe each city from the list below.

Useful Vocabulary: 山 *mountains*, うみ *sea*

1. Kyoto: _____

2. Sapporo: _____

   a. big
   b. old
   c. new
   d. beautiful
   e. a big population
   f. quiet
   g. lively
   h. old buildings
   i. famous
   j. close to the sea and mountains

F. Listen as Masao Hayashi asks Antonio Coronado about his home in Mexico. Then mark each statement either true (T) or false (F).

Useful Vocabulary: どうして *why,* 〜から *because* 〜

1. _____ Coronado comes from a small town near Mexico City.

2. _____ There is a train between the capital and Coronado's hometown.

3. _____ Coronado likes his town because it is quiet.

4. _____ He does not like the town he lives in now because it is too noisy.

5. _____ The town Coronado lives in is a college town.

G. Linda Brown is enjoying her vacation in Paris. She called her friend from Paris but her friend was not home. So she left a voice mail message. Listen to her message and complete the summary, filling in the blanks.

Linda is now in Paris which she thinks is _____. The city is _____ but the air is

_____. Yesterday she had dinner at one of the restaurants on the Champs-Élysées, which was

_____ but _____ and had good service. In particular, her waiter at the restaurant was

_____. Today she is going to the Louvre. It is _____ minutes by subway from her hotel. She

thinks the subway system in Paris is _____.

Vocabulary and Grammar 2B: Neighborhood

A. Linda Brown is asking her classmates, Takeshi Mimura, Henry Curtis, and John Kawamura, what kind of places are near their houses. Listen to the conversation, and indicate whose houses are close to the following places. Write the initials of their names. (M: Mimura, C: Curtis, K: Kawamura)

school _____   convenience store _____

bookstore _____   shops   _____

bank _____   restaurants   _____

park _____

B. Listen to the conversation between Linda Brown and Hitomi Machida about Machida's neighborhood, and fill in the blanks to complete the summary.

Machida's house is _____ minutes on foot to _____ station. It is close to a school and a

_____. Also, there are _____, supermarket, and _____

nearby. So it is a little _____.

C. John Kawamura is at a realtor looking for a new apartment. Listen to the conversation between John and the realtor, and fill in the chart below about the apartment mentioned:

	exist?	where?/proximity
Train station:	_____	_____
Convenience store:	_____	_____
Supermarket:	_____	_____
Laundromat:	_____	_____
Japanese-style eating place ("shokudoo"):	_____	_____
Coffee shop:	_____	_____
Family restaurant:	_____	_____

D. Masao Hayashi is from a small town. Listen to Masao's monologue and indicate what are in his village. If there is/are any of the facilities listed below, write in how many there are of each.

Useful Vocabulary: むら *village,* すんでいる人 *people who are living (there),* つくる *to make/build*

Department store	_____	Convenience store	_____
Shops	_____	Japanese-style eating place ("shokudoo")	_____
Restaurant	_____	Game center	_____
Movie theater	_____	Golf course	_____
Elementary school ("shoogakkoo")	_____	Junior high school ("chuugakkoo")	_____
High-rise building ("koosoo biru")	_____	Highway ("koosoku dooro")	_____

E. Listen to the following description of the Green Building, and then indicate on the drawing what is located on each floor.

Useful Vocabulary: ち下 *underground, basement,* おいしい *delicious*

6	
5	
4	
3	
2	
1	
B₁	

Vocabulary and Grammar 2C: Buildings and Places Around Town; Counting

A. Listen to the definition of each building or place and circle the most appropriate word for the definition.

Useful Vocabulary: たべもの *food,* いろいろな *various,* たくさん *a lot,* かりられます *can borrow,* できます *can*

1. こうえん えいがかん ぎんこう
2. 学こう びょういん ホテル
3. げきじょう てら ぎんこう
4. ブティック スーパー ガソリンスタンド
5. としょかん はくぶつかん びじゅつかん

B. Listen to these five short conversations and choose the appropriate answer in the parentheses.

1. There is a (movie theater / art museum) over there.

2. There is a (restaurant / restroom) in the neighborhood, but it is (clean / not clean).

3. There (is / is not) a Japanese (bank / school) nearby, but there is an American (bank / school), where the service is (good / not good).

4. There is a (hospital / museum) in Brown's town, where Brown (goes / does not go) often.

5. The hotel is located (5 minutes on foot / 15 minutes by train) from the place. And the restaurant in the hotel serves (inexpensive and tasty / expensive but not tasty) food.

C. Listen to the conversation between Takeshi Mimura and Linda Brown. Then complete the English summary by filling in the blanks.

Useful Vocabulary: げきじょう *theater*

Mimura and Brown are looking at a _____, which is a splendid-looking building. It is a

_____. _____ often goes there. There will be an

_____ held at the place next week. Brown seems a little worried about the price of the

_____, but Mimura offers to _____ it for her. So they decide to go there next

_____.

D. Listen as Professor Yokoi tells her students where to sit. Then write each name in the appropriate position on the seating chart. The top of the chart corresponds to the front of the room. NOTE: There will be three empty seats for three absent students.

	Professor	

E. Listen as a passerby asks Hitomi Machida for directions to the department store and the bank. Then write D after the phrases that describe the department store, and B after the phrases that describe the bank.

1. In front of the train station: _____

2. A tall building: _____

3. A small building: _____

4. between a coffee shop and a bookstore: _____

F. Listen to Henry Curtis describing his neighborhood. Then show the location of each building listed by writing its number in the appropriate blank space on the map.

1. my house   2. coffee shop   3. game center   4. supermarket   5. post office   6. sushi shop

G. Count the following items up to 10, counting on where the tape leaves off.

1. pieces of paper   2. pencils   3. oranges   4. books   5. shops

H. Hitomi Machida is stopped in front of a department store by a strange man who pretends to be a policeman. Listen as the man orders her to show him the contents of her backpack. Then indicate the quantity of each item he finds in her backpack.

> **Useful Vocabulary:** さいふ *wallet,* けいかん *policeman,* みせて下さい *Please show me.,* あけて下さい *Please open.*

How many of these items did Machida have in her backpack?

_____ book(s)   _____ pen(s)   _____ handkerchief(ves)   _____ credit card(s)

I. Listen as Heather Gibson talks about her roommate, Martha. Then list the things that each of them has.

Martha has: _____

Heather has: _____

J. Listen as Masaru Honda interviews the entertainer, Himiko. Then complete the English summary by filling in the blanks.

Himiko has _____ houses, and the closest one from here is in _____. In that house, there are

_____ rooms and _____ bathrooms. There are also _____ restaurants in which there are _____

cooks and _____ waiters. But after all, Himiko's favorite food is _____ and _____.

K. Listen as Linda Brown talks about the students in Professor Yokoi's class and write down the number of the students who best fit the following descriptions:

1. study hard: _____

2. don't like Professor Yokoi: _____

3. don't like the Japanese class: _____

4. don't like homework: _____

5. like homework: _____

6. like kanji: _____

7. don't like sushi: _____

8. like tempura and sukiyaki: _____

1 間 間	カン interval; space; between; (as suffix) between, among あいだ interval (of space or time); between, among ま space, room; pause; a rest (in music); time; leisure; luck etc.	
一時間：いちじかん　(one hour) ＡとＢの間：ＡとＢのあいだ　(between A and B)	間 間	
2 半 半	ハン、パン half, semi-; odd number なか-ば half, semi-; middle, halfway; partly	
一時間半：いちじかんはん　(one hour and a half) 四時間半：よじかんはん　(four hours and a half) 九時半：くじはん　(9:30)	半 半	
3 上 上	ジョウ upper, top, above, first volume / part (of a series); top-grade, etc. うえ up, upper part, top, above, over, besides, on top of, upon, etc. あげ-る to raise, to lift up, give　あが-る to rise; to go / come etc. 上：うえ　(upper part)	
本の上：ほんのうえ　(on the book)	上 上	
4 下 下	カ、ゲ low, lower, below, under ／した lower part, below, under さ-げる to hang, to suspend, to lower ／さ-がる to hand down, to fall, to go / come down; to step back ／くだ-る to come / go / get / step down; to be given; to be less than ／くだ-る／くだ-さる to bestow etc.	
下：した　(lower part) テレビの下：てれびのした　(under the TV) ち下てつ：ちかてつ　(subway) かいて下さい：かいてください　(Please write.)	下 下	
5 分 分	フン、-プン (of time / arc) ブン portion　ブ portion, 1 percent わ-ける／かつ divide, share, distinguish　わ-かれる be separated わ-かる understand	
一分：いっぷん　(one minute) 五分：ごふん　(five minutes) 十分：じゅっぷん／じっぷん　(ten minutes) 分かります：わかります　(understand)	分 分	

6	小 小	ショウ、ちいさい、こ-、お- little, small
	小さい：ちいさい　(small) 小さくありません：ちいさくありません　(is not small)	小 小
7	好 好	コウ、この-む、す-く、す-き good, favorite, all right; to like, be fond of …ず-き lover / fan of…
	好きです：すきです　((I) like (it)) 大好きです：だいすきです　((I) like (it) very much)	好 好
8	町 町	チョウ street, town; (unit of length, about 109 m); (unit of area, about 0.992 ha) まち street, town; quarter
	わたしの町：わたしのまち　(my town) 町田さん：まちださん　(Mr./Ms. Machida)	町 町
9	田 田	デン、た、-だ rice field, paddy
	山田さん：やまださん　(Mr./Ms. Yamada) 町田さん：まちださん　(Mr./Ms. Machida) 田中さん：たなかさん　(Mr./Ms. Tanaka)	田 田
10	左 左	サ、ひだり left
	左：ひだり　(left) 山田さんの左：やまださんのひだり　(the left of Mr./Ms. Yamada)	左 左
11	右 右	ウ、ユウ、みぎ right
	右：みぎ　(right) 山田さんの右：やまださんのみぎ　(the right of Mr./Ms. Yamada)	右 右

12	中	中	チュウ middle; China ／-チュウ、-ジュウ throughout, during, within なか inside; midst 中ごく：ちゅうごく (China)				
	中：なか (inside) 一日中：いちにちじゅう (all day)			中	中		
13	外	外	ガイ outside, external, foreign ／ゲ outside, external そと outside, outdoor ／ほか other ／はず-す to take off, to remove, to disconnect, to miss, etc.／はず-れる to come / slip off, to be / get out of place, to be disconnected, etc.				
	外：そと (outside) レストランの外：れすとらんのそと (outside the restaurant)			外	外		
14	前	前	ゼン、まえ before, front				
	前：まえ (front / before) 名前：なまえ (name) 大学の前：だいがくのまえ (in front of the university) ご前：ごぜん (A.M.)			前	前		
15	後	後	ゴ、のち after, later ／コウ、うし-ろ behind あと afterward, subsequent, back retro- おく-れる to be late, to lag behind				
	後ろ：うしろ (behind) たてものの後ろ：たてもののうしろ (behind the building ご後：ごご (P.M.)			後	後		
16	時	時	ジ、とき、-どき、と (as in とけい) time, hour				
	一時間：いちじかん (one hour) 何時ですか：なんじですか (What time is it?) 時けい：とけい (clock / watch)			時	時		
17	山	山	サン、-ザン、やま mountain				
	山：やま 山田さん：やまださん (Mr./Ms. Yamada) 山本さん：やまもとさん (Mr./Ms. Yamamoto)			山	山		

18	口 口	コウ、ク、くち、-ぐち　mouth				
	口：くち　(mouth) 人口：じんこう　(population) 山口さん：やまぐちさん　(Mr./Ms. Yamaguchi)		口	口		
19	千 千	セン、ゼン、ち　thousand				
	千：せん　(one thousand) 二千二百：にせんにひゃく　(two thousand two 　hundred) 三千：さんぜん　(three thousand)		千	千		
20	万 万	マン　ten thousand, myriad バン　countless, myriad, all よろず　ten thousand, all sorts of every...				
	一万：いちまん　(ten thousand) 二千二百万：にせんにひゃくまん　(twenty-two 　million)		万	万		
21	方 方	ホウ、-ボウ、-ポウ　direction, side; way, square かた、-がた　direction; person; method				
	この方：このかた　(this person) あの方：あのかた　(that person)		方	方		
22	近 近	キン、ちか-い、-ぢか　near, close, recent, near future				
	近い：ちかい　(close) 近じょ：きんじょ　(neighborhood) 近くの：ちかくの　(nearby) 近くに：ちかくに　(in the neighborhood)		近	近		
23	遠 遠	エン、オン、とお-い、-どお-い　far, distant				
	遠い：とおい　(close) 遠くに：とおくに　(in the distance)		遠	遠		

24	有	有	ユウ、ウ、あ-る　be, exist, have

有名：ゆうめい　(famous)
有名な人：ゆうめいなひと　(famous person)

Kanji Exercises

A. Match each kanji or kanji compound with the letter of its closest English equivalent.

1. 山＿＿＿
2. 千＿＿＿
3. 町＿＿＿
4. 外＿＿＿
5. 口＿＿＿
6. 半＿＿＿
7. 下＿＿＿
8. 間＿＿＿
9. 田＿＿＿

10. 前＿＿＿
11. 好＿＿＿
12. 人口＿＿＿
13. 百万＿＿＿
14. 近＿＿＿
15. 方＿＿＿
16. 後＿＿＿
17. 中＿＿＿
18. 五分＿＿＿

19. 時＿＿＿
20. 小＿＿＿
21. 上＿＿＿
22. 右＿＿＿
23. 二時間＿＿＿
24. 遠＿＿＿
25. 有名＿＿＿
26. 左＿＿＿

a. two hours　b. between/among　c. half　d. upper part　e. lower part　f. near　g. five minutes
h. small　i. like　j. town　k. rice field　l. left　m. right　n. inside　o. outside　p. front
q. far　r. behind　s. time　t. mountain　u. mouth　v. population　w. thousand　x. famous
y. one million　z. direction/person

B. Write hurigana for each kanji or kanji compound. Pay special attention to the changes in pronunciation that may occur when kanji are compounded.

1. 一時間半

2. としょかんの中

3. テーブルの下

4. 大学の前

5. 日本の人口

6. 山田さんの右

7. えいがかんの後ろ

8. 二千二百万人

9. 大きいびょういんの左

　　_____

10. いえの外

　　_____

11. スーパーとぎんこうの間

　　_____

12. つくえの上

　　_____

13. 大好きです

　　_____

14. 小さい町

　　_____

15. 近いです

　　_____

16. 遠いです

　　_____

17. 名前

　　_____

18. 有名です

　　_____

19. 四時五分

　　_____

20. あの方 (that person)

　　_____

C. Write the reading in hiragana in the blank boxes, using the number and the counters.

	GENERAL	PEOPLE	LONG, THIN ITEMS	MINUTES	HOURS	MONTHS
一	ひとつ					
二			にほん			
三						さんかげつ
四						
五		ごにん				
六						
七				ななふん／しちふん		
八					はちじかん	
九						
十	とお (without つ)					
(how many)	(no kanji) いくつ	[何人]	[何本]	[何分]	[何時間] なんじかん	[何か月 *]

*~ か月 is sometimes written ～ヶ月, which is still read as ～かげつ.

D. Fill in the blanks with the kanji for the words or phrases that are spelled out in hiragana below the lines.

1. わたしのうちは＿＿＿＿＿＿＿＿＿ から ＿＿＿＿＿＿＿＿＿ いです。
   　　　　　　　　だいがく　　　　　　　　　　　　　とお

2. でんしゃで＿＿＿＿＿＿＿＿＿ です。
   　　　　　いちじかんはん

3. ＿＿＿＿＿＿＿＿＿ の ＿＿＿＿＿＿＿＿＿ は ＿＿＿＿＿＿＿＿＿ ですか。
   　　にほん　　　　　　　　じんこう　　　　　　　　なんにん

4. ＿＿＿＿ おく＿＿＿＿＿＿＿＿＿ ぐらいです。
   　いち　　　にせんごひゃくまんにん

5. ＿＿＿＿＿＿＿＿＿ さんは、きょうしつの ＿＿＿＿＿＿＿＿＿ にいます。
   　　やまだ　　　　　　　　　　　　　　　　　　　　　　そと

6. スーパーはえきの ＿＿＿＿＿＿＿＿＿ にあります。
   　　　　　　　　　　　まえ

7. わたしの ＿＿＿＿＿＿＿＿＿ は ＿＿＿＿＿＿＿＿＿ さいですが、
   　　　　　　まち　　　　　　　　　　　ちい

   ＿＿＿＿＿＿＿＿＿ です。
   　　ゆうめい

8. こうえんは、＿＿＿＿ こうの ＿＿＿＿＿＿＿＿＿ ろにあります。
   　　　　　　　がっ　　　　　　　　　うし

9. カワムラさんの ＿＿＿＿＿＿＿＿＿ にブラウンさんがいます。
   　　　　　　　　　みぎ

10. カワムラさんの ＿＿＿＿＿＿＿＿＿ にギブソンさんがいます。
    　　　　　　　　　ひだり

11. カワムラさんは、＿＿＿＿＿＿＿＿＿ の ＿＿＿＿＿＿＿＿＿ にいます。
    　　　　　　　　　ふたり　　　　　　　　　あいだ

12. わたしはやさいが ＿＿＿＿＿＿＿＿＿ きです。
    　　　　　　　　　だいす

13. かばんの ＿＿＿＿＿＿＿＿＿ に ＿＿＿＿＿＿＿＿＿ があります。
    　　　　　なか　　　　　　　　　ほん

14. つくえの ＿＿＿＿＿＿＿＿＿ に ＿＿＿＿＿＿＿＿＿ きないぬがいます。
    　　　　　した　　　　　　　　　おお

15. いすの ＿＿＿＿＿＿＿＿＿ に ＿＿＿＿＿＿＿＿＿ さなねこがいます。
    　　　　うえ　　　　　　　　　ちい

16. いま、＿＿＿＿＿＿＿＿＿ です。
　　　　　　ごじごふん

17. あの ＿＿＿＿＿＿＿＿＿ はどなたですか。
　　　　　　　　かた

KANJI NOTE

Stroke Order

It is important that you write kanji following the prescribed stroke order. There are three reasons for this: your handwriting will look better, the shape of the kanji will not be distorted when you write fast, and if you practice the correct order enough to make it automatic, you will not accidentally leave strokes out when you write. Here are the basic rules of stroke order.

1. Write from top to bottom.
    三 (three)　　　一 二 三
    Related Principle: when a kanji consists of an upper and a lower part, the upper part is written first.
    今 (now)　　　ノ 今 今
    分 (minute)　　八 今 分
2. Write from left to right.
    川 (river)　　　丿 刂 川
    Related Principle: when a kanji consists of a left and a right part, or a left, a middle, and a right part, write in the order of left, middle, right.
    林 (woods)　　　木 林
    語 (language)　　言 語
    働 (to work)　　イ 俥 働
3. When a vertical and a horizontal line cross, the horizontal line is written before the vertical line.
    十 (ten)　　　一 十
    七 (seven)　　一 七
    大 (large)　　一 ナ 大
    Exceptions:
    (1)　田 and related kanji
    　　田 (rice paddy)　　门 冊 田
    　　町 (town)　　　　畕 畔 町
    　　男 (man)　　　　畕 畧 男
    (2)　王 and related kanji
    　　王 (king)　　　一 丁 王
    　　生 (life)　　　㇉ 牛 生
4. When a kanji consists of a left, a middle, and a right part and the left and right parts consist of one or two strokes each, the middle part is written first.
    小 (small)　　　亅 小 小
    Exception:
    火 (fire)　　　丶 丷 火
5. When a kanji has an enclosure, it is written first.
    日 (day)　　　丨 冂 月 日
    国 (country)　丨 冂 国 国

6. When two diagonal lines cross, the line from upper right to lower left is written first.

文 (sentence)　亠ナ文

人 (person)　ノ人

7. Lines that cross an entire kanji or part of it from top to bottom are written last.

中 (middle)　口中

書 (to write)　彐聿書

8. Lines that cross an entire kanji from left to right are written last.

子 (child)　了子

女 (woman)　く夕女

Exception:

世 (generation)　一廿世

9. In kanji including the radical *shinnyuu*, that radical is written last.

道 (street)　首首道

Exceptions:

起 (to get up)　走起

勉 (to study)　免勉

10. In kanji including the radical *tare*, that radical is written first.

店 (shop)　广店

庭 (garden)　广庭

Kanji in Everyday life

1. You and your host brother notice a note written by your host mother. It is lying next to some assorted candies on the table. It says 半分ずつ分けて食べて下さい. How much of each of them is it all right for you to eat?

   _____

2. There are two schools in your host family's neighborhood. One of them is a 小学校 and the other is a 中学校. Children of what age go to which school?

   _____

3. It's June now. The department store flyer you are looking at says 上半期に一度の大セール！, and the prices look much lower than during regular sales. How often do you think this department store has a big sale?

   _____

4. You saw an advertisement for eyeglasses (めがね). Some of them are 遠近両用めがね. What do you think 遠近両用 means? [Hint: 両用 means "for both".]

   _____

5. Your Japanese teacher gave you this semester's schedule on the first day. You noticed you are going to have a 中間テスト after several weeks. What is 中間テスト?

   _____

6. You saw a flyer about a クリスマスパーティー sponsored by your Japanese university. It says 日時：十二月二十一日（日）、午後四時. What does 日時 mean? Is 午後四時 4:00 a.m. or 4:00 p.m.?

_____

Writing Activities

Vocabulary and Grammar 2A: Commuting

A. Using the information in the chart on p. 130 in your main textbook, write a series of statements about the location, distance from school, and convenience of the homes of each of the following people. Activity 2 on p. 130 provides examples of the types of statements you could write.

1. カワムラさん：

_____

_____

_____

2. はやしさん：

_____

_____

_____

3. よこい先生：

_____

_____

_____

4. チンさん：

_____

_____

_____

5. 大の先生：

_____

_____

_____

6. Now tell about your own home:

_____

_____

_____

B. Fill in the blanks to create a meaningful sentence or phrase. Write in *X* if no additional word is needed.

1. 大^{おお}きい_____うち

2. 小^{ちい}さい_____アパート

3. しずか_____町^{まち}

4. にぎやか_____近^{きん}じょ

5. あたらしい_____くるま

6. おもしろい_____本^{ほん}

7. きれい_____大学^{だいがく}

8. わたしのうちはひろい_____。

9. 三^みむらさんのアパートはせまい_____。

10. わたしの大学^{だいがく}は有名^{ゆうめい}_____。

11. わたしの近^{きん}じょはしずか_____。

12. とうきょうのアパートはやすく_____。

13. ニューヨークはくるまがすくなく_____。

14. この本^{ほん}はおもしろく_____。

15. この町^{まち}はしずかでは_____。

16. わたしのアパートはきれいでは_____。

17. 先生^{せんせい}のうちは大^{おお}きいうち_____。

18. わたしのアパートはべんり_____アパートです。

C. Describe the following in at least three sentences. You may use either affirmative or negative statements, and you are encouraged to use adverbs such as とても and あまり, if you can.

1. your room _____

   _____

2. your advisor _____

   _____

3. your car or bicycle (If you don't have one, write about the one you would like to have.) _____

   _____

4. one of your family members _____

   _____

5. your girlfriend/boyfriend (actual or ideal) _____

   _____

Vocabulary and Grammar 2B: Neighborhood

A. Imagine that a Japanese student is asking you for information about various places in the United States. Tell this student at least three things about each place, making an effort to use the adjectives you have learned in this chapter.

EXAMPLE: JAPANESE STUDENT: ニューヨークはどんなところですか。

YOU: 大きい町です。おもしろいところですよ。でも (but) ちょっとうるさいです。

1. （イエローストーンパーク） _____

   _____

2. （サンフランシスコ） _____

   _____

3. （「イリノイの」ピオリア） _____

   _____

4. （ニューオーリンズ） _____

   _____

B. Complete each sentence with either あります or います.

1. きょうしつに先生が_____。

2. うちに小さいいぬが_____。

3. めじろにチンさんのアパートが_____。

4. この町に大きいスーパーが_____。

5. としょかんに本がたくさん_____。

C. A Japanese student wants to know where the following places are. Tell him or her which city or state they are located in.

EXAMPLE: JAPANESE STUDENT: イエローストーンパークはどこにありますか。
YOU: ワイオミングにありますよ。

1. (ホワイトハウス)

   JAPANESE STUDENT: _____

   YOU: _____

2. (ディズニーワールド)

   JAPANESE STUDENT: _____

   YOU: _____

3. (エンパイアステートビル)

   JAPANESE STUDENT: _____

   YOU: _____

4. (グランドキャニオン)

   JAPANESE STUDENT: _____

   YOU: _____

Vocabulary and Grammar 2C: Buildings and Places Around Town; Counting

A. Complete the following dialogues, using the information on the company message board pictured on p. 146 in your main textbook.

1. A: すみません。山田さんはいまどこにいますか。

    B: たか田さんのオフィスに_____。

    A: 何時にかえりますか。

    B: ご後 3 時ごろに_____。

2. A: すみません。田中さんはいまどこにいますか。

    B: レストラン_____ います。

    A: 何時_____ かえりますか。

    B: _____ 2 時ごろにかえります。

3. A: すみません。よし田さんはいま_____ にいますか。

    B: ニューヨーク_____ います。

    A: いつかえりますか。

    B: あした_____。

4. A: _____。さいとうさんは_____ どこに

    _____ か。

    B: _____ にいます。

    A: _____ かえりますか。

    B: ご後_____ ごろにかえります。

5. A: _____。さわいさんはいまどこに

    _____ か。

    B: ひろしま_____。

    A: いつ_____。

    B: らいしゅうの月よう日に_____。

B. The following is the seating chart for Professor Arai's classroom for the second term of the school year. Use it to figure out who the following five people are based on their descriptions of where they are. The top of the diagram corresponds to the front of the classroom.

先生

スミス	コロナド	クラウス	ジョンソン
ユー	キム	スコット	ペレス
オカダ	グリーン	マイヤー	トヤマ

1. わたしはクラスの後ろにいます。わたしの右にはマイヤーさんがいます。

   _____

2. わたしはユーさんとスコットさんの間にいます。

   _____

3. わたしのとなりにはクラウスさんがいます。わたしの後ろはペレスさんです。

   _____

4. わたしは先生のむかいにいます。わたしのとなりはスミスさんです。

   _____

5. わたしはきょうしつの一ばん前にいます。わたしは学生ではありません。

   _____

C. Answer the questions about the following drawing. Choose your answers from among the options listed.

本／バッグ／えんぴつ／つくえ／まど／ねこ／時けい／こくばん／いす／
先生のつくえ／先生／田中さん／まど／しんぶん／かさ

1. つくえの上に何がありますか。 _____

2. つくえの下に何がありますか。 _____

3. ショッピングバッグの中に何がありますか。 _____

4. ショッピングバッグの右に何がありますか。 _____

5. つくえの左に何がありますか。 _____

6. 外に何がいますか。 _____

7. 田中さんの前にだれがいますか。 _____

8. 田中さんの後ろに何がありますか。 _____

9. つくえのそばに何がありますか。 _____

10. こくばんの前に何がありますか。 _____

11. こくばんとまどの間に何がありますか。 _____

D. Add the following items to the drawing to match the descriptive sentences below. Don't worry about creating great art. A rough sketch will be sufficient.

1. 先生のつくえの上にノートがあります。

2. いすの下に大きいいぬがいます。

3. 時けいの下に大きいえ (picture) があります。

4. ねこのとなりに小さいねずみ (mouse) がいます。

5. ショッピングバッグの中にセータがあります。

6. 学生のつくえの上に小さいコンピュータがあります。

E. Complete the following dialogues according to the guidelines given in parentheses.

1. (A is looking for the post office, which is a small, white [しろい] building across from a bank.)

    A: すみません。_____ᵃ はありますか。

    B: ええ、_____ᵇ にありますよ。

    A: どんなたてものですか。

    B: _____ᶜ たてものです。

    A: どうもありがとうございました。

    B: どういたしまして。

2. (A is looking for a certain coffee shop, which is a pretty, blue [あおい] building near the university.)

    A: すみません。_____ᵃ はありますか。

    B: ええ、_____ᵇ にありますよ。

    A: どんなたてものですか。

    B: _____ᶜ たてものです。

    A: どうもありがとうございました。

    B: _____ᵈ。

3. (A is looking for the police box, which is a small, black [くろい] building in front of the station.)

    A: すみません。_____ᵃ。

    B: ええ、_____ᵇ。

    A: どんなたてものですか。

    B: _____ᶜ たてものです。

    A: _____ᵈ。

    B: どういたしまして。

F. Complete the following dialogues according to the guidelines given in parentheses

1. (A is looking for a good coffee shop. There is one called Kasaburanka near the university.)

    A: この近じょにいいきっさてんはありますか。

    B: ええ、ありますよ。

    A: どこに_____ᵃ か。

B: 大学の _____ ᵇ にあります。

A: 名前は。

B: 「カサブランカ」です。

2. (A is looking for a large department store. There is one called Daitoku across from the subway station.)

A: この近じょに _____ ª はありますか。

B: ええ、ありますよ。

A: どこにありますか。

B: _____ ᵇ のえきの _____ ᶜ

にあります。

A: _____ ᵈ は。

B: 「だいとく」_____ ᵉ 。

3. (A is looking for a cheap parking lot. There is one south of the hospital, but B doesn't know its name.)

A: この近じょに _____ ª はありますか。

B: ええ、ありますよ。

A: _____ ᵇ にありますか。

B: びょういんの _____ ᶜ にあります。

A: _____ ᵈ は。

B: さあ、わかりません。

4. (A is looking for the new hotel. It's east of the restaurant, and it's called the Hotel Miyako.)

A: この近じょに _____ ª 。

B: ええ、ありますよ。

A: _____ ᵇ にありますか。

B: レストランの _____ ᶜ にあります。

A: _____ ᵈ は。

B: 「ホテルみやこ」です。

5. (A is looking for a quiet park. There is one called Chuuoo Kooen behind the library.)

A: この _____ ᵃ。

B: ええ、ありますよ。

A: _____ ᵇ。

B: _____ ᶜ の _____ ᵈ。

A: _____ ᵉ は。

B: 「ちゅうおうこうえん」_____ ᶠ。

G. Write dialogues in which you ask a Japanese person for directions. Follow the guidelines given in parentheses.

1. (You'd like to know where the JR station is. It is next to a large supermarket.)

   YOU: _____

   JAPANESE: _____

2. (You want to know what kind of building the post office is. It's a large building.)

   YOU: _____

   JAPANESE: _____

3. (You want to know what that big, white building is. It's a hotel.)

   YOU: _____

   JAPANESE: _____

4. (You'd like to find out where the big park is. It's in front of the university.)

   YOU: _____

   JAPANESE: _____

5. (You'd like to know what is above the station building. There's a department store.)

   YOU: _____

   JAPANESE: _____

6. (You'd like to know if there is a convenient parking lot nearby. It's behind the movie theater.)

   YOU: _____

   JAPANESE: _____

7. (You want to find out if there is a big hospital around here. You also want to know its name. It's between the park and the university, and it's called Meeji Byooin.)

YOU: _____

JAPANESE: _____

YOU: _____

JAPANESE: _____

H. Answer the following questions based on your actual situation.

1. あなたのかぞく (family) はいまどこにいますか。

_____

2. ボーイフレンド／ガールフレンドはいますか。いまどこにいますか。

_____

3. ルームメートはいますか。いまどこにいますか。

_____

4. あなたの日本語（にほんご）の先生（せんせい）はどこにいますか。 (Guess if you don't know.)

_____

5. あなたのへや(or アパート or いえ)にだれがいますか。左（ひだり）のへや (or アパート or いえ) には。じゃあ、前（まえ）のへや (or アパート or いえ) には。

(へや／アパート／いえ) _____

(左（ひだり）) _____

(前（まえ）) _____

I. How many people do you need to play the following games? Answer in hiragana. Then see if you can write the answer in kanji.

	HIRAGANA	KANJI
EXAMPLE: やきゅう	じゅうはちにん	十八人
1. バスケットボール	_____	_____
2. バレーボール	_____	_____
3. サッカー	_____	_____
4. マージャン	_____	_____

5. アイスホッケー _____ _____

6. テニス（シングルス） _____ _____

7. アメリカンフットボール _____ _____

8. ラケットボール _____ _____

9. ジョギング _____ _____

J. Answer the following questions about your home.

1. あなたのいえにへやはいくつありますか。_____

2. いすはいくつありますか。_____

3. テレビは何だいありますか。_____

4. 人は何人いますか。_____

5. 本は何さつありますか。(If you don't know, guess.) _____

6. ペットは何びきいますか。_____

K. Complete the following dialogues according to the guidelines given in parentheses.

1. (There are three men and two women on the basketball team.)

   A: 町田さんのバスケットボールのチームに学生は何人いますか。

   B: 5人です。

   A: みんなおとこの人ですか。

   B: いいえ、おとこの人が_____ とおんなの人が_____ です。

2. (There are three Japanese and one Chinese mah-jongg players. All of them are students.)

   A: 三むらさんのマージャンのメンバーに学生は_____ いますか。

   B: _____ です。

   A: みんな日本人ですか。

   B: いいえ、日本人が_____ と中ごく人が_____ です。

3. (There are five teachers and 35 students in the orchestra.)

A: 山口さんのオーケストラにメンバーは _____ か。

B: _____ です。

A: みんな学生ですか。

B: いいえ、学生が _____ と先生が _____ です。

L. Make up a statement based on the information given.

EXAMPLE: books/in my room/50

わたしのへやに本が５０さつあります。

1. students / in the library / 2

   _____

2. instructor / in front of the classroom / 1

   _____

3. banks / in this town / 4

   _____

4. cafeterias / at the university / 5

   _____

5. hospital / next to the post office / 1

   _____

M. Using your local telephone book, answer the following questions about the people and businesses in your community.

あなたの町に：

1. ぎんこうは何けんありますか。 _____

2. ファミリーレストランは何けんありますか。 _____

3. すしやは何けんありますか。 _____

4. 大きいスーパーは何けんありますか。 _____

5. 田中さんは何人いますか。 _____

6. ブラウンさんは何人いますか。 _____

N. Answer the following questions, giving as many details as possible.

EXAMPLE: どんな人が好きですか。

しんせつな人が好きです。まじめな人も好きです。

1. どんなくるまが好きですか。_____

2. どんな先生が好きですか。_____

3. どんな町が好きですか。_____

4. どんな大学が好きですか。_____

O. Brown polled her classmates and instructor on their likes and dislikes and wrote up the results on the following chart. Answer the questions using the information presented on the chart.

	たばこ	おさけ	さかな	やさい	コーヒー
ブラウン	きらい	きらい	好き	好き	好き
カーティス	きらい	好き	きらい	好き	きらい
カワムラ	きらい	好き	好き	きらい	好き
ギブソン	きらい	きらい	好き	好き	きらい
よこい	きらい	好き	きらい	好き	好き
はやし	好き	好き	きらい	好き	好き

1. たばこがきらいな人は何人いますか。_____

2. おさけがきらいな人は何人いますか。_____

3. さかなが好きな人は何人いますか。_____

4. やさいがきらいな人は何人いますか。_____

5. コーヒーが好きな人は何人いますか。_____

Now write two statements based on the information on the chart.

6. _____

7. _____

P. Form a study group of five people (or call up five of your classmates on the phone if you can't get together), and report on the following after asking the members of your group appropriate questions in Japanese.

EXAMPLE: How many people like ice cream? How many people dislike it?

アイスクリームが好きな人は5人います。

アイスクリームがきらいな人はいません。

1. How many people like the current President (だいとうりょう) of the U.S.A.? How many dislike the President?

大とうりょうが好きな人は _____

大とうりょうがきらいな人は _____

2. How many people like your favorite musical group? How many people dislike them?

_____

_____

3. How many people like broccoli? How many dislike it?

_____

_____

4. How many people like New York as a place to live? How many dislike it?

_____

_____

Now make up four similar questions of your own, ask the members of your group, and write up the results.

5. _____

_____

6. _____

_____

7. _____

_____

8. _____

_____

Chapter 2 Review

A. Fill in each blank with a hiragana to make a phrase. Write *X* if nothing is necessary.

EXAMPLE: 田中さんの<ruby>田中<rt>たなか</rt></ruby>さんのアパート

1. わたし＿＿＿＿＿ でん<ruby>話<rt>わ</rt></ruby>ばんごう

2. おいしい＿＿＿＿＿ バナナ

3. おもしろい＿＿＿＿＿ <ruby>本<rt>ほん</rt></ruby>

4. <ruby>有名<rt>ゆうめい</rt></ruby>＿＿＿＿＿ <ruby>学<rt>がっ</rt></ruby>こう

5. やすい＿＿＿＿＿ くるま

6. <ruby>日本<rt>にほん</rt></ruby>＿＿＿＿＿ おちゃ

7. きれい＿＿＿＿＿ うち

8. べんり＿＿＿＿＿ かばん

9. チンさん＿＿＿＿＿ ともだち

10. <ruby>好き<rt>す</rt></ruby>＿＿＿＿＿ やさい

11. きらい＿＿＿＿＿ スポーツ

B. Write dialogues in which you ask Kawamura whether his home is near various places. After he answers, add a comment on whether the distance is convenient or inconvenient. Use the information in the following chart.

PLACES	TRANSPORTATION	TIME
station	on foot	six minutes
supermarket	on foot	fifteen minutes
movie theater	bus	thirty minutes
bus stop	on foot	one minute
bank	electric train	fifteen minutes
post office	bus	one hour

EXAMPLE:　　　YOU: カワムラさんのうちはえきに<ruby>近い<rt>ちか</rt></ruby>ですか。

KAWAMURA: ええ、あるいて6<ruby>分<rt>ぶん</rt></ruby>です。

YOU: それはべんりですね。

1.　　YOU: ＿＿＿＿＿＿＿＿＿＿＿＿＿＿＿＿＿＿＿＿＿＿＿＿＿＿

KAWAMURA: ＿＿＿＿＿＿＿＿＿＿＿＿＿＿＿＿＿＿＿＿＿＿＿＿＿＿

YOU: ＿＿＿＿＿＿＿＿＿＿＿＿＿＿＿＿＿＿＿＿＿＿＿＿＿＿

2.　　YOU: ＿＿＿＿＿＿＿＿＿＿＿＿＿＿＿＿＿＿＿＿＿＿＿＿＿＿

KAWAMURA: ＿＿＿＿＿＿＿＿＿＿＿＿＿＿＿＿＿＿＿＿＿＿＿＿＿＿

YOU: ＿＿＿＿＿＿＿＿＿＿＿＿＿＿＿＿＿＿＿＿＿＿＿＿＿＿

3.   YOU: _____

     KAWAMURA: _____

         YOU: _____

4.   YOU: _____

     KAWAMURA: _____

         YOU: _____

5.   YOU: _____

     KAWAMURA: _____

         YOU: _____

C. John Kawamura is moving into his new room. He would like to have certain furniture and other things placed according to his directions. Please help him move in by drawing pictures of the various items in the appropriate places on the drawing. (おいて下^{くだ}さい means "Please place/put it.") Again, you don't have to produce great art.

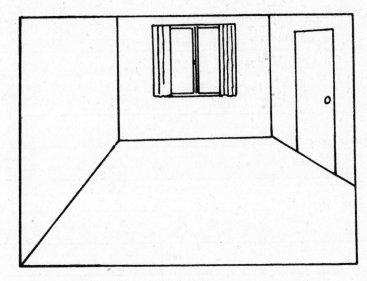

EXAMPLE: このへやの右^{みぎ}のコーナーにベッドをおいて下^{くだ}さい。

1. ベッドの左^{ひだり}に小^{ちい}さいテーブルをおいて下^{くだ}さい。ラジオはそのテーブルの上^{うえ}において下^{くだ}さい。

2. まどの前^{まえ}に大^{おお}きいつくえをおいて下^{くだ}さい。つくえの上^{うえ}にスタンド (lamp) とでん話^わをおいて下^{くだ}さい。あ、コンピュータとキーボードもおねがいします。

3. そのいすはつくえの前^{まえ}において下^{くだ}さい。

4. ドアのむかいのかべのところに、テレビと本^{ほん}だなをおいて下^{くだ}さい。あ、すみません。テレビと本^{ほん}だなの間^{あいだ}にステレオをおいて下^{くだ}さい。

D. Now draw a diagram of your room. Describe the locations of at least six items. Remember the difference between X はY にあります (The X is in location Y) and Y にX があります (In location Y there is an X).

1. _____

2. _____

3. _____

4. _____

5. _____

6. _____

E. Write as much as you can about each of the items below, following the example.

      EXAMPLE: your favorite drink

わたしの好きなのみものはコーヒーです。わたしはあついのみものが
大好きです。

1. your favorite food _____

_____

2. your favorite city in the U.S.

_____

3. your least favorite subject at college _____

_____

4. your least favorite instructor _____

_____

5. your favorite car _____

_____

EVERYDAY LIFE

日常生活

Listening Comprehension Activities

Vocabulary and Grammar 3A: Schedules

A. Looking at Heather Gibson's schedule in the calendar below, listen to the questions on the tape and answer yes or no by circling はい or いいえ.

S	M	T	W	Th	F	S
			January			
						1
2 ski club	3	4	5 **today**	6 part-time job	7	8
9	10	11	12	13 part-time job	14 exam	15 party
16 ski club	17	18 exam	19	20 part-time job	21	22
23	24	25	26 exam	27 part-time job	28	29
30	31					

1. はい／いいえ

2. はい／いいえ

3. はい／いいえ

4. はい／いいえ

5. はい／いいえ

6. はい／いいえ

7. はい／いいえ

8. はい／いいえ

9. はい／いいえ

10. はい／いいえ

11. はい／いいえ

B. Listen to Masao Hayashi ask his friends when their birthdays are and write down their answers.

	Month	Day	Year
1. Chin:			
2. Curtis:			
3. Brown:			
4. Kawamura:			
5. Machida:			

C. Listen to the passage about Takada's typical week. Then mark each of the following statements either true (T) or false (F).

1. _____ Takada is from Los Angeles.

2. _____ Takada is not a student.

3. _____ During the week, Takada is very busy at work.

4. _____ On Sundays, Takada does a variety of things.

5. _____ Takada goes out on Sunday nights.

D. Listen to the conversation between Antonio Coronado and Takako Matsui. Then complete the English summary by filling in the blanks. Some blanks may need more than one word.

Takako Matsui has a _____ this afternoon, and she is busy tomorrow and the day after

tomorrow because she has to _____. Saturday, April _____, is her

birthday. So Antonio decides to _____ Saturday night, which

will be at _____ o'clock. Takako _____ his invitation.

E. Professor Yokoi's students have planned a party for her. Listen to the conversation in which they tell her about it. Then complete the sentences below by circling the correct answer.

Useful Vocabulary: どうして *why,* ～から *because* ～

1. Professor Yokoi is usually busy in the (a. morning   b. afternoon   c. evening) every day.

2. Today is (a. August   b. September   c. October) 2nd.

3. Tomorrow is (a. Wednesday   b. Thursday   c. Friday).

4. September 4th is (a. Wednesday   b. Thursday   c. Friday).

5. Professor Yokoi's birthday is (a. today   b. tomorrow   c. the day after tomorrow).

Vocabulary and Grammar 3B: Daily Activities

A. Listen as Henry Curtis, Hitomi Machida, and John Kawamura describe their morning activities. Then complete each sentence by filling in the initial of the person it best describes.
(C: Curtis, M: Machida, K: Kawamura)

Getting up:

1. _____ gets up at 7:00.

2. _____ gets up at 6:30.

Morning activities:

3. _____ take(s) a shower.

4. _____ jogs.

5. _____ studies before leaving home.

Breakfast:

6. _____ has toast and yogurt.

7. _____ has no breakfast.

8. _____ drinks orange juice.

9. _____ drinks coffee.

Getting to school:

10. _____ drives to school

11. _____ goes to school by bus.

B. Professor Yokoi has assigned Henry Curtis and Heather Gibson to be conversation partners. Listen to their conversation, and then complete each sentence by writing in the initial of the person it refers to.
(C: Curtis, G: Gibson, M: Mimura)

Useful Vocabulary: 〜から *because* 〜, たいてい *mostly*

EXAMPLE: <u>C and M</u> eat at home during the week.

1. _____ is good at cooking.

2. _____ eats out on weekends.

3. _____ practices Japanese a lot.

4. _____ prefers washing dishes to cooking.

5. _____ prefers staying at home on weekends.

6. _____ is lucky to live with a good cook.

C. Professor Yokoi and John Kawamura run into each other one afternoon on campus. Listen to their conversation, and answer the following questions briefly in English.

Useful Vocabulary: おそく *late* (adv.), しけん *exam*

1. Why did Kawamura miss class this morning? _____

2. What did he do last night? _____

3. What is he going to do this evening? _____

4. What is he going to do tomorrow? _____

5. When is the exam? _____

D. Listen to John Kawamura talk about what he did and did not do yesterday. Then circle the correct answer in the parentheses.

Yesterday, Kawamura:

1. (took / did not take) a shower in the morning.

2. (did / did not do) exercise at the gym.

3. (ate / did not eat) breakfast.

4. (called / did not call) his friend.

5. (took / did not take) a bus.

6. (worked / did not work) from 4:00 to 9:00.

7. (went / did not go) to economics class.

8. (drank / did not drink) beer at home.

9. (returned / did not return) home late.

E. Listen to the questions on the tape and give your own answers, circling the affirmative if you did the activity yesterday or the negative if you did not do it.

1. はやく(起きました／起きませんでした)。

2. ねぼう (しました／しませんでした)。

3. 朝、コーヒーを(飲みました／飲みませんでした)。

4. 朝、はを (みがきました／みがきませんでした)。

5. 朝、学こうへ (行きました／行きませんでした)。

6. 学こうでともだちと (話しました／話しませんでした)。

7. かいものを (しました／しませんでした)。

8. カフェテリアで昼ごはんを (食べました／食べませんでした)。

9. 日本語のきょうかしょを (読みました／読みませんでした)。

10. 日本語のテープを (聞きました／聞きませんでした)。

F. Hitomi Machida has received a letter from her friend Noriko, who is studying in Sapporo about what she did and did not do. You will hear Noriko's letter read out loud. After listening to the letter, list four things she did and two things she did not do.

What Noriko did:

1. _____

2. _____

3. _____

4. _____

What Noriko did not do:

1. _____

2. _____

G. There was a robbery last night at the company where Miss Yamaguchi works. Listen as the police officer questions Miss Yamaguchi. Then mark the following statements true (T) or false (F).

Useful Vocabulary: (...の) 間 between, だれも (+ negative) no one, はんたい opposite, へん strange

1. _____ Yesterday, at 7 P.M., both Yamaguchi and Takada were still at work.

2. _____ Yamaguchi left work later than Takada.

3. _____ Yamaguchi took a train to Tokyo Station.

4. _____ Yamaguchi didn't go home directly.

5. _____ Yamaguchi ate dinner at a restaurant last night.

6. _____ Yamaguchi didn't see anyone after she left work.

7. _____ Takada was in Shinjuku around 10 P.M.

8. _____ Takada and Yamaguchi live far away from each other.

9. _____ Takada took a train going in the opposite direction from his home.

10. _____ Yamaguchi and the police officer are suspicious of Takada.

H. Professor Yokoi is asking her students about their athletic activities. Listen to the conversation, and find out what sports each person does and how frequently he/she does them.

	sport	how often	sport	how often
1. Kawamura:	_____	_____	_____	_____
2. Curtis:	_____	_____	_____	_____
3. Chin:	_____	_____		

I. Listen as Masaru Honda continues interviewing Himiko. Then complete the following sentences by circling the correct answer.

Useful Vocabulary: びょういん *beauty shop*

1. Himiko usually gets up at around (a. 8 b. 10 c. 12) o'clock.

2. Himiko brushes her teeth (a. once b. twice c. three times) a day.

3. Himiko takes a bath (a. more often b. as often as c. less often than) she brushes her teeth every day.

4. Himiko goes to the beauty shop (a. every day b. every week c. every month).

5. Himiko practices dancing (a. once b. twice c. three times) a day.

6. Honda eats (a. twice b. three times c. five times) a day.

7. Himiko drinks a (a. glass b. bottle c. case) of champagne every day.

8. Honda (a. sometimes b. seldom c. never) drinks champagne.

9. Honda watches movies (a. very often b. once in a while c. never).

Vocabulary and Grammar 3C: Weekends and Holidays

A. The last sentence of each of the following five dialogues is incomplete. You will hear each dialogue twice. Then choose the best way to complete the dialogue from the right-hand column and write its letter in the appropriate blank in the left-hand column. Use each option only once.

1. _____
2. _____
3. _____
4. _____
5. _____

   a. ひまです。
   b. します。
   c. よるおそくまで見ます。
   d. ねぼうします。
   e. よく行きます。

B. Listen as Henry Curtis and Takako Matsui talk about their weekend activities. Find out which one of the two (C: Curtis, M: Matsui) does the following.

Useful Vocabulary: しゅくだい *homework assignment*

1. _____ goes to the movies frequently.

2. _____ goes to parties.

3. _____ does some housework on weekends.

4. _____ is active on Saturday afternoons.

5. _____ often drinks sake on Saturday nights.

6. _____ relaxes on Sundays.

7. _____ studies on Sunday nights.

C. The last sentence of each of the following five dialogues is incomplete. You will hear each dialogue read twice. Then choose the best way to complete the dialogue from the right-hand column and write its letter in the appropriate blank in the left-hand column. Use each option only once.

1. _____   a. 今、あらいましょう。
         b. もうすこしまちましょう。
2. _____   c. ジュースをかいましょうか。
3. _____   d. うみへ行きましょうか。
         e. としょかんでべんきょうしましょう。
4. _____

5. _____

D. It is Sunday afternoon. John Kawamura and Mei Lin Chin, who have finished the weekend's homework, are sitting around, wondering how to pass the time. Listen to their conversation, and then mark each of the following statements either true (T) or false (F).

1. _____ Kawamura and Chin decide not to go to the movies because they have no money.

2. _____ They decide to invite Curtis and Machida over for dinner.

3. _____ They are going to have dinner at a restaurant.

4. _____ Chin really likes Kawamura's spaghetti sauce.

5. _____ Chin has some drinks at home.

6. _____ Kawamura and Chin are going shopping at a supermarket.

1	朝	朝	チョウ morning; dynasty あさ morning
	朝：あさ (morning) 朝ごはん：あさごはん (breakfast)		

2	明	明	メイ light/ミョウ light; next, following/ミン Ming (dynasty) あ-かり light, clearness/あか-るい bright/あき-らか clear あ-ける、あか-るむ／らむ to become light/あ-く to be open/visible あ-かす to pass (the night)/あ-くる next, following
	明日：あした／みょうにち／あす (tomorrow)		

3	午	午	ゴ、うま seventh horary sign (horse); noon
	午前：ごぜん (A.M.) 午後：ごご (P.M.)		

4	昼	昼	チュウ、ひる daytime, noon
	昼：ひる (daytime) 昼ごはん：ひるごはん (lunch)		

5	来	来	ライ to come; (as prefix) next (week); (as suffix) since く-る to come き-ます to come/こ-ない not come き-たる this coming (Sunday); be due to
	来週：らいしゅう (next week) 来る／来ない：くる／こない (to come/not to come) 来ます／ません：きます／ません ((will) come/ (will) not come)		

6	行 行	コウ　to go, to proceed, to do, to carry out; bank ギョウ　line (of text), row; to walk along; to do, to carry out い-く、ゆ-く　to go おこな-う　to do, to carry out, to conduct etc.		
	行く：いく　(to go) 大学へ行きます：だいがくへいきます ((will) go to the university) ぎん行：ぎんこう　(bank)	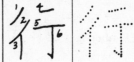	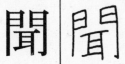	
7	聞 聞	ブン、モン、き-く　to hear, to listen to, to heed, to ask き-こえる　to be heard / audible き-こえ　reputation, publicity		
	聞く：きく　(to listen / ask) ラジオを聞きます：らじおをききます　((will) 　listen to the radio) しん聞：しんぶん　(newspaper)			
8	食 食	ショク、ショッ、ジキ　food, eating た-べる　to eat く-う／らう　to eat, to drink, to receive (a blow) く-える　can eat		
	食べる：たべる　(to eat) 朝ごはんを食べます：あさごはんをたべます 　((will) eat breakfast)	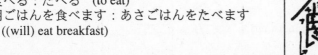		
9	出 出	シュツ、シュッ-、スイ、で-る　to go/come out, to appear, to emerge で　one's turn; origin だ-す　to put/take out, to send; (as verb suffix) begin to...		
	出かける：でかける　(to go out) 出る：でる　(to leave (home) / attend (class)) 出しん：しゅっしん　(hometown)	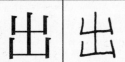		
10	飲 飲	イン、の-む　to drink		
	飲む：のむ　(to drink) コーヒーを飲みました：こーひーをのみました 　((I) drank coffee.)			
11	入 入	ニュウ、ジュ、はい-る、い-る　to go/come in, to enter い-れる　to put/let in		
	入る：はいる　(to go in) 入ります：はいります　((will) go in) 入れる：いれる　(to put in) 入れます：いれます　((will) put in)	 		

12	休 休	キュウ、やす-む　to rest, to take time off やす-める　to rest, to set at ease やす-まる　to be rested, to feel at ease やす-み　rest, break, vacation; absence			
	休む：やすむ　(to rest) 休みましょう：やすみましょう　(Let's take a rest.) 休みの日：やすみのひ　(holiday)	休	休		
13	夕 夕	セキ、ゆう、ゆう-べ　evening			
	夕ごはん：ゆうごはん　(supper) 夕方：ゆうがた　(evening)	夕	夕		
14	今 今	コン、キン、now, the present, this いま　now　いま-や　now			
	今、何時ですか：いま、なんじですか　(What time is it now?) 今日：きょう　(today)　今朝：けさ　(this morning) 今月：こんげつ　(this month)	今	今		
15	週 週	シュウ　week			
	一週間：いっしゅうかん　(one week) 今週：こんしゅう　(this week) 来週：らいしゅう　(next week) 先週：せんしゅう　(last week)	週	週		
16	曜 曜	ヨウ　day of the week			
	日曜日：にちようび　(Sunday) 月曜日：げつようび　(Monday) 何曜日ですか：なんようびですか　(What day of the week is it?)	曜	曜		
17	毎 毎	マイ、-ごと、-ごと-に　every, each			
	毎日：まいにち　(every day) 毎週：まいしゅう　(every week) 毎月：まいつき　(every month) 毎年：まいねん／まいとし　(every year)	毎	毎		

192　　　Chapter Three

18	回	回	カイ、エ (how many) times; (which) round/inning; to go round まわ-る to go/turn around まわ-り turning around; surrounding; vicinity まわ-す to turn, to send around		
	三回：さんかい (three times) 何回：なんかい (how many times) 回り：まわり (surrounding)			回	回	
19	見	見	ケン、み-る to see み-える to be visible, can see み-せる to show		
	見る：みる (to watch / see) テレビを見ます：てれびをみます ((will) watch 　TV)			見	見	
20	起	起	キ awakening, rise, beginning お-きる to get/wake/be up; to occur お-こる to occur, to happen お-こす to wake (someone) up; to begin/start to create; to cause		
	起きる：おきる (to wake/get up) 午前四時に起きます：ごぜんよじにおきます 　((will) get up at 4:00 A.M.)			起	起	
21	読	読	ドク、トク、トウ、よ-む to read		
	読む：よむ (to read) 本を読みます：ほんをよみます ((will) read a 　book)			読	読	
22	火	火	カ fire; Tuesday ひ、ほ fire		
	火曜日：かようび (Tuesday)			火	火	
23	水	水	スイ water, Wednesday みず water		
	水曜日：すいようび (Wednesday) （お）水：（お）みず (water)			水	水	

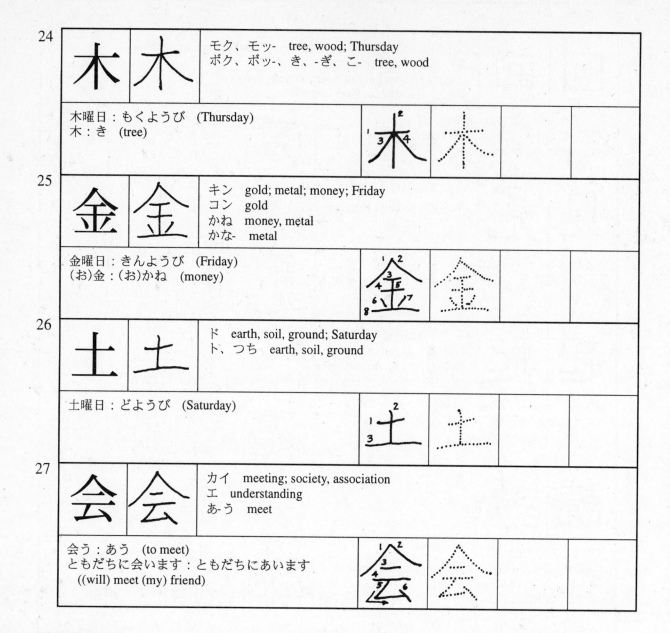

24	木　木	モク、モッ- tree, wood; Thursday ボク、ボッ-、き、-ぎ、こ- tree, wood
	木曜日：もくようび　(Thursday) 木：き　(tree)	
25	金　金	キン　gold; metal; money; Friday コン　gold かね　money, metal かな-　metal
	金曜日：きんようび　(Friday) （お）金：（お）かね　(money)	
26	土　土	ド　earth, soil, ground; Saturday ト、つち　earth, soil, ground
	土曜日：どようび　(Saturday)	
27	会　会	カイ　meeting; society, association エ　understanding あ-う　meet
	会う：あう　(to meet) ともだちに会います：ともだちにあいます 　((will) meet (my) friend)	

KANJI NOTE

The Chinese character 々 which is called 同の字点 (どうのじてん), does not have a sound or meaning of its own. Its function is to repeat the preceding character, and its sound is determined by the preceding character, so in effect, it's a sort of ditto mark for kanji. Thus, instead of writing 日日 and 人人, you can write 日々(ひび: day in and day out) and 人々 (ひとびと: people). The following are some kanji compounds that include 々.

佐々木 (ささき: *a family name*)
月々 (つきづき: *every month*)
個々 (ここ: *each*)
多々 (たた: *many*)
少々 (しょうしょう: *a little*)
時々 (ときどき: *sometimes*)

The stroke order of 々 is as follows:

Not every repeated syllable is written with 々. For the time being, use it only to write words that you have actually seen written in kanji in your main textbook or workbook.

Kanji Exercises

A. Match each kanji or compound with the letter of its closest English equivalent.

1. 曜 _____
2. 読 _____
3. 飲 _____
4. 食 _____
5. 見 _____
6. 聞 _____
7. 会 _____
8. 行 _____
9. 休 _____
10. 出 _____
11. 来 _____
12. 昼 _____
13. 朝 _____
14. 明日 _____
15. 今 _____
16. 夕方 _____
17. 週 _____
18. 午後 _____
19. 毎 _____
20. 入 _____
21. 起 _____
22. 三回 _____

a. morning b. evening c. tomorrow d. now e. afternoon f. week g. daytime h. to come i. to meet j. to go k. to enter l. to listen m. to watch n. to eat o. to get up p. to read q. three times r. day of a week s. every t. to rest u. to drink v. to go/come out

B. The following kanji represent the days of the week (column A) although each of them has its original meaning (column B). Connect each word of each column.

	A	B
火	Sunday	fire
金	Monday	gold
月	Tuesday	moon
水	Wednesday	soil
土	Thursday	sun
日	Friday	tree
木	Saturday	water

C. Write the hurigana for each kanji or compound.

1. 毎朝 _____
2. 夕方 _____
3. 午前 _____
4. 読む _____
5. 休む _____
6. 飲む _____
7. 出かける _____
8. 見る _____
9. 入る _____
10. 昼 _____
11. 行く _____
12. 聞く _____

13. 会う _____
14. 食べる _____
15. 起きる _____
16. 来週 _____
17. 今 _____
18. 時々 _____
19. 午後 _____
20. 二、三回 _____
21. 金曜日 _____
22. 明日 _____
23. 今日 _____
24. 毎日 _____

25. 来ます _____
26. 来る _____
27. 来ない _____
28. 今年 _____
29. 今週 _____
30. 今月 _____
31. 一週間 _____
32. 何回 _____
33. 土曜日 _____
34. 木曜日 _____
35. 水曜日 _____
36. 火曜日 _____

D. Write the appropriate kanji for the hiragana under the lines.

1. _____ の _____ はひまです。
　　　あした　　　　　　　　　ごご

2. _____ の _____ は _____ ですか。
　　　らいしゅう　　　　　げつようび　　　　　なんにち

3. _____ _____ に _____ きます。
　　　まいにち　　　　　ごじはん　　　　　　お

4. _____ に _____ ごはんを _____
　　　ろくじ　　　　　　　　あさ　　　　　　　　　　　　　　た

べました。

5. _____ は、しん _____ を _____ み
　　　きょう　　　　　　　　　　ぶん　　　　　　　　　　よ

ませんでした。

6. _____ きっさてんでコーヒーを _____ みます。
　　　ときどき　　　　　　　　　　　　　　　　　　　の

7. _____ に _____ おふろに _____ り
　　いっしゅうかん　　　　　なんかい　　　　　　　　　　　はい

ますか。

8. _____ ごはんを _____ べましょう。
　　　ひる　　　　　　　　　　　た

9. _____ みの _____ は _____ を
　　　やす　　　　　　　　ひ　　　　　　　　なに

しますか。

10. _____ 、ともだちがうちへ _____ ました。
　　　ゆうがた　　　　　　　　　　　　　　　き

11. _____ _____ ですか。
　　　いま　　　　　なんじ

12. おんがくを _____ きましょう。
　　　　　　　　き

13. バスで _____ へ _____ きます。
　　　　　だいがく　　　　　　　い

14. きのう、えいがを _____ ました。
　　　　　　　　　　み

15. あにはカワムラさんと _____ かけました。
　　　　　　　　　　　　　で

16. わたしはフランス _____ を _____ します。
　　　　　　　　　　ご　　　　　　　　はな

17. _____ ともだちに _____ います。
　　　あした　　　　　　　　　　あ

Kanji in Everyday Life

1. It is getting close to the end of the year and you often see the phrase 今年の十大ニュース！ on TV and in the newspaper. What does 今年の十大ニュース mean?

   _____

2. When you are looking at a science book, you see the kanji 月, 火, 水, 木, 金, 土 in the solar system diagram below. What do you think the names of these planets are in English? Write the English names in the brackets under each kanji compound.

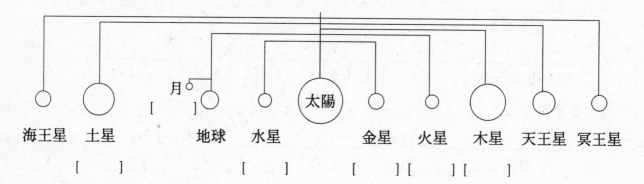

海王星　土星　　　　地球　水星　　　金星　火星　木星　天王星　冥王星

　[　　　]　　　　　　　[　　　]　　[　　][　　][　　]

3. On a power pole near your host family's house, you saw a poster 行方不明です！さがして下さい！ under which there is a picture of a dog. What is this poster for?
   (Hint: 不 means "not" or "un-".)

   _____

4. There is a proverb 百聞は一見に如かず in Japanese. What do you think is the English equivalent of this proverb?

   _____

5. Pupils and students in Japan go to school from Monday to Saturday. But the Ministry of Education has adopted 週休二日制 for some Saturdays. What kind of system is 週休二日制?

   _____

6. You went to a culture center near your host family's house to get some information about classes the center offers. You were given a brochure and found out that you need 入会金 plus tuition in order to take a class there. What is 入会金?

   _____

Writing Activities

Vocabulary and Grammar 3A: Schedules

A. Answer the following questions, based on this year's calendar.

1. クリスマスは何月何日ですか。

   _____

2. バレンタインデーは何月何日ですか。

   _____

3. エープリルフールは何月何日ですか。

   _____

4. 今年の 5 月 5 日は何曜日ですか。

   _____

5. 今年の 9 月 8 日は何曜日ですか。

   _____

6. 今年の 7 月 8 日は何曜日ですか。

   _____

7. 今年の 8 月 24 日は何曜日ですか。

   _____

8. 今年の 10 月 31 日は何曜日ですか。

   _____

9. 今年の 10 月 3 日は何曜日ですか。

   _____

10. 今年の 6 月 9 日は何曜日ですか。

    _____

11. 来週の水曜日は何日ですか。

    _____

12. 今週の土曜日は何日ですか。

    _____

13. 来月の 13 日は何曜日ですか。

_____

14. 今月の 29 日は何曜日ですか。

_____

15. 先週の木曜日は何日でしたか。

(でした *it was,* past tense form of です.)

_____

16. 先週の日曜日は何日でしたか。

_____

17. あなたのたん生日は何月何日ですか。

_____

18. あなたは何年生まれですか。

_____

B. Today is Friday. Kawamura and three of his classmates have decided to go on a picnic, and they need to find a day when all of them are free. Fill in the schedule according to each person's description of his or her activities. Then decide what the best day for the picnic would be.

	THIS SATURDAY	THIS SUNDAY	NEXT SATURDAY	NEXT SUNDAY
Kawamura				
Brown				
Hayashi				
Machida				

カワムラ：わたしは明日はひまですが、あさってはクラブのミーティングが
あります。来週は土曜日も日曜日もひまです。

ブラウン：今週も来週も土曜日はいいですけど、日曜日はきょう会へ
行きます。

はやし：明日はクラスがあります。午後3時ごろからはひまです。あさって
もひまですよ。来週の土曜日はクラスがありませんけれども、日曜
日はデートをしますから、ちょっと…。

町田： ごめんなさい。今週はとうきょうにいません。来週の金曜日のよる
かえります。そして、日曜日もまた出かけます。

The best day for the picnic is: _____.

C. Using this year's calendar, make up short dialogues about the dates and the days of the week of the following holidays. For Japanese holidays, you may refer to Chapter 3, p. 217, of your main text.

EXAMPLE: (U.S.) (どくりつきねん日) (Independence Day)
Q: どくりつきねん日は何月何日ですか。今年のどくりつきねん日
は何曜日です／でしたか。
A: ７月４日です。今年はＸ曜日でした。

1. マーティン・ルーサー・キング・デー (U.S.)

Q: _____

A: _____

2. あなたのたん生日 (Not really a holiday, but...)

Q: _____

A: _____

3. サンクスギビングデー (U.S.)

Q: サンクスギビングデーは何曜日ですか。今年のサンクスギビングデーは何月
何日です／でしたか。

A: _____

4. こどもの日 （日本）

Q: _____

A: _____

5. けいろうの日 （日本）

Q: _____

A: _____

6. ぶんかの日 （日本）

Q: _____

A: _____

D. How would you ask questions in the following situations? Make up questions using such time expressions as 何年（なんねん）、何月（なんがつ）、何日（なんにち）etc.

You'd like to know:

1. when Linda's birthday is. _____

2. in what year she was born. _____

3. in which month she is returning to the U.S. _____

4. on which days of the week she has classes. _____

5. which day she has free time. _____

E. Looking at John's schedule for this month, ask when the following events took place/are going to take place. Then answer the questions about his schedule. Assume that today is the 8th.

日	月	火	水	木	金	土
	1 しけん	2	3	4 バイト	5 プール	6 デート
7 バイト	8 たん生日（じょうび）	9	10 はいしゃ	11	12	13
14	15 休み（やす）	16	17	18 バイト	19 プール	20 パーティー
21	22	23	24 しけん	25	26	27
28	29	30	31 コンサート			

Useful Vocabulary: しけん *exam, test,* でした *it was* (past tense form of です), はいしゃ *dentist*

バイト is short for アルバイト and is a slang term used by college students.

EXAMPLE:　　(exam)

YOU:　しけんは何日（なんにち）の何曜日（なんようび）ですか。

JOHN:　1日（ついたち）の月曜日（げつようび）でした。それから、２４日（か）の水曜日（すいようび）にもあります。

1. (work)

   YOU: _____

   JOHN: _____

2. (swimming)

   YOU: _____

   JOHN: _____

3. (dentist's appointment)

   YOU: _____

   JOHN: _____

4. (date)

   YOU: _____

   JOHN: _____

5. (day off)

   YOU: _____

   JOHN: _____

6. (concert)

   YOU: _____

   JOHN: _____

F. To which classes do the following verbs belong? Write the numbers in the blanks.

1. _____ 食べる

2. _____ 見る

3. _____ 読む

4. _____ 入る

5. _____ でん話する

6. _____ 来る

7. _____ 行く

8. _____ シャワーを
        あびる

9. _____ うちを出る

10. _____ 起きる

11. _____ ねる

12. _____ かえる

13. _____ 出かける

14. _____ ある

15. _____ いる

16. _____ あそぶ

17. _____ かく

18. _____ およぐ

19. _____ まつ

20. _____ 会う

21. _____ 話す

G. The non-past, plain, negative forms of all the verbs listed can be found in the array of syllables. Find them and circle them. They may be written top to bottom, left to right, or diagonally starting from the top.

は	と	か	さ	な	い	き	で	つ	あ
た	い	え	そ	ら	な	い	か	し	び
ら	あ	ら	わ	な	い	れ	け	な	な
か	れ	な	な	や	な	ゆ	な	い	い
な	た	い	な	い	す	ね	い	き	ぬ
い	み	べ	ふ	は	き	ま	な	な	も
の	が	ほ	な	の	お	が	な	い	み
ら	か	さ	ま	い	き	る	え	い	な
な	な	な	ぬ	が	な	い	で	な	い
い	い	い	か	な	い	よ	ま	な	い

きく	おきる	でかける
でる	はいる	はたらく
かえる	いる	あらう
とかす	あびる	たべる
ねる	のむ	つかれる
いく	のる	きがえる
する	みがく	そる
よむ	ぬぐ	みる
きる	はなす	やすむ
		ほす

Vocabulary and Grammar 3B: Daily Activities

A. Look at Maria Nakajima's schedule and answer the following questions.

MARIA NAKAJIMA'S SCHEDULE

6:00 A.M.	get up
6:20	jogging
7:00	read the newspaper
8:00	drink juice
8:10	study English
9:30	leave for English class
12:00 P.M.	eat lunch
1:00	leave for work
8:00	go back home
9:00	eat dinner
10:00	watch TV
12:00	go to bed

1. 中じまさんは、毎日何時に起きますか。

_____

2. 中じまさんは、毎日朝ごはんを食べますか。

_____

3. 毎日6時20分に何をしますか。

_____

4. 毎日午前7時に何をしますか。

_____

5. 毎日ジュースを飲みますか。

_____

6. 何時に出かけますか。

_____

7. 毎日何をべんきょうしますか。

_____

8. 午後1時から午後8時まで何をしますか。

_____

9. 午後10時から12時まで何をしますか。

_____

10. 毎日何時にねますか。

_____

11. 毎日何時間べんきょうしますか。

_____

12. 毎日何時間ねますか。

_____

B. Answer the questions, based on Maria Nakajima's schedule as shown in Exercise A.

1. 中じまさんは、何時にしん聞を読みますか。

_____

2. それから、何をしますか。

_____

3. その後、何をしますか。

_____

4. 中じまさんは、何時に昼ごはんを食べますか。

   _____

5. その後、何をしますか。

   _____

6. 中じまさんは、何時にうちへかえりますか。

   _____

7. それから、何をしますか。

   _____

8. その後、何をしますか。

   _____

C. Answer the following questions based on your actual situation.

1. あなたは毎日何時に起きますか。 _____

2. 何時に朝ごはんを食べますか。 _____

3. 何時に大学へ行きますか。 _____

4. 日曜日は何時に起きますか。 _____

5. 土曜日は何時にねますか。 _____

6. たいてい(mostly)よる何時からべんきょうしますか。_____

D. On a separate sheet of paper jot down four or five things you plan to do tomorrow afternoon. Then write your plans in connected narrative form in the space below, remembering to use conjunctions such as

それから、そして、and その後 to make your paragraph flow smoothly.

_____

_____

_____

_____

E. Read each of the questions in the left-hand column and choose *the best* answer from the right-hand column. Some of the possible answers in the right-hand column will not be used.

1. _____ 何を飲みましたか。

2. _____ うんどうをしましたか。

3. _____ だれにでん話しましたか。

4. _____ どこへ行きましたか。

5. _____ テレビを見ましたか。

6. _____ 朝、ねぼうしましたか。

7. _____ シャワーをあびましたか。

8. _____ 本を読みましたか。

a. 8時に行きました。

b. ともだちにでん話しました。

c. いいえ、見ませんでした。

d. いいえ、コーヒーを飲みました。

e. はい、本を読みました。

f. おいしいお茶を飲みました。

g. はい、うんどうしました。

h. はい、でん話しました。

i. いいえ、ねぼうしませんでした。

j. としょかんへ行きました。

k. はい、シャワーをあびました。

F. Here is a schedule of what Peggy Yu did yesterday. Use the information in the schedule to answer the questions.

PEGGY YU'S SCHEDULES

7:00 A.M.	got up
7:10	exercised
7:45	took a shower
8:30	ate breakfast
9:00	left home
10:10	went to her political science class
12:00 P.M.	went to her literature class
1:30	ate a banana
1:45	went to her friend's apartment
2:00	cooked spaghetti with her friend
2:30	ate spaghetti
5:00	returned home
5:15	phoned her friend
7:00	watched TV
9:00	listened to music
10:30	took a bath
11:00	went to bed

1. ユーさんはきのう何時に起きましたか。

_____

2. きのうの朝、何分うんどうしましたか。

_____

3. きのう、シャワーをあびましたか。

_____

4. おふろに入りましたか。

_____

5. 昼ごはんを食べましたか。何を食べましたか。

_____

6. ともだちに会いましたか。

_____

7. 何のクラスに行きましたか。

_____

8. 何をつくりましたか。

_____

9. 何時にうちへかえりましたか。

_____

10. ともだちにでん話しましたか。

_____

11. 何時間ともだちと話しましたか。

_____

12. えいがを見ましたか。

_____

13. 何時間テレビを見ましたか。

_____

14. しん聞を読みましたか。

_____

15. 何時にねましたか。

_____

G. Interview three classmates (in Japanese) and find out if each of them did the following activities yesterday. If the answer is yes, ask what time s/he did it and record the time in the chart. If the answer is no, leave the box blank.

	NAME	TOOK SHOWER	PHONED FRIEND	LISTENED TO MUSIC	STUDIED	WENT TO LIBRARY
1						
2						
3						

H. On a separate piece of paper jot down four or five things you did yesterday afternoon. Then write a connected account in narrative form in the space below, remembering to use conjunctions such as

それから、そして、and その後 to make your paragraph flow smoothly.

_____

_____

_____

_____

_____

I. Complete each sentence with a verb. Be sure that the verb you choose makes sense in terms of meaning and in terms of the time words used.

1. きのう、としょかんで本を_____。

2. 明日、かいものを_____。

3. 先週、ともだちにでん話を_____。

4. 来週、田中さんとテニスを_____。

5. 来月、クラスが_____ (to start)。

6. 先月、クラスが_____ (to end)。

7. きょ年、日本へ_____。

8. 来年、スペイン語をべんきょう_____。

9. おととい、ぜんぜんテレビを_____。

10. 今週、あまりコーヒーを_____。

11. 毎週、シャワーを_____。

12. 毎週、デートを ＿＿＿＿＿＿＿＿＿＿＿＿＿＿＿＿＿＿＿。

13. 毎日、おんがくを ＿＿＿＿＿＿＿＿＿＿＿＿＿＿＿＿＿＿＿。

14. 時々、てがみを ＿＿＿＿＿＿＿＿＿＿＿＿＿＿＿＿＿＿＿。

J. How often do you do the following activities? Read through the list of activities in the left-hand column and write in the letter of the time phrase which best describes how often you do each activity. You may use a time phrase more than once if it describes your actual situation.

EXAMPLE: ___f___ 大学へ行きます。

1. _____ 朝ごはんを食べます。

2. _____ シャワーをあびます。

3. _____ かおをあらいます。

4. _____ デートをします。

5. _____ かいものをします。

6. _____ そうじをします。

7. _____ ひげをそります。

8. _____ おさけを飲みます。

9. _____ りょうりをします。

10. _____ えいがを見ます。

11. _____ くるまをうんてんします。

12. _____ せんたくをします。

13. _____ さんぽします。

14. _____ はをみがきます。

a. 1日に1回
b. 1日に2回
c. 1日に3回
d. 1週間に1回
e. 1ヵ月に1回
f. 毎日
g. 毎週
h. 毎月
i. いつも
j. よく
k. 時々
l. たまに
m. あまりしない
n. ぜんぜんしない

K. Interview a classmate in Japanese and find out how often he or she does the following things. State the answer in terms of number of times per day, week, month, or year. Then give your opinion of the frequency of the action, using words such as いつも、よく、たまに、ぜんぜん、and others.

EXAMPLE: *Your conversation:*

YOU: スミスさんは1日何回ぐらいはをみがきますか。

SMITH: 1日3回ぐらいみがきます。

Your report: スミスさんは1日3回ぐらいはをみがきます。よくはをみが
きます。

The name of the person you are reporting on: _____

1. (taking bath) _____

2. (changing clothes) _____

3. (driving a car) _____

4. (doing laundry) _____

5. (cooking) _____

6. (cleaning room) _____

7. (oversleeping) _____

8. (dating) _____

L. You have learned a number of particles up to this point. Test yourself to see how well you have mastered the new ones and remember the old ones by filling in the blanks in the sentences below. Use *X* if no particle is needed.

1. わたし _____ 日本人です。

2. レストラン _____ ハンバーガー _____ 食べましょう。

3. 毎日 _____ 8時 _____ シャワー _____ あびます。

4. としょかん _____ 何 _____ 読みますか。

5. バス _____ のりましょう。

6. きのう _____ 、大学 _____ ともだち _____ 会いました。

7. にく _____ 好きですか。

8. びょういん _____ どこ _____ ありますか。

9. 日曜日 _____ せんたく _____ します。

10. 明日 _____ かいもの _____ 行きましょう。

11. えき _____ 前 _____ ぎん行 _____ あります。

12. 毎日 _____ おふろ _____ 入りますか。

13. 10時 _____ でんしゃ _____ のります。

14. 先生は何時 _____ うち _____ かえりましたか。

15. 学こう _____ はたらきます。

16. うち _____ テレビ _____ 見ましょう。

17. うち＿＿＿ 学こう＿＿＿ でんしゃ＿＿＿10分です。

18. わたし＿＿＿ でん話ばんごう＿＿＿ 342＿＿＿ 6801 です。

19. わたしは、えい語を話します。日本語＿＿＿ 話します。

20. かばん＿＿＿ 中＿＿＿ 本＿＿＿ ノート＿＿＿ あります。

21. カワムラさん＿＿＿ こうえん＿＿＿ さんぽしました。

22. コンピュータ＿＿＿ てがみ＿＿＿ かきます。

23. さかな＿＿＿ きらいですか。

Vocabulary and Grammar 3C: Weekends and Holidays

A. Write down your typical weekday and weekend schedules, following the examples shown on p.215 of Mr. Takada's schedules. Then compare the two and make 8 statements. Practice using "On weekdays I do X, but on weekends I do Y/do not do X," statements and "Both on weekdays and weekends I do X," statements.

WEEKDAY SCHEDULE	WEEKEND SCHEDULE

EXAMPLES: へい日は朝6時に起きますが、週まつは9時に起きます。

へい日も週まつも朝ごはんを食べません。

1. ＿＿＿＿＿＿＿＿＿＿＿＿＿＿＿＿＿＿＿＿＿＿＿＿＿＿＿

2. ＿＿＿＿＿＿＿＿＿＿＿＿＿＿＿＿＿＿＿＿＿＿＿＿＿＿＿

3. ＿＿＿＿＿＿＿＿＿＿＿＿＿＿＿＿＿＿＿＿＿＿＿＿＿＿＿

4. ＿＿＿＿＿＿＿＿＿＿＿＿＿＿＿＿＿＿＿＿＿＿＿＿＿＿＿

5. ＿＿＿＿＿＿＿＿＿＿＿＿＿＿＿＿＿＿＿＿＿＿＿＿＿＿＿

6. ＿＿＿＿＿＿＿＿＿＿＿＿＿＿＿＿＿＿＿＿＿＿＿＿＿＿＿

7. _____

8. _____

B. What suggestions would you make if the person you were with made the following comments? Choose an appropriate response for each comment from among the options below. Not all the responses will be used.

1. _____ おなかがすきましたね。

2. _____ のどがかわきましたね。

3. _____ わたしは、今日はひまです。

4. _____ 明日は日曜日ですね。

5. _____ あさっては日本語のしけんです。

6. _____ つかれましたね。

7. _____ このレストランはおいしいですよ。

8. _____ このえいがはあたらしいですね。

   a. じゃ、一しょに見ましょう。

   b. じゃ、ジュースを飲みましょう。

   c. じゃ、明日、一しょにゴルフをしましょう。

   d. じゃ、このレストランに入りましょう。

   e. じゃ、りょうりしましょう。

   f. じゃ、おさけを飲みましょう。

   g. じゃ、今日の午後、かいものに行きましょう。

   h. じゃ、ともだちにでん話をしましょう。

   i. じゃ、一しょにべんきょうしましょう。

   j. じゃ、しごとをしましょう。

   k. じゃ、休みましょう。

C. A classmate of yours is inviting you to do the following. Decide whether you want to accept or not and give an appropriate response.

1. 今ばんディスコへ行きませんか。 _____

_____

2. 今週の金曜日にえいがに行きませんか。 _____

_____

3. 明日の朝5時から一しょにジョギングをしませんか。 _____

_____

4. 明日の午後、一しょに日本語をべんきょうしませんか。_____

_____

5. 一しょにマクドナルドへ行きましょう。_____

_____

6. 一しょにコーヒーを飲みましょう。_____

_____

D. Make suggestions in Japanese in response to the following situations.

1. Your friend says that she's hungry but doesn't want to eat alone.

_____

2. Your friend is bored and is looking for something interesting to do.

_____

3. A classmate has fallen behind in Japanese class, and he complains that he doesn't know what is going on.

_____

4. A friend tells you that she doesn't think she should walk home from the library alone at midnight.

_____

E. Which would you use in the following situations, 〜ませんか or 〜ましょうか? Ask an appropriate question for each, then write what you would answer if you were asked the question in that situation. Remember, 〜ましょうか is used when you are offering to do something for someone ("Shall I do 〜?") and when you are pretty sure that the listener wants to do the activity you are going to suggest ("Shall we do 〜?"). On the other hand, use 〜ませんか when you are inviting someone to do something or when you don't know how s/he feels about what you are going to suggest.

EXAMPLE: An old lady is carrying a big and heavy suitcase. You want to help her.
Q: それ、もちましょうか。 ("Shall I carry it for you?")
A: どうもありがとうございます。

1. John has invited you and your classmates to a birthday party. You don't know what everyone is planning to do for John's birthday gift, but you want to suggest that everyone contribute money and buy a big gift together.

Q: _____

A: _____

2. You and your classmate are waiting for Heather to show up at the station and it's 20 minutes later than the decided time. You don't want to wait much longer, so you suggest that you call Heather.

Q: _____

A: _____

3. You are interested in going camping next weekend. Find out if your classmate wants to join you.

Q: _____

A: _____

4. Your roommate is studying in your room. It's very hot and your roommate is sweating, but s/he is so involved in her/his work that s/he doesn't realize that the window is closed. Suggest that you open the window for her/him.

Q: _____

A: _____

5. Your classmate told you that s/he wanted to do something with you this coming weekend, and listed a few things s/he is interested in doing, such as playing tennis, going to a movie, or playing a video game. Suggest that you go to a movie.

Q: _____

A: _____

Chapter 3 Review

A. Complete the sentences, telling what people do in each of the following places.

1. としょかんで_____

2. 大学（だいがく）で_____

3. レストランで_____

4. ランゲージラボで_____

5. えいがかんで_____

6. デパートで_____

7. きょうしつで_____

8. うちで_____

B. Fill in the blanks with particles, paying close attention to the overall meaning of each sentence. Write *X* if nothing is necessary.

わたし＿＿＿＿¹ ボストン大学＿＿＿＿² 学生です。きょ年＿＿＿＿³、日本＿＿＿＿⁴ 来ました。とうきょう＿＿＿＿⁵ 日本語＿＿＿＿⁶ べんきょうしています。

きのう＿＿＿＿⁷、わたしは日本語＿＿＿＿⁸ クラス＿＿＿＿⁹ ともだち＿＿＿＿¹⁰ 一しょに日本りょうり＿＿＿＿¹¹ レストラン＿＿＿＿¹² 行きました。レストランはち下てつ＿＿＿＿¹³ えき＿＿＿＿¹⁴ 前＿＿＿＿¹⁵ あります。しずか＿＿＿＿¹⁶ レストランです。大きい＿＿＿＿¹⁷、しろい＿＿＿＿¹⁸ ビルです。

レストラン＿＿＿＿¹⁹ すきやき＿＿＿＿²⁰ すし＿＿＿＿²¹ 食べました。ともだち＿＿＿＿²² すきやき＿＿＿＿²³ すし＿＿＿＿²⁴ 食べました。わたしははし (chopsticks)＿＿＿＿²⁵ すし＿＿＿＿²⁶ 食べました。ともだち＿＿＿＿²⁷ て (hand)＿＿＿＿²⁸ 食べました。

レストラン＿＿＿＿²⁹ 先生＿＿＿＿³⁰ 会いました。先生は日本＿＿＿＿³¹ ビール＿＿＿＿³² 飲みました。わたし＿＿＿＿³³ ビール＿＿＿＿³⁴ あまり好きではありません。おちゃ＿＿＿＿³⁵ 好きです。

9 時＿＿＿＿³⁶ レストラン＿＿＿＿³⁷ 出ました。レストラン＿＿＿＿³⁸ うち＿＿＿＿³⁹ でんしゃ＿＿＿＿⁴⁰ かえりました。10 時＿＿＿＿⁴¹ うち＿＿＿＿⁴² かえりました。それから、10 時＿＿＿＿⁴³ 11 時＿＿＿＿⁴⁴ テレビ＿＿＿＿⁴⁵ 見ました。11 時＿＿＿＿⁴⁶ ねました。

C. Ask a classmate the following questions in Japanese. Then write down both your question and your classmate's answers.

> EXAMPLE: what he bought yesterday.
>
> > YOU: きのう何をかいましたか。
> >
> > CLASSMATE: あたらしいノートをかいました。

1. what s/he is going to wear tomorrow.

    YOU: ＿＿＿＿＿＿＿＿＿＿＿＿＿＿＿＿＿＿＿＿＿＿＿＿＿＿＿＿＿＿＿＿＿＿＿

    CLASSMATE: ＿＿＿＿＿＿＿＿＿＿＿＿＿＿＿＿＿＿＿＿＿＿＿＿＿＿＿＿＿＿＿＿

2. what time s/he left home today.

    YOU: ＿＿＿＿＿＿＿＿＿＿＿＿＿＿＿＿＿＿＿＿＿＿＿＿＿＿＿＿＿＿＿＿＿＿＿

    CLASSMATE: ＿＿＿＿＿＿＿＿＿＿＿＿＿＿＿＿＿＿＿＿＿＿＿＿＿＿＿＿＿＿＿＿

3. what time s/he ate breakfast this morning.

    YOU: _____

    CLASSMATE: _____

4. where her/his Japanese textbook is.

    YOU: _____

    CLASSMATE: _____

5. where s/he is planning to go next Saturday.

    YOU: _____

    CLASSMATE: _____

6. where s/he eats lunch every day.

    YOU: _____

    CLASSMATE: _____

7. by what means of transportation s/he comes to campus.

    YOU: _____

    CLASSMATE: _____

8. from what time to what time s/he studied Japanese yesterday.

    YOU: _____

    CLASSMATE: _____

9. if s/he likes ice cream, too. (The assumption is that you like ice cream.)

    YOU: _____

    CLASSMATE: _____

10. if s/he likes both *sushi* and *sashimi.*

    YOU: _____

    CLASSMATE: _____

11. with whom s/he ate dinner last night.

    YOU: _____

    CLASSMATE: _____

D. Write questions for which the following sentences could be the answers. It may be possible to make up more than one question for some of the items. Do not write yes-no questions.

1. _____

おんがくを聞きます。

2. _____

先生がいます。

3. _____

おもしろいです。

4. _____

10 時にねます。

5. _____

来月行きます。

6. _____

きっさてんに行きました。

7. _____

うちでべんきょうします。

8. _____

ぎん行の前にあります。

9. _____

9つ食べました。

10. _____

1本かいましょう。

11. _____

10分です。

12. _____

4かいです。

13. _____

4月9日です。

14. _____

9時15分です。

15. _____

バスで行きます。

16. _____

28さいです。

17. _____

3,000えんです。

18. _____

とうきょうの出しんです。

19. _____

よこい先生のうちです。

20. _____

せんこうはぶん学です。

21. _____

れきしの本です。

E. Someone is interviewing you in Japanese. Answer the questions based on your actual situation.

1. お名前は何ですか。 _____

2. おしごとは何ですか。 _____

3. 何さいですか。 _____

4. 出しんはどこですか。

5. どこの大学の学生ですか。 _____

6. せんこうは何ですか。 _____

7. 日本語のクラスは毎日ありますか。 _____

8. 日本語のクラスは何時からですか。 _____

9. 日本語のクラスに学生が何人いますか。 _____

10. おとこの学生は何人ですか。おんなの学生は何人ですか。 _____

11. 大学からうちまで近いですか。 _____

12. あなたのうちのそばにどんなみせがありますか。 _____

13. たいてい (mostly) 何で大学へ行きますか。 _____

14. 何分ぐらいかかりますか。_____

15. 何時に起きますか。_____

16. 何時にねますか。_____

17. 週まつもおなじ (same) ですか。_____

18. 夕ごはんは何時ごろ食べますか。_____

19. たん生日は何月何日ですか。_____

20. きのうクラスに出ましたか。_____

21. 先週の週まつには何をしましたか。_____

22. どんな食べものが好きですか。_____

_____

WEATHER AND CLIMATE

天気・気候

Listening Comprehension Activities

Vocabulary and Grammar 4A: Weather Reports

A. Listen to the weather report for seven cities and fill in the blanks with appropriate words.

1. さっぽろは今日は _____ です。寒いです。

2. ながのは _____ です。_____ が強いです。

3. 東きょうは _____ です。

4. 名ごやは _____ です。ちょっと _____ でしょう。

5. 大さかは _____ です。

6. かごしまは _____ です。

7. おきなわは _____ です。_____ です。

B. You are in a Japanese geography class. Looking at the following chart, answer the questions.

	AVERAGE TEMPERATURE	PRECIPITATION IN SEPTEMBER
Nagano	15°C	95 mm
Kyoto	20°C	82 mm
Kagoshima	23°C	67 mm

1. _____

2. _____

3. _____

4. _____

C. Listen to the weather reports for four cities in Japan. Then fill in the blanks in the chart below.

CITY	WEATHER	°C	TEMPERATURE	WIND
Sapporo	clear	1.	2.	3.
Tokyo	4.	20 °C	5.	6.
Osaka	7.	8.	humid	9.
Nagasaki	10.	11.	12.	none

D. Listen to Heather Gibson talk about her trip to Lake Michigan last weekend, and fill in the blanks to complete the following English summary.

Last weekend, Heather and _____ went _____ at Lake Michigan. The weather in the

morning was not very good, because it was _____ and cold, and the wind was _____.

But in the afternoon, it _____ and the temperature went up to _____ degrees.

Heather and her friend went _____ in the lake. They had a big _____ for their

dinner. At night it was very _____, and they had a campfire. Heather thought it was

_____.

E. Professor Yokoi and her class have just returned to school after the summer vacation. Listen to the conversation and complete each statement with the initials of the person it refers to.

(HC: Henry Curtis, MC: Mei Lin Chin, HG: Heather Gibson, Y: Professor Yokoi)

1. _____ traveled a long distance by car.

2. _____ worked at a supermarket.

3. _____ spent a hot and humid summer in Osaka and Kyoto.

4. _____ was in a cold place most of the summer.

5. _____ spent a cool summer in Hokkaido.

6. _____ had a boring summer.

F. Listen as Antonio Coronado tells Hitomi Machida about the weather in Mexico. Then mark each statement below either true (T) or false (F).

1. _____ Antonio went home during the summer.

2. _____ The weather in Mexico was hot at all times.

3. _____ It is more humid here than in Mexico in summer.

4. _____ It is warmer here in winter than in Mexico.

5. _____ It rains more here than in Mexico.

6. _____ Antonio wants to go to the warmest place possible in winter.

G. Listen to the conversation between Henry Curtis and Masao Hayashi. Then mark each statement either true (T) or false (F).

1. _____ Hayashi was not home yesterday because he had to work late.

2. _____ Many people went to the beach yesterday.

3. _____ Curtis phoned Hayashi because he had nothing to do then.

4. _____ Kawamura celebrated his birthday yesterday.

5. _____ Curtis went to a movie with Kawamura yesterday.

6. _____ Hayashi is not working today.

Vocabulary and Grammar 4B: Enjoying the Four Seasons

A. What season are these months in (northern hemisphere)? Write 春、夏、秋、or 冬 for each month you hear.

1. _____   3. _____   5. _____   7. _____

2. _____   4. _____   6. _____   8. _____

B. Listen to Heather Gibson read the composition she wrote for her Japanese class, and then mark (T) for the true statements and (F) for the false ones.

1. _____ Heather Gibson is almost never home in summer because she is busy with outdoor activities.

2. _____ She is busy on weekends in winter because she goes skating with her friends.

3. _____ She enjoys spring and autumn as well because she goes cycling.

4. _____ She enjoys all kinds of sports all year around.

5. _____ She apologizes to her teacher for not inviting her to join her in sports.

C. Listen to the following four descriptions, and in English identify each thing or person described.

Useful Vocabulary: たのしい *fun*

1. _____   3. _____

2. _____   4. _____

D. Listen as Hitomi Machida and Heather Gibson talk about Michigan. Then fill in the blanks to complete the following English summary.

Heather Gibson likes Michigan even in winter when it _____, because it is very

_____. In summer, it sometimes _____, but it is not as

_____ as in Japan. It is a good place for outdoor summer activities such as

_____, _____, and _____ in Lake Michigan. In

autumn, you can see beautiful _____ on the University of Michigan campus.

Vocabulary and Grammar 4C: Forecasting

A. Listen as Kawamura and Machida, who are in Tokyo, talk about vacation plans. Then fill in the blanks to complete the English summary.

Kawamura thinks the weather in Los Angeles is probably very _____ now. It may

already be _____ there. Kawamura is thinking of going to _____ this

_____. Summer in Hokkaido is pleasant, but it is still _____ now.

There may still be _____ in the mountains in Hokkaido. In the end, Kawamura and

Machida think _____ is a good time to travel in Hokkaido.

B. Listen to a fortune teller reading Hitomi Machida's palm. Circle the appropriate descriptions based on the palm reader's insights.

1. Machida is (nice, smart, beautiful, lucky).

2. She will be a good (housekeeper, educator, businesswoman, newscaster).

3. She (will be, may become, will not be) a company president.

4. Her future husband is a (rich, handsome, nice, intelligent) man.

5. He is a(n) (good cook, athlete, musician, artist).

6. They will be very (compatible, quarrelsome, healthy, happy).

Kanji Practice and Exercises

1	天 天	テン sky, the heavens; heaven, nature, God あめ sky, heaven あま- heavenly			
	天気：てんき　(weather)		天	天	
2	気 気	キ、ケ spirit, mind, heart; intention; mood; temperament, disposition; attention; air, atmosphere; flavor, smell			
	天気：てんき　(weather) 気こう：きこう　(climate) 気おん：きおん　(air temperature)		気	気	
3	雨 雨	ウ、あめ、あま-、-さめ (as in こさめ)　rain			
	雨：あめ　(rain) 大雨：おおあめ　(heavy rain) 小雨：こさめ　(light rain) にわか雨：にわかあめ　(shower)		雨	雨	
4	雪 雪	セツ、ゆき snow			
	雪：ゆき　(snow) 大雪：おおゆき　(heavy snow)		雪	雪	
5	度 度	ド、タク、ト degree; extent, measure, limit; (how many) times たび time, occasion			
	何度：なんど　(how many degrees) 10度：じゅうど　(10 degrees)		度	度	

6	風 風	フウ、フ wind; appearance; style; custom かぜ、かざ- wind; a cold	
	風：かぜ (wind) 台風：たいふう (typhoon) 風ろ：ふろ (bath)	風 風	
7	台 台	ダイ、タイ stand, platform, base; tableland, heights; level, mark, price; (counter for vehicles or machines)	
	台風：たいふう (typhoon) テレビが五台あります：てれびがごだいあります (There are 5 TV sets.)	台 台	
8	番 番	バン keeping watch; one's turn; number, order	
	一番：いちばん (number one) 一番好きです：いちばんすきです (I like it best)	番 番	
9	春 春	シュン spring, beginning of the year はる spring	
	春：はる (spring)	春 春	
10	夏 夏	カ、ゲ、なつ summer	
	夏：なつ (summer)	夏 夏	
11	秋 秋	シュウ、あき autumn, fall	
	秋：あき (fall)	秋 秋	

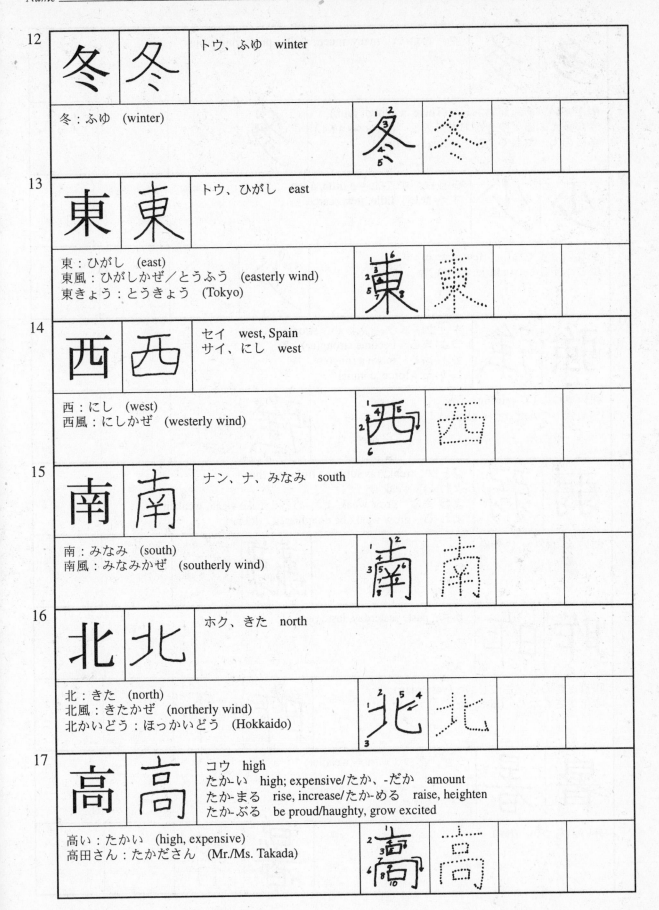

12	冬 冬	トウ、ふゆ winter
	冬：ふゆ （winter）	

13	東 東	トウ、ひがし east
	東：ひがし （east） 東風：ひがしかぜ／とうふう （easterly wind） 東きょう：とうきょう （Tokyo）	

14	西 西	セイ west, Spain サイ、にし west
	西：にし （west） 西風：にしかぜ （westerly wind）	

15	南 南	ナン、ナ、みなみ south
	南：みなみ （south） 南風：みなみかぜ （southerly wind）	

16	北 北	ホク、きた north
	北：きた （north） 北風：きたかぜ （northerly wind） 北かいどう：ほっかいどう （Hokkaido）	

17	高 高	コウ high たか-い high; expensive／たか、-だか amount たか-まる rise, increase／たか-める raise, heighten たか-ぶる be proud/haughty, grow excited
	高い：たかい （high, expensive） 高田さん：たかださん （Mr./Ms. Takada）	

18	多 多	夕、おお-い　many, much, multi-, poly-, numerous				
	雨が多い：あめがおおい　(There is a lot of rain.) 雪が多くふる：ゆきがおおくふる　(It snows a lot.) 多くの人：おおくのひと　(many people)		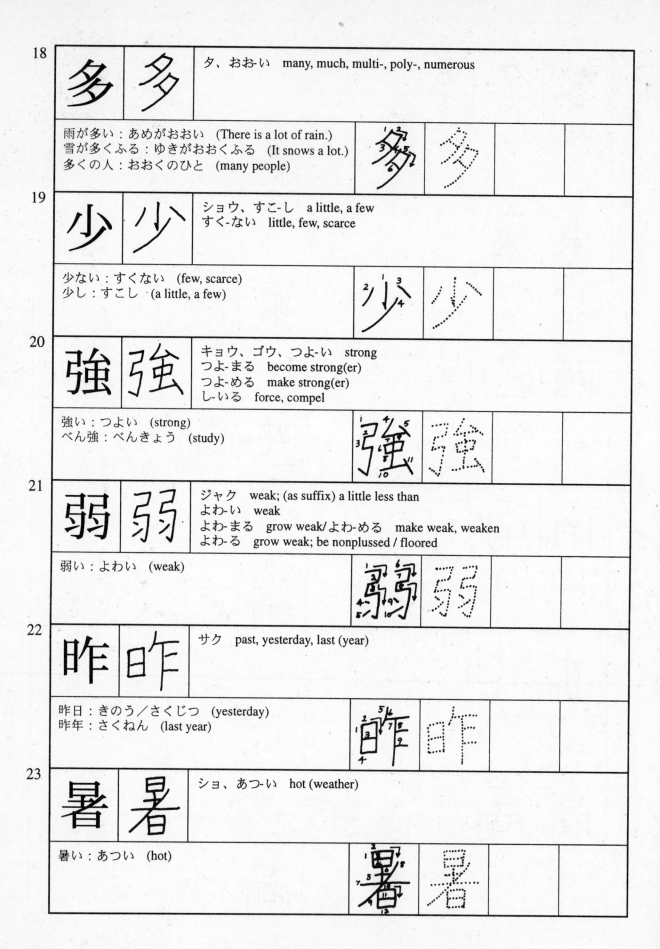			
19	少 少	ショウ、すこ-し　a little, a few すく-ない　little, few, scarce				
	少ない：すくない　(few, scarce) 少し：すこし　(a little, a few)					
20	強 強	キョウ、ゴウ、つよ-い　strong つよ-まる　become strong(er) つよ-める　make strong(er) し-いる　force, compel				
	強い：つよい　(strong) べん強：べんきょう　(study)					
21	弱 弱	ジャク　weak; (as suffix) a little less than よわ-い　weak よわ-まる　grow weak/よわ-める　make weak, weaken よわ-る　grow weak; be nonplussed / floored				
	弱い：よわい　(weak)					
22	昨 昨	サク　past, yesterday, last (year)				
	昨日：きのう／さくじつ　(yesterday) 昨年：さくねん　(last year)					
23	暑 暑	ショ、あつ-い　hot (weather)				
	暑い：あつい　(hot)					

24	寒 寒	カン　cold, midwinter さむ-い　cold (weather), chilly			
	寒い：さむい　(cold)		寒	寒	
25	空 空	クウ　sky, empty ／そら、-ぞら　sky す-く、あ-く　be empty/unoccupied あ-ける　empty, leave bleak ／から、から-っぽ　empty むな-しい　empty, vain, futile ／うつ-ろ　hollow, blank			
	空：そら　(sky) 空気：くうき　(air) 空オケ：からおけ　(karaoke: singing to a pre- 　　recorded accompaniment)		空	空	

Kanji Exercises

A. Match each kanji or compound with the letter of its closest English equivalent. Not all the definitions will be used.

1. 番 _____
2. 雨 _____
3. 空 _____
4. 強 _____
5. 弱 _____
6. 昨 _____
7. 高 _____
8. 秋 _____
9. 春 _____
10. 少 _____
11. 雪 _____
12. 多 _____
13. 台風 _____
14. 冬 _____
15. 天気 _____
16. 度 _____
17. 東 _____
18. 南 _____
19. 風 _____
20. 北風 _____
21. 小雨 _____
22. 暑 _____
23. 寒 _____
24. 西 _____
25. 夏 _____

a. weather　b. rain　c. light rain　d. snow　e. hot　f. cold　g. wind　h. typhoon　i. past　j. number　k. spring　l. summer　m. autumn　n. winter　o. east　p. east wind　q. west　r. west wind　s. south　t. south wind　u. north　v. north wind　w. high/expensive　x. many/much　y. little/few　z. strong　aa. weak　bb. degree　cc. sky

B. Write the hurigana for each kanji or kanji compound.

1. 台風
   _____

2. 大雨
   _____

3. 風
   _____

4. 弱い
   _____

5. 高い
   _____

6. 強い
   _____

7. 暑い
   _____

8. 多い
   _____

9. 寒い
   _____

10. 少し
    _____

11. 少ない
    _____

12. 一番
    _____

13. 冬
    _____

14. 南
    _____

15. 秋
    _____

16. 北
    _____

17. 何度
    _____

18. 夏
    _____

19. 西
    _____

20. 春
    _____

21. 東
    _____

22. 天気
    _____

23. 北風
    _____

24. 十度
    _____

25. 昨日
    _____

26. 雪
    _____

27. 空
    _____

C. Write the appropriate kanji for the hiragana under the lines.

1. _____ の _____ は _____ でしょう。
   あした　　　　　てんき　　　　　あめ

2. _____ は _____ が _____ いです。
   ことし　　　　ゆき　　　　おお

3. _____ い _____ より _____ い _____ の
   あつ　　　　なつ　　　　　　さむ　　　　ふゆ

   _____ が _____ きです。
   ほう　　　す

4. _____ の _____ おんは _____ ですか。
   きょう　　　　き　　　　　　なんど

5. _____ が _____ いです。_____ が _____ ます。
   かぜ　　　つよ　　　　　たいふう　　　き

6. _____ の _____ はとてもきれいです。
   あき　　　　　そら

7. _____ きょうの _____ に _____ がありますか。
   とう　　　　　　　　　　にし　　　　なに

8. _____ の _____ にその _____ があります。
   やま　　　　みなみ　　　　　　　まち

9. この _____ は _____ し _____ いです。
   ほん　　　　すこ　　　　たか

10. _____ がふいて、_____ いです。
    きたかぜ　　　　　　　　さむ

11. _____ は _____ が _____ かったです。
    きのう　　　　かぜ　　　　よわ

12. きせつの _____ で _____ が _____ _____ きです。
    なか　　　　　はる　　　　いちばん　　　す

13. その _____ は _____ が _____ ないです。
    まち　　　　じんこう　　　　すく

Kanji in Everyday Life

1. You were invited to your friend's picnic next Sunday. The invitation card says 小雨決行 because the weather is a little bit unpredictable around this time of the year. What do you think 小雨決行 means?

   _____

2. You saw the words 春分の日 and 秋分の日 in the calendar. What are their English equivalents?

   春分の日：_____

   秋分の日：_____

3. Can you list the countries that are collectively called 中近東諸国?

   _____

4. 大西洋（たいせいよう）is one of the five biggest oceans in the world. What is it in English?

   _____

5. There are many Japanese family names containing 東、西、南、北. Do you know someone whose family name contains one of these kanji? If you do, write his/her/their family name(s).

   _____

6. During the summer, you received a post card saying 暑中お見舞い申し上げます from a Japanese friend. For what purpose do you think he/she sent this to you?

_____

Writing Activities

Vocabulary and Grammar 4A: Weather Reports

A. Answer each question based on the following table.

PLACE	WEATHER	TEMPERATURE	WIND
Tokyo	Snow	0 degrees, cold	no wind
Osaka	Cloudy	10 degrees, cold	light wind
Naha	Clear	19 degrees, warm	strong wind

1. なはは、今日はどんな天気ですか。

_____

2. 大さかは、今日はどんな天気ですか。

_____

3. 東きょうの気おんは何度ですか。

_____

4. 大さかの気おんは何度ですか。寒いですか。

_____

5. 東きょうは、風がありますか。

_____

B. Answer the following questions about the summer weather in your hometown. Use these time adverbs in your answer, if appropriate: いつも／よく／時々／たまに／ほとんど／ぜんぜん

1. あなたはどこの出しんですか。 _____

_____

2. よくはれますか。 _____

_____

3. よくくもりますか。 _____

　_____

4. よく雨^{あめ}がふりますか。 _____

　_____

5. 暑^{あつ}いですか。 _____

　_____

6. 強^{つよ}い風^{かぜ}がふきますか。 _____

　_____

7. 台風^{たいふう}が来^きますか。 _____

　_____

C. Write statements about the following items or people, using both affirmative and negative adjectives in the same sentence. You may want to use a "good news–bad news" format. Be creative!

EXAMPLE:　(most recent Japanese homework)
　　　多^{おお}かったですけど、むずかしくありませんでした。

1. (your Japanese teacher) _____

　_____

2. (your last Japanese class) _____

　_____

3. (yesterday's dinner) _____

　_____

4. (your dream car) _____

　_____

5. (your next-door neighbor) _____

　_____

6. (the last movie you saw) _____

　_____

7. (your most recent summer vacation) _____

　_____

8. (the last date you had) _____

_____

D. Fill in the blanks with the choices given to create a true sentence.

EXAMPLE: _____ は _____ より大きいです。(日本、アメリカ)

アメリカは日本より大きいです。

1. _____ は _____ より寒いです。(ボストン、フロリダ)

2. _____ は _____ よりやすいです。(ステーキ、ハンバーガー)

3. _____ は _____ より小さいです。(メロン、レモン)

4. _____ は _____ より東にあります。(東きょう、大さか)

5. _____ は _____ よりやさしいです。(ひらがな、かんじ)

E. Make up questions comparing two items, using the words suggested. Then answer the questions truthfully.

EXAMPLE: てんぷら／すし／好き

てんぷらとすしとどちら(の方)が好きですか。

てんぷらの方が好きです。

1. べん強／えいが／おもしろい

_____ a

_____ b

2. オレゴン／カリフォルニア／雨がたくさんふる

_____ a

_____ b

3. ニューヨーク／マイアミ／雪がたくさんふる

_____ a

_____ b

4. くるま／バス／べんり

_____ a

_____ b

5. りょう／アパート／しずか

a _____

b _____

6. 日本りょうり／中かりょうり／よく食べる

a _____

b _____

7. コーヒー／コーラ／おいしい

a _____

b _____

8. 4月／10月／好き

a _____

b _____

F. Compare the two drawings below and find at least five differences between them besides the one given in the example. Then explain how they are different, using comparative sentences containing the より structure.

A.

B.

EXAMPLE: Aのおとこの人は、Bのおとこの人よりせが高い(tall)です。

1. _____ .

2 _____ .

3 _____ .

4 _____ .

5 _____ .

G. Do the same as in F. but use the ほど structure.

> EXAMPLE: Ｂのおとこの人はＡのおとこの人ほどせが高くないです。

1. _____.
2. _____.
3. _____.
4. _____.
5. _____.

H. Study the table of temperature and rainfall in Tokyo on p. 258 of your textbook, and then answer the following questions, comparing the climate of your community to that of Tokyo.

1. あなたの町と東きょうとどちらの方が冬は寒いですか。 _____
   _____

2. 夏はどちらの方が暑いですか。 _____
   _____

3. 夏はどちらの方が雨が多いですか。 _____
   _____

4. 秋はどちらの方がすずしいですか。 _____
   _____

5. 春はどちらの方があたたかいですか。 _____
   _____

I. Make up questions comparing three or more items, using the words suggested. Then answer the questions truthfully.

> EXAMPLE: てんぷら／すし／すきやき／好き
> てんぷらとすしとすきやきの中で、どれが一番好きですか。
> てんぷらが一番好きです。
> or 町／好き
> 町の中でどこが一番好きですか。
> サンフランシスコが一番好きです。

1. トヨタ／ホンダ／ベンツ／高い

   _____ a
   _____ b

2. アンカレッジ／東きょう／ホンコン／寒い

_____ a

_____ b

3. ビール／コーヒー／ジュース／よく飲む

_____ a

_____ b

4. 日本語／フランス語／えい語／むずかしい

_____ a

_____ b

5. ラスベガス／ニューヨーク／デンバー／にぎやか

_____ a

_____ b

6. スポーツ／おもしろい

_____ a

_____ b

7. 日本のえいが／好き

_____ a

_____ b

8. おんがく／よく聞く

_____ a

_____ b

J. Your Japanese pen pal has asked you the following questions about the climate of your home state. Please answer them as accurately as you can.

Useful Vocabulary: しゅう *state,* こう水りょう *amount of precipitation*

1. あなたのしゅうはアメリカのどこにありますか。_____

_____

2. そこは何月が一番寒いですか。_____

_____

3. ７月と８月とどちらが暑いですか。_____

_____

4. １月と７月とどちらがこう水りょうが多いですか。_____

_____

5. ６月と７月と８月のうちで何月が一番雨がふりますか。_____

_____

6. 何月が一番こう水りょうが多いですか。_____

_____

7. 何月が一番気おんが高いですか。_____

_____

8. 何月が一番気おんがひくいですか。_____

_____

K. The following is an actual weather report from Tokyo's *Yomiuri Shinbun* for January 31. Study the hints provided, and then answer the questions.

Name of Cities Listed:

東京 （とうきょう）

札幌 （さっぽろ）	大阪 （おおさか）
仙台 （せんだい）	広島 （ひろしま）
長野 （ながの）	高松 （たかまつ）
新潟 （にいがた）	福岡 （ふくおか）
金沢 （かなざわ）	鹿児島 （かごしま）
名古屋 （なごや）	那覇 （なは）

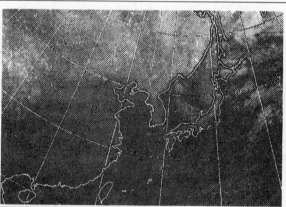

Courtesy of *The Yomiuri Shimbun* and the Japan Meteorological Agency

Useful Vocabulary: 時々 *sometimes*, 晴れ *clear skies*, 曇 *cloudy skies*

1. The numbers in circles from left to right indicate the chance of rain in percentages for 6:00 A.M.–12 Noon, 12 Noon–6:00 P.M., and 6:00 P.M.–12:00 Midnight respectively.

2. The two numbers to the right of the chances of rain are the expected high temperature for the day and the lowest temperature for that morning.

EXAMPLE: 今日の東きょうの天気はどうですか。

はれです。

1. 今日東きょうは雨がふりますか。 _____

    _____

2. 今日はどこが一番あたたかいですか。どこが一番寒いですか。 _____

    _____

3. 今朝はどこが一番寒かったですか。どこが一番あたたかかったですか。

    _____

4. 今日の金ざわの天気はどうですか。雨はふりますか。 _____

    _____

5. 今日はどこで雨がふりますか。 _____

    _____

6. 今日の天気がおなじ (same) 町はありますか。(Hint: Check the chance for precipitation,

    too) _____

    _____

7. 今朝のふくおかの気おんは何度でしたか。 _____

    _____

8. 今朝、どことどこの気おんが2度でしたか。 _____

    _____

L. The following is a U.S.A. weather forecast from a newspaper. Pretend that you are doing this exercise on Thursday, and make up questions and answers according to the cues below.

City	Wed. HI/Lo/Sky	Thu. HI/Lo/Sky	Fri. HI/Lo/Sky	City	Wed. HI/Lo/Sky	Thu. HI/Lo/Sky	Fri. HI/Lo/Sky
Albuquerque	51/30s	45/25c	50/25pc	Los Angeles	70/46s	74/54pc	72/50pc
Albany	41/8pc	31/17pc	38/22pc	Louisville	58/25s	53/30s	56/38pc
Anchorage	5/-18s	0/-15pc	-3/-18sn	Memphis	63/31s	60/36pc	58/35c
Atlanta	56/30s	61/36s	57/38pc	Miami Beach	73/63pc	74/58pc	74/62pc
Austin	59/54r	57/47r	55/37r	Milwaukee	48/26s	43/30pc	47/21pc
Baltimore	55/17s	45/26pc	54/30pc	Minneapolis	38/21pc	40/26pc	42/16pc
Billings	44/20s	51/29s	50/21pc	Nashville	59/24s	58/31s	57/38pc
Birmingham	58/32s	60/33pc	61/34c	New Orleans	64/41pc	61/47c	62/43c
Bismarck	37/20s	48/18s	33/13pc	New York	51/21s	41/28pc	48/34pc
Boston	38/19pc	30/20s	39/23pc	Norfolk	54/24s	50/30s	57/37pc
Buffalo	36/15pc	33/28pc	43/21pc	Oklahoma City	53/48c	46/36r	53/34sh
Burlington	33/5c	20/13pc	29/6sf	Omaha	40/34c	41/28pc	51/20pc
Charleston, SC	57/27s	61/38s	61/43pc	Orlando	69/45pc	70/51pc	71/55pc
Charleston, WV	53/17s	49/25s	56/37pc	Palm Springs	74/45pc	72/45pc	68/38pc
Chicago	46/24s	45/30pc	50/22pc	Philadelphia	52/21s	47/30pc	51/32pc
Cheyenne	30/23sn	41/21pc	56/19pc	Phoenix	72/45s	72/49s	73/50s
Cincinnati	52/20s	50/29s	55/35pc	Pittsburgh	47/19s	42/26pc	53/30pc
Cleveland	47/25s	39/27pc	48/24pc	Portland, ME	33/3s	27/11pc	33/18pc
Dallas	53/49r	56/42r	55/37r	Raleigh	55/20s	59/29s	59/38pc
Denver	34/26sn	44/22c	59/23pc	Rapid City	33/27sn	44/25pc	58/22pc
Des Moines	45/24pc	42/29pc	50/23pc	Red Bluff	62/46c	63/49r	60/45sh
Detroit	48/25s	40/28s	44/26pc	Redding	62/44c	61/48r	58/44sh
Duluth	44/24s	37/20pc	31/7sf	Reno	40/30pc	50/31c	50/24c
El Paso	64/30s	56/34pc	55/34s	Richmond	60/19s	54/26s	58/36pc
Fairbanks	-36/-56c	-35/-52pc	-31/-46pc	Sacramento	61/43pc	61/47c	58/46sh
Fargo	27/19c	43/18s	28/5pc	Salt Lake City	33/24sn	37/19c	40/16c
Flagstaff	42/12s	50/23s	45/20s	San Antonio	62/56r	60/47r	56/37r
Fresno	60/45pc	67/46c	63/44c	San Diego	69/49pc	71/54pc	68/51pc
Grand Rapids	41/26s	40/29pc	44/21pc	San Francisco	63/49pc	63/51r	57/49sh
Hartford	43/16pc	33/18s	42/25pc	Santa Fe	47/23s	38/20c	45/19pc
Helena	36/16s	42/13s	38/10c	St. Louis	55/30s	50/33pc	55/29pc
Honolulu	79/62pc	80/62pc	82/64pc	Syracuse	40/5pc	31/21pc	41/17pc
Houston	66/50pc	68/50r	59/37r	Tampa	71/44s	70/51pc	71/55pc
Indianapolis	50/22s	47/29pc	52/29pc	Topeka	48/36sh	43/31c	53/22pc
Jackson, MS	66/31s	63/36pc	59/36c	Tucson	69/36s	73/47s	71/44s
Juneau	17/15sn	24/14sn	26/16sf	Tulsa	54/43c	48/36c	52/30sh
Kansas City	49/34sh	42/32pc	49/22pc	Wash. DC	57/22s	50/32pc	55/34pc
Las Vegas	60/38pc	64/42pc	62/39pc	Wichita	45/41r	42/32c	52/25c
Little Rock	61/31s	55/36c	55/34sh	Yuma	73/52pc	77/51s	73/56s

EXAMPLE: (coldest city yesterday)

Q: 昨日(きのう)一番(ばんさむ)寒かったのはどこですか。

A: フェアバンクスです。

1. (warmest city tomorrow)

Q: _____

A: _____

2. (cities where it snowed yesterday)

Q: _____

A: _____

3. (warmest city yesterday)

Q: _____

A: _____

4. (coldest city today)

    Q: _____

    A: _____

Make up your own questions and answers for 5 and 6.

5. Q: _____

    A: _____

6. Q: _____

    A: _____

M. Interview two of your classmates in Japanese about the following matters. Then report the results in writing as directed below.

Name of the two people you interviewed:

_____

1. Ask what time each one of your interviewees got up this morning. Tell which one got up earlier.

_____

What time did you yourself get up this morning? Tell which of the three of you got up earliest.

_____

2. Find out from each of them which ice cream flavor they like better, vanilla or chocolate.

_____

_____

_____

3. Find out which of the two studied more last night. (Ask them how many hours they studied, and then compare their answers.) Be sure to use the より + affirmative structure.

_____

_____

Which person did not study as much as the other? Answer using the ほど + negative structure.

_____

_____

How much did you study last night? Compare your answer with your classmates' and indicate who of the three of you studied the most.

_____

_____

4. Find out from one of them what his/her least favorite food is.

_____

_____

Find out from the other person if s/he dislikes the food that was mentioned above. If the answer is yes, ask him/her if s/he dislikes it as much as your least favorite food. (Use おなじぐらい). If the answer is no, find out what his/her least favorite food is.

_____

_____

N. Complete the dialogues, using the appropriate form of the cue word given in parentheses.

EXAMPLE: クラスに＿＿＿行かない＿＿＿んですか。（行きません）

ええ、しごとが＿＿＿ある＿＿＿んです。（あります）

1. 本を＿＿＿＿＿＿＿＿んですか。（読みます）

ええ、時間がたくさん＿＿＿＿＿＿＿＿んです。（あります）

2. 一日中＿＿＿＿＿＿＿＿んですか。（およぎます）

ええ、＿＿＿＿＿＿＿＿んです。（暑いです）

3. 昨日、たくさん＿＿＿＿＿＿＿＿んですか。（かいものをしました）

ええ、＿＿＿＿＿＿＿＿んです。（やすかったです）

4. 先週、ピクニックに＿＿＿＿＿＿＿＿んですか。（行きました）

ええ、天気が＿＿＿＿＿＿＿＿んです。（よかったです）

5. 学こうへ＿＿＿＿＿＿＿＿んですか。（行きません）

ええ、クラスが＿＿＿＿＿＿＿＿んです。（ありません）

6. 昨日、きっさてんで＿＿＿＿＿＿＿＿んですか。（おちゃを飲みました）

ええ、ともだちに＿＿＿＿＿＿＿＿んです。（会いました）

7. ともだちが＿＿＿＿＿＿＿＿んですか。（来ます）

ええ、パーティーを＿＿＿＿＿＿＿＿んです。（します）

8. どうしてレストランで朝_{あさ}ごはんを _____ んですか。(食_たべます)

   りょうりが _____ んです。(きらいです)

9. どうしてあたらしいくるまを _____ んですか。(かいます)

   わたしのくるまは _____ んです。(ふるい)

10. どうして今朝_{けさ}は朝_{あさ}ごはんを _____ んですか。(食_たべませんでした)

    朝_{あさ}、ねぼう _____ んです。(しました)

11. どうして昨日_{きのう}は _____ んですか。(つかれました)

    一日中_{じゅう} _____ んです。(はたらきました)

12. どうしてビールを _____ んですか。(飲_のみません)

    ビールが _____ んです。(きらいです)

O. Match the phrases to make sentences. There may be more than one possible ending for each sentence.

1. _____ 雪_{ゆき}がふったので
2. _____ ひまだったので
3. _____ いい天気_{てんき}なので
4. _____ 今日は寒_{きょう さむ}いから
5. _____ ベンツは高_{たか}いから
6. _____ 日本語はむずかしいので
7. _____ 午前_{ごぜん} 2 時_じにねたので
8. _____ さかながきらいだから
9. _____ ともだちが来_くるので

a. さんぽをしました。
b. スキーをしました。
c. セーターをきます。
d. そうじしました。
e. テレビを見_みました。
f. ともだちにでん話_わをしました。
g. すしを食_たべません。
h. 朝_{あさ}ねぼうしました。
i. 毎日_{まい}べん強_{きょう}します。
j. かいません。
k. おふろに入_{はい}りました。

P. How would you handle these situations?

1. You have forgotten to do your Japanese homework. Your strict Japanese teacher requires a good reason for not handing in your homework on time. Come up with three possible excuses and write them down. (Be sure to use …から or …ので or …んです。)

   _____

   _____

   _____

2. You're invited to a classmate's birthday party, but you really don't like that person and don't want to go. Think of three good excuses for turning down the invitation. Then write them down. (Be sure to use …から or …ので or …んです.)

    _____

    _____

    _____

3. Your Japanese acquaintance wants to know why you are interested in Japan. Give three reasons. (Be sure to use …から or …ので or …んです.)

    _____

    _____

    _____

Q. Ask questions in the following situations. You will have to decide if you need to use the の／んです structure for each situation. Give a possible answer to the question also.

EXAMPLE: 1. You have just gotten up in the morning. Ask your roommate if it's cold this morning.

    Q: 今朝は寒いですか。

    A: ええ、とても寒いですよ。

    2. You have just gotten up in the morning, and you see your roommate getting ready to go out. S/he is all bundled up. Ask a question regarding the temperature.

    Q: 今朝は寒いんですか。

    A: ええ、とても寒いんですよ。

1. It's Friday, but a classmate of yours does not look happy. You wonder if the reason is that s/he has a lot of work to do.

    Q: _____

    A: _____

2. You are at a stationery store. You would like to know the price of the pen you have picked up.

    Q: _____

    A: _____

3. Your classmate was going to move to a new apartment, but you heard that s/he decided against it because s/he didn't like one feature. Ask for an explanation of what s/he doesn't like.

    Q: _____

    A: _____

4. You want to invite Yoshida-san out, but you have reason to suspect that s/he might already have a boy/girl friend, so you ask one of your classmates.

   Q: _____

   A: _____

5. You would like to know tomorrow's weather out of simple curiosity.

   Q: _____

   A: _____

6. You invited Yoshimura-san to a party, but at the last minute she called and said she could not make it. She sounded a bit subdued. Find out if she is ill.

   Q: _____

   A: _____

Vocabulary and Grammar 4B: Enjoying the Four Seasons

A. Match the phrases to make complete sentences. One possible ending will not be used.

1. _____ コーヒーはやすいですけれども、
2. _____ 雨はよくふりますけれども、
3. _____ 雪はぜんぜんふりません。
4. _____ 夏は暑いですが、
5. _____ 今年の気おんは高いです。
6. _____ 昨年の冬は寒かったです。
7. _____ てんぷらは好きです。
8. _____ 学こうは近いですが、

a. 雪はほとんどふりません。
b. 好きです。
c. けれども、すしはきらいです。
d. ビールは高いです。
e. でも、寒いです。
f. スーパーは近くありません。
g. でも、えきは近いです。
h. しかし、昨年はひくかったです。
i. けれども、雪はふりませんでした。

B. Comment on the following, using two or more adjectives and/or nouns in one sentence.

   EXAMPLE: your roommate

   わたしのルームメートは、おもしろくて、しんせつです。

1. Your next-door neighbor _____

2. One of your family members (choose anyone you like or dislike) _____

3. Your hometown _____

4. Your university _____

5. Your room _____

C. Criticize the following by using two or more adjectives and/or nouns. Be tactful by saying something nice at the beginning, followed by a negative comment.

      EXAMPLE: your roommate

          わたしのルームメートは、とてもしんせつですけれど、うるさいです。

1. Your Japanese class _____

2. One of your parents _____

3. Your advisor _____

4. Japanese cars _____

5. A grocery store you go to often _____

D. Respond to the following offers and suggestions with the te-form of a verb + 下^{くだ}さい.

      EXAMPLE: そうじしましょうか。→

          ええ、すみませんが、そうじして下さい。

1. 日本語で話しましょうか。

   ええ、すみませんが、_____

2. もう一度^どいいましょうか。

   ええ、すみませんが、_____

3. 一しょに行きましょうか。

   ええ、すみませんが、_____

4. 明日^{あした}もう一度^ど来^きましょうか。

   ええ、すみませんが、_____

5. かんじをかきましょうか。

   ええ、すみませんが、_____

6. かんじを読^よみましょうか。

   ええ、すみませんが、_____

7. もう少したちまちましょうか。

   ええ、すみませんが、_____

8. くるまをあらいましょうか。

   ええ、すみませんが、_____

9. うんてんしましょうか。

   ええ、すみませんが、_____

E. Make up sentences describing sequences of actions, using the suggested verbs.

    EXAMPLE: 朝ごはんを食べる→出かける

           朝ごはんを食べてから、出かけました。

1. しん聞を読む→でん話をかける

   _____ ました。

2. コーヒーを飲む→せんたくをする

   _____ ましょう。

3. テレビを見る→かいものに行く

   _____ かもしれません。

4. 日本語をべん強する→日本へ行く

   _____ でしょう。

5. きょうかしょを読む→テープを聞く

   _____ ます。

6. 学こうに行く→先生に会う

   _____ ました。

7. はをみがく→ねる

   _____ て下さい。

8. いえにかえる→りょうりをする

   _____ ます。

9. シャワーをあびる→ビールを飲む

   _____ ましょう。

10. 日本に来る → 日本語をべん強する

_____ ました。

11. かおをあらう → ふくをきる

_____ ます。

F. The following chart tells you what John Kawamura's classmates did last weekend. Describe each person's activity in one sentence, using the te-form for the first verb.

EXAMPLE: Heather Gibson　　went to the sea　　fished

ギブソンさんはうみへ行って、つりをしました。

1. Linda Brown　　　　slept late　　　　　　　　　　　　watched TV all day
2. Takeshi Mimura　　went to a disco　　　　　　　　　danced all night
3. Masao Hayashi　　was at home　　　　　　　　　　　studied all weekend
4. Henry Curtis　　　went to a country club with a friend　played golf
5. Hitomi Machida　went to Chin's apt.　　　　　　　　cooked Chinese food together

1. _____

2. _____

3. _____

4. _____

5. _____

G. Write what you would do in the following situations, using at least two verbs connected with the te-form.

EXAMPLE: Tomorrow is a holiday and the weather is expected to be very nice.

うみへ行って、およぎます。それから、レストランでばんごはんを
食べてかえります。

1. You have received $300 for your birthday, and you want to spend it all!

_____

2. At last it's Friday, but the weather forecast says that it'll be raining all weekend.

_____

3. A guest is coming to dinner tomorrow night.

_____

4. Your least favorite relative is going to come and stay at your place for a week.

_____

5. You are going to meet your girl/boyfriend's parents for the first time.

_____

H. Write down two or more things you did:

EXAMPLE: this morning.

コーヒーを飲んで、ゆっくりしん聞を読みました。

1. last night. _____

2. last Thanksgiving Day. _____

3. last Saturday. _____

4. during yesterday's Japanese class. _____

5. during the most recent football game you attended. _____

I. You are an executive at a company, and you have a secretary. What would you ask her/him to do in the following situations?

EXAMPLE: You have written a letter in longhand.

このてがみをタイプして、出して (mail) 下さい。

1. You are out of pens and writing pads (レポートようし).

_____

2. You don't know what your schedule is tomorrow: all you know is that you'll be awfully busy.

_____

3. You need to withdraw (おろす) some money from the bank.

_____

4. You need to call Mr. Iwata, but you don't have his phone number.

_____

5. You are going to have an important meeting at 7:00 A.M. tomorrow, and you need your secretary to be there.

_____

Vocabulary and Grammar 4C: Forecasting

A. Write a brief paragraph about each of the four seasons in your hometown. Tell how long they last, what the weather is like, and what sorts of activities are typical of each season.

EXAMPLE: ここの冬はとてもながくて寒いです。冬はふつう (usually) 11 月から 4 月までです。雪がたくさんふります。ここの人はよくスケートとクロスカントリースキーをします。

1. _____
   _____
   _____

2. _____
   _____
   _____

3. _____
   _____
   _____

4. _____
   _____
   _____

B. Change the sentence endings.

EXAMPLE: 明日は雨がふります。→ 明日は雨がふるかもしれません。

1. はやしさんはこのえいがを見ました。

   _____

2. 三むらさんは 9 時ごろ起きます。

   _____

3. あの人は日本人です。

   _____

4. その町はきれいです。

   _____

5. 日本語のしけんはむずかしいです。

_____

6. 東きょうは昨日ちょっと寒かったです。

_____

7. 先生は昨日げん気ではありませんでした。

_____

8. ブラウンさんはあのバスにのりました。

_____

9. カワムラさんは3時ごろに来ます。

_____

10. カーティスさんは、町田さんと一しょにテニスをしました。

_____

C. What do you think you will be doing in 20 years? Write three sentences that describe you 20 years from now. If you are pretty sure of some things, use でしょう; otherwise, use かもしれません。

1. _____

_____

2. _____

_____

3. _____

_____

D. How would you handle the following situations?

1. You receive a phone call from an acquaintance in Japan during the evening. Your acquaintance asks you how the weather was today. Describe the local weather conditions for the day, including temperature, sky conditions, and precipitation.

_____

_____

_____

2. You have Japanese visitors staying with you. They would like to know what the weather is going to be like tomorrow. Check the actual forecast from your local newspaper or local radio and television broadcasts, and write a summary in Japanese, including temperature, sky conditions, and precipitation.

_____

_____

_____

Chapter 4 Review

A. Choose the right expression for each situation.

1. _____ When you want to know the pronunciation of a word.

2. _____ When you want to know how to read a kanji.

3. _____ When you want to know how to write a kanji.

4. _____ When you want to know the meaning of a word.

5. _____ When you want someone to teach you something.

6. _____ When you want to have someone write something down.

7. _____ When you have a question.

8. _____ When you want to know if a certain word is different from the some other word.

9. _____ When someone has taught you something.

 a. ありがとうございます。
 b. すみません。これはどうはつおんしますか。
 c. ちょっと、かいて下さいませんか。
 d. すみません。「雪」はどういういみですか。
 e. ちょっとすみません。おしえて下さいませんか。
 f. すみません。このかんじはどう読みますか。
 g. すみませんが、ちょっとしつもんがあるんですが。
 h. すみません。「にほん」はかんじでどうかきますか。
 i. 「しつ度」は「おん度」とは、ちがいますか。

B. The following is information on the available seats at a theater. You are working at the ticket counter. Write down 5 comparative or superlative questions that you anticipate from your customers, and then answer them. Here are some hints: people may want to know, for instance, which section of seats is most expensive, which section has the most seats available, and which section has the best seats.

Seating and ticket information for theater

SECTION	PRICE	TOTAL # OF SEATS	# OF SEATS LEFT	LOCATION
S	¥10,000	30	2	Center, very close to stage
A	¥8,000	80	15	Center and sides, close to stage
B	¥5,000	100	45	Center and sides, halfway back
C	¥3,000	100	60	Center and sides, back

EXAMPLES: 1. Q: A と B とどちらのほうがステージに近いですか。
A: A のほうが近いです。
2. Q: どのせき (seat) が一番ステージに近いですか。
A: S です。

1. Q: _____ 1
   A: _____ 1
2. Q: _____ 1
   A: _____ 1
3. Q: _____ 1
   A: _____ 1
4. Q: _____ 1
   A: _____ 1
5. Q: _____ 1
   A: _____ 1

C. Paul, a high school senior, has to decide which college he will attend. By looking at the chart below, compare the three colleges he is interested in and write as many statements as you can about their location, tuition, Japanese language program, availability of scholarships, and the size of the college. Then decide which college you would choose if you were Paul. Write down why you would choose that particular school.

NAME	LOCATION	TUITION	JAPANESE PROGRAM	SCHOLARSHIPS	# OF STUDENTS
1. Western State University	in town	$3,500	poor	many	18,000
2. Friendship College	3 hours away by plane, 700 miles	$12,000	excellent	some	2,000
3. East-West College	300 miles	$8,000	good	some	5,000

EXAMPLE: (location)

1が一番近いので、べんりです。2は一番ふべんです。3は2よりべんりですが、1ほどべんりではありません。

1. (tuition) _____

2. (Japanese language program) _____

3. (scholarships) _____

4. (size of the school) _____

5. Which school would you choose (use "go to") and why? (Answer in Japanese.)

_____

_____

_____

D. The following maps indicate the average temperature and rainfall in different areas of Japan. Study them carefully, noting the eight regions of Kyushu, Shikoku, Chugoku, Chubu, Kinki, Kanto, Tohoku, and Hokkaido. Then answer the questions that follow.

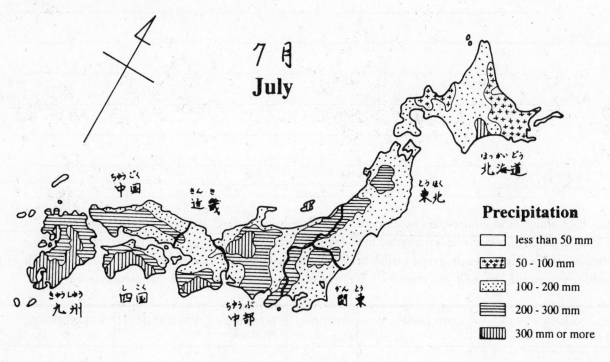

7月
July

北海道

中国

近畿

東北

九州

四国

中部

関東

Precipitation

less than 50 mm

50 - 100 mm

100 - 200 mm

200 - 300 mm

300 mm or more

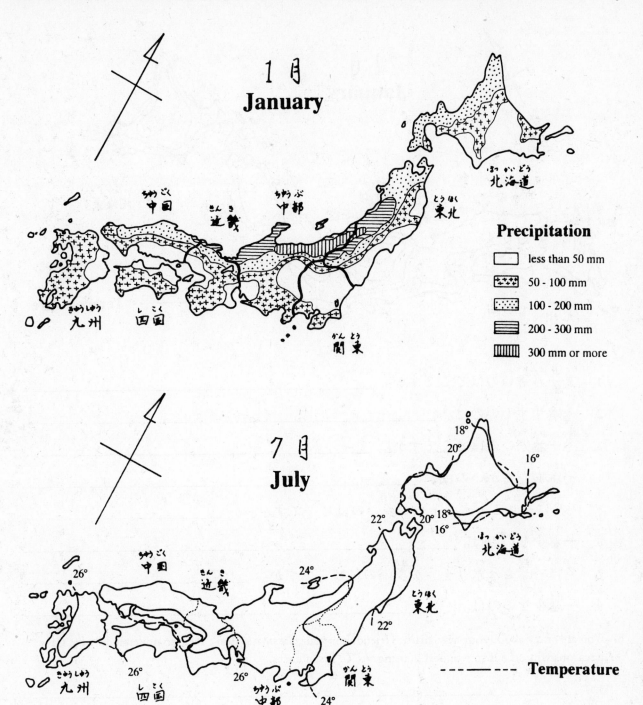

1月
January

Precipitation

less than 50 mm

50 - 100 mm

100 - 200 mm

200 - 300 mm

300 mm or more

中国

近畿

中部

東北

北海道

九州

四国

関東

7月
July

中国

近畿

北海道

東北

九州

四国

中部

関東

- - - - - - **Temperature**

18°
20°
16°
22°
20° 18°
16°
24°
22°
26°
26°
26°
24°

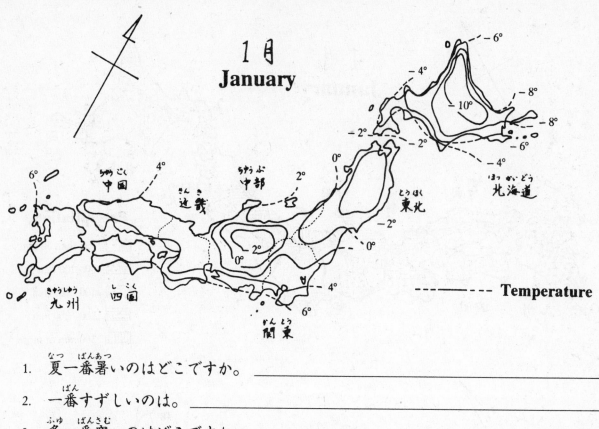

1月
January

中国 ちゅうごく
近畿 きんき
中部 ちゅうぶ
東北 とうほく
北海道 ほっかいどう
九州 きゅうしゅう
四国 しこく
関東 かんとう

- - - - - - **Temperature**

1. 夏一番暑いのはどこですか。 _____

2. 一番すずしいのは。 _____

3. 冬一番寒いのはどこですか。 _____

4. 一番あたたかいのは。 _____

5. 7月に一番こう水りょうが多いのはどこですか。 _____

6. 一番少ないのは。 _____

7. 冬に一番こう水りょうが多いのはどこですか。 _____

8. 一番少ないのは。 _____

E. You are crazy about your new girl/boyfriend, but your classmates don't seem to understand why. Give three reasons why s/he is so wonderful, using んです sentences.

1. _____

2. _____

3. _____

F. Respond to the following questions, using explanatory sentences with んです. Use your imagination.

1. 明日じゅぎょう (class) に出ないんですか。

   _____

2. とても高いステレオをかったんですねえ。

   _____

3. あたらしいくるまがいる (is needed) んですか。

   _____

4. そのアパートはうるさいんですか。

   _____

5. あの先生はしんせつ (kind) じゃないんですか。

   _____

HOBBIES AND LEISURE ACTIVITIES

趣味・余暇
<small>しゅみ・よか</small>

Listening Comprehension Activities

Vocabulary and Grammar 5A: Hobbies and Pastimes

A. Listen to the five persons' statements and identify their hobbies by circling the appropriate word from the three given for each answer.

1. りょうり　　　スポーツ　　　きってあつめ
2. 読書<small>どくしょ</small>　　　かいが　　　音楽<small>おんがく</small>
3. えんげい　　　りょうり　　　えいが
4. クラブ　　　スポーツ　　　楽<small>がっ</small>きえんそう
5. つり　　　りょ行<small>こう</small>　　　しゃしん

B. Listen as Masao Hayashi and Heather Gibson talk about their interests. Then complete each of the following sentences by writing in the name of the person it refers to. (H for Hayashi, G for Gibson, and B for Both)

Useful Vocabulary: 今度<small>こんど</small> *next time*

1. _____ has/have many hobbies.
2. _____ likes/like any kind of music.
3. _____ likes/like classical music.
4. _____ is/are busy this week.
5. _____ will go to a university concert.
6. _____ will call this weekend.

C. Listen as Linda Brown and Takeshi Mimura talk about their interests. Then complete each of the English sentences by filling in the blanks.

1. Brown has _____ particular hobbies.

2. Brown likes both _____ and _____.

3. Brown has not seen either _____ or _____.

4. Mimura would be willing to go to _____.

5. Brown can go _____ day.

6. Mimura suggests going to the musical on _____.

7. _____ says it doesn't matter where they meet.

8. They will meet in _____ at _____ before going to the show.

D. Heather Gibson wants to learn more about Japanese culture. She decides to call the Fuji Culture Center to ask about their ikebana (flower arrangement) class. Listen to the dialogue and complete the English summary by filling in the blanks.

Useful Vocabulary: 書道 (しょどう) *Japanese calligraphy,* おなじ *same*

At the Fuji Culture Center, the _____ class meets at 6 P.M. on

_____. In the morning, there are _____ classes at 10

A.M., and the teacher is _____. It meets on the _____ floor of the Kita (North) Building.

Heather ends up deciding to take a calligraphy class on _____ at the Fuji

Culture Center.

E. The survey results shown below indicate how Japanese adults and children like to spend their leisure time. Listen to the questions on the tape and answer them in Japanese, following the example given.

じゅんい (RANK)	大人 (おとな) (ADULT)	人ずう (にん) (NUMBER OF PEOPLE)	子ども (こ) (CHILD)	人ずう (にん)
1	りょ行(こう)をする	46	テレビを見(み)る	48
2	テレビを見(み)る	43	ファミコンをする	45
3	読書(どくしょ)をする	32	ともだちとあそぶ	30
4	音楽(おんがく)を聞(き)く	25	スポーツをする	28
5	スポーツをする	19	コンピュータを使(つか)う	24

EXAMPLE: <u>りょ行をすることです。</u>

1. _____

2. _____

3. _____

4. _____

5. _____

Vocabulary and Grammar 5B: Sports

A. As you listen to the questions about your sports activities and skills, answer each question orally, then stop the tape and write your answer in Japanese.

1. _____

2. _____

3. _____

4. _____

5. _____

6. _____

7. _____

B. Professor Yokoi and her students are talking about their favorite pastimes in class. Listen to the conversation, and then mark each statement true (T) or false (F).

1. _____ The sport Kawamura is best at is skiing.

2. _____ Both Kawamura and Curtis like sports.

3. _____ The sport Curtis is good at is swimming.

4. _____ Kawamura is a better swimmer than Curtis.

5. _____ Chin cannot swim because she didn't have a chance to swim.

6. _____ Chin is good at winter sports since she is from a cold region.

7. _____ Sports are not Chin's favorite pastime.

C. Professor Yokoi has asked the students to talk about their special areas of skill, and John Kim and Takako Matsui are conversation partners. Listen to their conversation and then mark each of the following sentences true (T) or false (F).

Useful Vocabulary: ほかに *besides*, じつは *to tell the truth*

1. _____ Matsui is interested in learning martial arts.

2. _____ Both Kim and Matsui like dancing.

3. _____ Matsui enjoys cooking.

4. _____ Kim wants to take cooking lessons from Matsui.

5. _____ Kim prefers sports to cooking.

D. John Kim has received his first letter from a new pen pal in Tokyo. Listen to the letter, and circle the correct answer for each sentence.

Mariko:

1. is a _____ in Tokyo now.
   a. college student   b. company worker   c. housewife

2. often goes abroad because of _____.
   a. her language training   b. her job   c. her research

3. _____ traveling.
   a. enjoys   b. is afraid of   c. is tired of

4. is good at _____.
   a. English and French   b. English and Chinese   c. French and Chinese

5. finds it difficult to _____ Chinese.
   a. study   b. write   c. speak

6. _____ sports.
   a. does not do any   b. prefers watching to doing   c. is good at most

7. likes to _____ on weekends.
   a. go out   b. stay home   c. work

8. likes to _____.
   a. cook   b. eat   c. both cook and eat

E. The following chart shows how Professor Yokoi, John Kawamura, and Mei Lin Chin compare in some activities. First, listen to the questions on the tape and answer each question orally, referring to the chart. When each question is read the second time, stop the tape and write the answer.

(○ = able to do × = unable to do)

ACTIVITIES	PROF. YOKOI	KAWAMURA	CHIN
cook well	○	×	○
speak Spanish	×	○	○
get up early	○	×	×
run 10 km	×	○	×
play musical instruments	○	×	○
sing well	×	○	○

EXAMPLE: はい、（上手に）作れます。

1. _____

2. _____

3. _____

4. _____

5. _____

6. _____

7. _____

8. _____

F. Listen as John Kawamura talks about the American Culture Club and circle things that he can do at the club.

speak in English   write English   listen to English speeches

cook American food   eat American food   play the banjo

go to concerts   meet college students from America

Vocabulary and Grammar 5C: Family

A. Listen as Takao Matsui describes her family, and write (in English) that person's relationship to Takako beside each person's name or description.

Kazuo _____

Yoshiko _____

Noisy but cute _____

Pretty and smart graduate student _____

25-year-old company employee _____

B. Listen to the description of Takako Matsui's family again and first, answer the questions orally. Then, when the questions are read the second time, stop the tape and write the answers in Japanese.

1. _____

2. _____

3. _____

4. _____

5. _____

6. _____

C. Listen as Antonio Coronado talks about his family in Mexico. Then mark each of the following statements true (T) or false (F).

1. _____ Coronado is the only son in his family.

2. _____ He is the oldest of the children.

3. _____ His mother plays some musical instruments.

4. _____ Coronado is very artistic.

5. _____ His sisters are both students.

6. _____ One of his sisters is a good cook.

7. _____ He can speak English with his other sister.

8. _____ Coronado's home is a very pleasant and interesting place.

D. Takeshi Mimura is showing a picture of his family to Henry Curtis. Listen to their conversation. Then complete each sentence with the name of the person it best describes.

Useful Vocabulary: かの女 *she*

Mimura's:

1. _____ is fifty-four years old.

2. _____ is a company employee.

3. _____ is a homemaker.

4. _____ is 80 years old.

5. _____ is tall.

6. _____ is a graduate student.

7. _____ is wearing a black dress.

8. _____ is a teacher.

9. _____ works for a bank.

10. _____ will meet Curtis in the summer.

E. During Professor Yokoi's office hours, Henry Curtis stop by to ask some questions. Listen to their conversation, and then choose the correct answer from among the options given.

1. Your おい is your _____.
   a. uncle's or aunt's son   b. brother's or sister's son   c. brother's or sister's daughter

2. Your めい is your _____.
   a. uncle's or aunt's daughter   b. brother's or sister's daughter   c. parent's sister

3. Curtis has _____ cousins.
   a. 4   b. 36   c. 40

4. Your まご is your _____.
   a. parent's child   b. child's child   c. cousin's child

5. Your きょうだい are your _____.
   a. brothers   b. sisters   c. both a and b

F. Listen to the statements about what each person in the picture is doing now. Then write the name of the person described. (To refresh your memory, check back to p. xviii.)

1. _____ 3. _____ 5. _____

2. _____ 4. _____ 6. _____

G. Listen to John Kawamura describe the people in a photograph taken at his birthday party last year. Then complete each sentence by stating what each person is doing.

     Useful Vocabulary: わらっています *is smiling,* やいていた *was baking*

1. John Kawamura is in the center and is _____

2. His girlfriend is sitting to his right and is _____

3. His sister is behind him and is _____

4. His sister's boyfriend is beside her and is _____

5. John's father is also in the back and is _____

6. John's brother is to his left and is _____

7. His mother is not in the picture. She was _____

H. Listen as Professor Yokoi and John Kawamura talk about various people they see at a reception for a visiting scholar from the U.S. Then circle all the choices from a-d that describe the four people mentioned.

Useful Vocabulary: おしえている *is teaching*

1. Professor Yamashita:
   a. tall   b. young   c. teaches Japanese literature   d. talking with Smith

2. Professor Yamashita's wife:
   a. young   b. long-haired   c. in a green sweater   d. by the window

3. Professor Yamashita's son:
   a. strange   b. by the door   c. drinking juice   d. teaches Japanese literature

4. Professor Yokoi's older brother:
   a. long-haired
   b. drinking juice
   c. wearing dark glasses
   d. looking at Professor Yokoi and Kawamura

I. Listen to the radio advertisement for Orange University. Then complete the following sentences by filling in the blanks.

Useful Vocabulary: いろいろな *various*, ところ *place*

1. At Orange University, there are many students who _____ Japanese.

2. There are many buses that _____.

3. Around the university, there are many places of business, including _____

   and _____ .

4. At the university, there are game centers, _____, and a student center where

   you can _____.

5. The town is near _____ where you can _____ .

J. The last part is missing in each of five dialogues between Mei Lin Chin and Takeshi Mimura. You will hear each dialogue twice. Listen, then choose the phrase that best completes each dialogue.

Useful Vocabulary: できた *was built*

1. _____
2. _____
3. _____
4. _____
5. _____

a. 上手になりました。
b. 大学生になります。
c. べんりになりました。
d. あかくなるんです。
e. あたたかくなるでしょう。

K. Listen as Masaru Honda interviews Himiko about her educational background. Then circle the correct answer for each sentence.

> **Useful Vocabulary:** つもり *intention*, えをかく *to draw/paint a picture*, が^か家 *a painter/artist*, か^{しゅ}手 *singer*

1. As a child, Himiko was very talented in _____.
    a. singing   b. dancing   c. both a and b

2. Himiko wanted to work after finishing high school because she _____.
    a. needed money   b. didn't like school   c. wanted to become a star

3. Himiko did not get a job because _____.
    a. she had no skills   b. she was too lazy   c. her family didn't want her to

4. Himiko tried to _____.
    a. learn typing and computer skills   b. become a painter   c. run an art school

5. Besides dancing, Himiko took lessons in _____ at the dance school she attended.
    a. painting   b. singing   c. both a and b

6. She _____ her ambition in art.
    a. fulfilled   b. continued with   c. gave up

7. Honda is glad Himiko did not become a painter because he _____.
    a. knows she has no artistic talent
    b. knows it is hard to become a painter
    c. loves her singing

Kanji Practice and Exercises

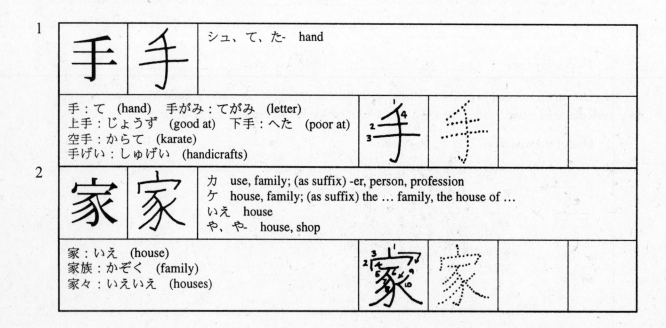

1	手 手	シュ、て、た- hand			
	手：て (hand)　手がみ：てがみ (letter) 上手：じょうず (good at)　下手：へた (poor at) 空手：からて (karate) 手げい：しゅげい (handicrafts)				
2	家 家	カ　use, family; (as suffix) -er, person, profession ケ　house, family; (as suffix) the … family, the house of … いえ　house や、や-　house, shop			
	家：いえ (house) 家族：かぞく (family) 家々：いえいえ (houses)				

3

族 族　　ゾク　family, tribe

家族：かぞく　(family)
ご家族は何人ですか：ごかぞくはなんにんですか
　(How many people are there in your family?)

4

男 男　　ダン、ナン、おとこ　man, male

男：おとこ　(male)
男の人：おとこのひと　(man)
男の方：おとこのかた　(man [polite])

5

女 女　　ジョ、ニョ、ニョウ、おんな、め-　woman, female

女：おんな　(female)
女の人：おんなのひと　(woman)
女の方：おんなのかた　(woman [polite})

6

子 子　　シ、ス　child
　　こ　child, offspring; (female name suffix)

子ども：こども　(child)
お子さん：おこさん　(child [honorific form])
男の子：おとこのこ　(boy)
女の子：おんなのこ　(girl)

7

父 父　　フ、ちち、お-とう-さん　father

父：ちち　([one's own] father)
お父さん：おとうさん　(father [polite])

8

母 母　　ボ、はは、お-かあ-さん　mother

母：はは　([one's own] mother)
お母さん：おかあさん　(mother [polite])

9	兄 兄	ケイ、キョウ、あに elder brother お-にい-さん elder brother; young man		
	兄：あに ([one's own] elder brother) お兄さん：おにいさん (elder brother [polite])	兄	兄	
10	姉 姉	シ、あね elder sister お-ねえ-さん elder sister; young lady ねえ-や maid		
	姉：あね ([one's own] elder sister) お姉さん：おねえさん (elder sister [polite])	姉	姉	
11	弟 弟	テイ、ダイ、デ younger brother, pupil, disciple おとうと younger brother		
	弟：おとうと ([one's own] younger brother) 弟さん：おとうとさん (younger brother [polite]) 兄弟：きょうだい (siblings) ご兄弟：ごきょうだい (siblings [polite])	弟	弟	
12	妹 妹	マイ、いもうと、いも younger sister		
	妹：いもうと ([one's own] younger sister) 妹さん：いもうとさん (younger sister [polite])	妹	妹	
13	勉 勉	ベン diligence つと-める make efforts, work hard, be diligent		
	勉強：べんきょう (study)	勉	勉	
14	道 道	ドウ、トウ、みち way, path, road, street		
	道：みち (street) さ道：さどう (tea ceremony) じゅう道：じゅうどう (judo) けん道：けんどう (Japanese fencing)	道	道	

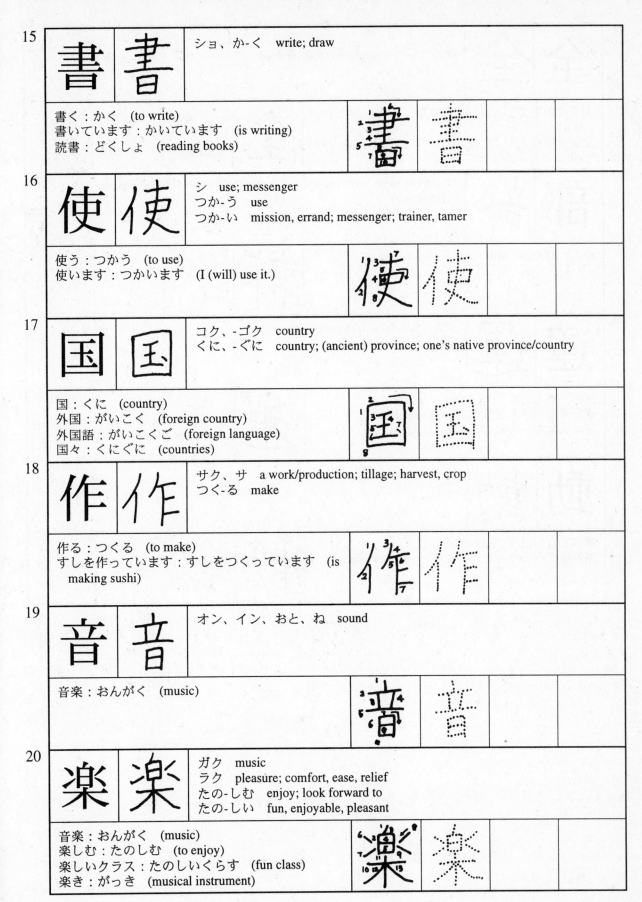

15	書 書	ショ、か-く　write; draw
	書く：かく　(to write) 書いています：かいています　(is writing) 読書：どくしょ　(reading books)	

16	使 使	シ　use; messenger つか-う　use つか-い　mission, errand; messenger; trainer, tamer
	使う：つかう　(to use) 使います：つかいます　(I (will) use it.)	

17	国 国	コク、-ゴク　country くに、-ぐに　country; (ancient) province; one's native province/country
	国：くに　(country) 外国：がいこく　(foreign country) 外国語：がいこくご　(foreign language) 国々：くにぐに　(countries)	

18	作 作	サク、サ　a work/production; tillage; harvest, crop つく-る　make
	作る：つくる　(to make) すしを作っています：すしをつくっています　(is making sushi)	

19	音 音	オン、イン、おと、ね　sound
	音楽：おんがく　(music)	

20	楽 楽	ガク　music ラク　pleasure; comfort, ease, relief たの-しむ　enjoy; look forward to たの-しい　fun, enjoyable, pleasant
	音楽：おんがく　(music) 楽しむ：たのしむ　(to enjoy) 楽しいクラス：たのしいくらす　(fun class) 楽き：がっき　(musical instrument)	

21	全 全	ゼン　all まった-く　completely; truly, indeed				
	全くにが手です：まったくにがてです　(truly poor at it) 全部分かります：ぜんぶわかります　(I understand all)		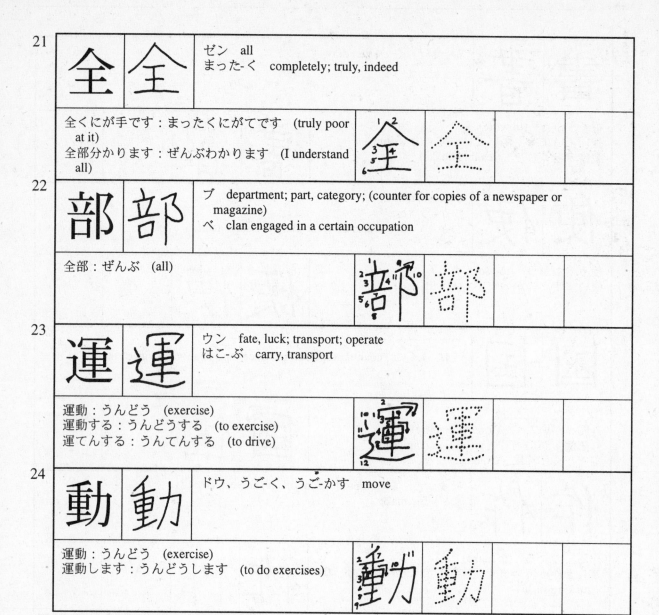			
22	部 部	ブ　department; part, category; (counter for copies of a newspaper or magazine) べ　clan engaged in a certain occupation				
	全部：ぜんぶ　(all)					
23	運 運	ウン　fate, luck; transport; operate はこ-ぶ　carry, transport				
	運動：うんどう　(exercise) 運動する：うんどうする　(to exercise) 運てんする：うんてんする　(to drive)					
24	動 動	ドウ、うご-く、うご-かす　move				
	運動：うんどう　(exercise) 運動します：うんどうします　(to do exercises)					

8. あの _____ の _____ は _____ の
　　　　　おんな　　　　　　　　こ　　　　　　　　　　あに

　　_____ どもです。
　　　　　こ

9. _____ はカメラを _____ もっています。
　　　　ちち　　　　　　　　　　よんだい

10. _____ _____ いのは _____ えんです。
　　　いちばん　　　　たか　　　　　　　　じゅうごまん

11. _____ _____ しています。
　　　まいあさ　　　　　うんどう

12. _____ を _____ くのが _____ きです。
　　　おんがく　　　　　　き　　　　　　　　　す

13. りょうりは_____ くにが _____ です。
　　　　　　　　まった　　　　　　　　　て

14. _____ に _____ がたくさんいます。
　　　みち　　　　　　ひと

Kanji in Everyday Life

1. You see an advertisement in the newspaper for a local culture center which is offering a new class. It says あなたも手話を習いませんか. What would you learn in this class?

　　_____

2. You are in the map section of a bookstore and see a thick atlas which says 日本全国道路地図 on the front cover. What is this atlas for?

　　_____

3. You are about to go through the ticket gate to a bullet train (しんかんせん) platform at Tokyo Station to meet your friend who is coming from Kobe, and you notice a sign that says 運休のお知らせ. You realize that there is a big typhoon coming from the western area. Are you going to take a look at this sign or not? Why?

　　_____

4. Who is the author of 雪国? (Hint: He received the Nobel Prize in Literature in 1968.)

　　_____

5. You are at the door of a study room in the library and see a sign 使用中 on the door. Can you use the room?

    _____

6. You are asked to fill out a questionnaire written in Japanese. One of the questions is あなたの母国語は何ですか. What would you write?

    _____

Writing Activities

Vocabulary and Grammar 5A: Hobbies and Pastimes

A. Match each question in Column 1 with the most appropriate response in Column 2.

COLUMN 1

1. _____ 何か飲みましたか。
2. _____ 何を飲みますか。
3. _____ だれかいますか。
4. _____ だれがいますか。
5. _____ どこへ行きましたか。
6. _____ どこかへ行きましたか。
7. _____ いつ日本へ行きますか。
8. _____ いつか日本へ行きますか。
9. _____ どれを読みますか。
10. _____ どれか読みますか。
11. _____ どちらが好きですか。
12. _____ どちらか好きですか。

COLUMN 2

a. 学生がいます。
b. はい、行きました。
c. はい、こちらが好きです。
d. デパートへ行きました。
e. これを読みます。
f. はい、飲みました。
g. はい、読みます。
h. はい、だれかいます。
i. 来年日本へ行きます。
j. はい、いつか行きます。
k. こちらが好きです。
l. コーヒーを飲みます。

B. Ask your classmates what their hobbies are. Then list the five most popular hobbies, adding a statement about how many people pursue each one.

EXAMPLE: 音楽（おんがく）が好きな人は 15 人いました。

スポーツの好きな人は 12 人でした。

1. _____

_____

2. _____

_____

3. _____

_____

4. _____

_____

5. _____

_____

C. A new student from Japan is interested in non-credit classes offered by a nearby community college. Look at the information given on the catalogue page and tell him/her the titles of the courses, the time and day of the week they are offered, the names of the instructors, the fees for each, and the beginning and the ending dates.

EXAMPLE: キルティングのクラスは月曜日（よう）の 8 時から 10 時までです。先生は スミス先生で、50 ドルです。このクラスは 1 月 4 日（か）から 3 月 15 日ま でです。

```
┌─────────────────────────────────────────────────────────┐
│              NON-CREDIT SPECIAL INTEREST COURSES          │
│                      WINTER QUARTER                        │
│                                                            │
│   COURSE          TIME           INSTRUCTOR          FEE   │
│                                                            │
│   Aerobics        MWF            Jennifer Blake    $60.00  │
│                   12:00–12:45                              │
│                   1/4–3/19                                 │
│                                                            │
│   English         T TH           Richard Finnegan $120.00 │
│   Conversation    6:30–9:00                               │
│                   1/6–3/18                                 │
│                                                            │
│   French for      W              Monique Dutoit    $75.00 │
│   Travelers       6:30–9:00                               │
│                   1/6–2/17                                 │
│                                                            │
│   Origami         Sat            Kimiko Nakamura   $10.00  │
│   Workshop        9:00–12:00                              │
│                   2/13 only                               │
│                                                            │
│   Photography     Sat      George "Flash" Gordon  $120.00 │
│                   9:00–12:00                              │
│                   1/9–3/20                                 │
│                                                            │
│   Quilting        M              Abigail Smith     $50.00 │
│                   8:00–10:00                              │
│                   1/4–3/15                                 │
│                                                            │
│   Yoga            MWF            Andrew Mills      $60.00  │
│                   5:30–6:30                               │
│                   1/4–3/19                                 │
└─────────────────────────────────────────────────────────┘
```

1. エアロビクス _____

   _____

2. ヨガ _____

   _____

3. おりがみ _____

   _____

4. えい語 _____

   _____

5. フランス語 _____

   _____

   _____

6. しゃしん _____

   _____

Vocabulary and Grammar 5B: Sports

A. If you were interviewing a newly arrived Japanese exchange student for your school paper, what questions would you ask to get the following information?

1. If there is any sport that she is good at and likes.

    _____

2. If there is any academic subject that she is poor at and dislikes.

    _____

3. If there are any musical instruments she can play.

    _____

4. If there is any foreign language she is good at and likes.

    _____

B. If you were the exchange student interviewed in the previous exercise, how would you answer the questions? Base the answers on your own skills and preferences.

1. _____

2. _____

3. _____

4. _____

C. Ask three of your classmates what sports they like, if they play them and how often, if they watch them on television, if they are good or poor at them, etc. Then write their answers in paragraph form below.

       EXAMPLE: スミスさんはバスケットボールが好きです。でも、とくいじゃ ありませんから、あまりしません。いつもテレビで見ます。

1. _____

    _____

    _____

2. _____

    _____

    _____

3. _____

    _____

    _____

4. Now write about yourself.

_____

_____

_____

D. Fill in the blanks with a nominalized verb with either こと or の.

EXAMPLE: 日本語を ＿＿＿＿＿＿＿＿ はむずかしいです。(読みます)

日本語を読むこと／のはむずかしいです。

1. やきゅうを ＿＿＿＿＿＿＿＿ が好きです。(します)

2. すもうを ＿＿＿＿＿＿＿＿ はおもしろくありません。(見ます)

3. 日本で＿＿＿＿＿＿＿＿ はむずかしいです。(運てんします)

4. ひらがなを ＿＿＿＿＿＿＿＿ はやさしいです。(書きます)

5. ＿＿＿＿＿＿＿＿ はきらいです。(そうじをします)

6. ＿＿＿＿＿＿＿＿ と ＿＿＿＿＿＿＿＿ とどちらの方が好きですか。(食べます) (ねます)

7. リンカーンがそう＿＿＿＿＿＿＿＿ は有名です。(いいました)

8. はやしさんがイギリスに＿＿＿＿＿＿＿＿ はしりませんでした。(行きました)

9. カワムラさんがスポーツが＿＿＿＿＿＿＿＿ は有名です。(上手です)

10. 日本の家が＿＿＿＿＿＿＿＿ はだれでもしっています。(高いです)

E. Answer questions 1 through 3 truthfully. For items 4 through 7, make up your own questions and then answer them.

1. バスケットボールは見るのとするのとどちらの方が好きですか。

_____

2. りょうりは作るのと食べるのとどちらの方が好きですか。

_____

3. えはかくのと見るのとどちらの方が好きですか。

_____

4. しゃしんは

_____

5. えんげきは

_____

6. ダンスは

_____

7. うたは

_____

F. Linda Brown is trying to decide what to give some of her friends for Christmas. Using the table below, suggest a gift for each person that will be in line with his or her interests.

	NAME	HOBBIES
1.	Hitomi Machida	cooking, cycling
2.	Heather Gibson	skiing, skating, hiking
3.	Henry Curtis	reading, stamp collecting
4.	Mei Lin Chin	movies, brush collecting
5.	Takeshi Mimura	partying
6.	Sayuri Yamamoto	watching TV, music

EXAMPLE: 町田さんはりょうりをすることが好きですから、
りょうりの本はどうですか。

1. _____

2. _____

3. _____

4. _____

5. _____

G. You live in an apartment complex in Japan where a number of foreigners live. There was a murder on the fourth floor last night, and a Japanese detective is going around to see if some of you have seen or heard anything. Since some of the foreigners cannot speak Japanese, help the detective out by telling him what the others say they heard or saw.

	NAME	LIVE(S) ON THE...	CLAIMS TO HAVE...
1.	Mr. Green	third floor	seen a man go to the fourth floor
2.	Ms. Smith	fourth floor	heard someone cry (なく)
3.	Mr. and Mrs. Li	third floor	heard someone scream (さけぶ)
4.	Mr. Young	fourth floor	seen an odd-looking (へんな) man go downstairs
5.	Ms. Kim	first floor	seen a car drive away (はしって行く)

EXAMPLE: 3かいのグリーンさんは、<ruby>男<rt>おとこ</rt></ruby>の人が4かいへ<ruby>行<rt>い</rt></ruby>くのを<ruby>見<rt>み</rt></ruby>ました。

1. _____

2. _____

3. _____

4. _____

5. (Now write what you yourself saw or heard.) _____

_____

H. Continuing the situation described in the previous exercise, the detective has found more witness. Now he is reporting to his boss about the witnesses. Pretending that you are the detective, answer the following questions, using the ⋯も⋯も structure if necessary as you study the chart.

	GREEN	SMITH	LI	YOUNG	KIM	YAMADA	KITA	TAKADA	YOSHIDA
Saw a man go to the 4th floor	×						×	×	
Heard someone cry		×				×	×		
Heard someone scream			×				×		
Saw a strange man go downstairs				×					×
Saw a car drive away					×	×			

EXAMPLE: Q: だれが男の人が４かいへ行くのを見ましたか。

A: グリーンさんが見ました。それから、北さんと高田さんも
見ましたよ。

1. Q: スミスさんも高田さんもだれかがなく (to cry) のを聞きましたか。

A: _____

2. Q: リーさんとよし田さんがだれかがさけぶ (to scream) のを聞きましたか。

A: _____

3. Q: ヤングさんだけ (only)、へんな男の人が下へ行くのを見ましたか。

A: _____

4. Q: キムさんも山田さんもくるまがはしって行く (to drive away) のを見ましたか。

A: _____

5. Q: 北さんはだれかがなくのだけ (only) 聞きましたか。

A: _____

I. A Japanese acquaintance would like to know more about you. Answer the following questions using one of the following patterns: 1) も…も + affirmative 2) も…も + negative 3) …は affirmative …は negative.

EXAMPLE: Q: あなたはバレーボールとバスケットボールをしますか。

A: はい、バレーボールもバスケットボールもします。
スポーツは大好きですから。
OR
いいえ、バレーボールもバスケットボールもしません。スポーツは
にが手ですから。
OR
いいえ、バレーボールはしますけれど、バスケットボールは
しません。

1. Q: あなたは日本語も中国語もできますか。

A: _____

2. Q: あなたはビールもワインも飲みますか。

A: _____

3. Q: あなたは土曜日も日曜日も勉強しますか。

A: _____

4. Q: あなたはレバーもほうれんそう (spinach) も食べますか。

   A: _____

5. Q: あなたの家にはねこ (cat) かいぬ (dog) がいますか。

   A: _____

6. Q: あなたはコーヒーもおさけも飲みますか。

   A: _____

J. What would a person such as those described below say? Make up sentences with も used to mean "not even."

   EXAMPLE: (a person who has insomnia)
   昨日のよるは1時間もねられませんでした。

1. (a student who is healthy, diligent, and so interested in Japanese that he or she has never missed a class)

   _____

2. (a person who is allergic to alcohol) (hint: one drop = 一てき)

   _____

3. (a person who is so afraid of flying that he or she has never dared to try it)

   _____

4. (a stationery store manager who has sold out all the pens and pencils)

   _____

K. Answer these questions, using the potential form, either positive or negative, depending on whether the answer blank begins with はい or いいえ.

   EXAMPLE: 日本語で話すことができますか。
   はい、話せます。

1. カメラを使うことができますか。

   はい、_____

2. りょうりをすることができますか。

   いいえ、_____

3. 何か楽きをえんそうすることができますか。

   はい、_____

4. 上手にかんじを書くことができますか。

  いいえ、_____

5. 一日中、読書をすることができますか。

  いいえ、_____

6. 10キロおよぐことができますか。

  いいえ、_____

7. 日本のうたをうたうことができますか。

  はい、_____

8. 明日コンサートに行くことができますか。

  はい、_____

9. 一人ですしを作ることができますか。

  いいえ、_____

10. 明日もう一度、ここに来ることができますか。

  はい、_____

L. Answer these questions truthfully.

1. 何語が話せますか。

  _____

2. どんな日本りょうりが作れますか。

  _____

3. どんな楽きがえんそうできますか。

  _____

4. くるまが運てんできますか。

  _____

5. やきゅうができますか。

  _____

6. 生けばな かさ道ができますか。

  _____

7. 空手かじゅう道ができますか。

_____

8. テニスかゴルフができますか。

_____

9. どんなうたがうたえますか。

_____

10. どこでキャンプができますか。

_____

11. だれが上手に日本語を話せますか。

_____

M. The following are a few examples of amazing people. Tell your Japanese acquaintance what they can do, first using the potential verb form and then using こ と が で き る structure.

1. Takeuchi: can swim as much as 20 kilometers
2. Masuda: can eat as many as 15 hamburgers
3. Aoki's son: can write as many as 1500 *kanji* although he is 7 years old.
4. You: ???

EXAMPLE: Sakamoto: can drink as much as 2 liters of cola
   a.   さか本さんはコーラが 2 リットルも飲めます。
   b.   さか本さんはコーラを 2 リットルも飲むことができます。

1. a. _____

   b. _____

2. a. _____

   b. _____

3. a. _____

   b. _____

4. a. _____

   b. _____

Vocabulary and Grammar 5C: Family

A. Here is Toshio Minami's description of his family. Read it through, and then draw the Minami family tree. (Use squares to indicate males and ovals to indicate females.)

わたしは、南としおです。南はるおは、わたしの兄です。南まゆみは、兄のつまです。兄は、子どもが二人います。むす子はよしのりで、むすめはかずよです。南えみは、わたしの妹です。南まさるは、わたしの父です。母の名前は、ゆう子です。東じろうは、母の弟です。南あい子は、わたしの父の姉です。南くに子は、わたしのそぼです。そふの名前は、南いちろうです。これが、わたしの家族です。

B. All the people in this portrait of Midori Momoi and her family are labeled with numbers. After reading Midori's description of the portrait, write the identity of each person after the appropriate number.

あかいドレスの女の人はわたしの姉です。姉のとなりのせの高い男の人は姉のおっとです。姉の後ろの男の人と女の人はわたしのりょうしんです。一番右のしろいブラウスの女の子はわたしのめいです。そのとなりはわたしの弟です。弟の前の男の人は姉のおっとの兄です。まん中はわたしです。

EXAMPLE: 1. お姉さんのごしゅ人（ぎりのお兄さん）

2. _____   6. _____

3. _____   7. _____

4. _____   8. _____

5. _____

C. Assume that this is the family tree of your friend Terry. Study the family tree, and then write statements about how each person is related to Terry.

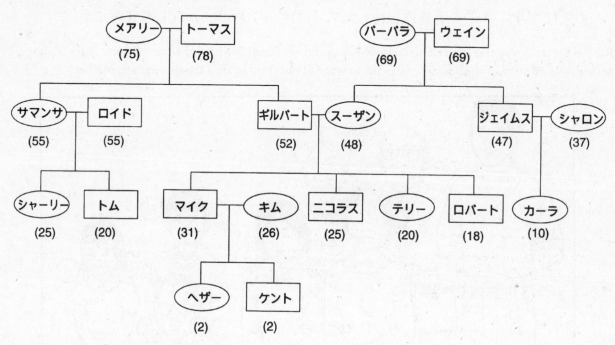

EXAMPLE: (Mary and Barbara)
　　　メアリーさんとバーバラさんはテリーさんのおばあさんです。

1. (Thomas and Wayne) _____

2. (Samantha and Sharon) _____

3. (Gilbert) _____

4. (Susan) _____

5. (James and Lloyd) _____

6. (Shirley and Tom) _____

7. (Mike) _____

8. (Kim) _____

9. (Nicholas) _____

10. (Robert) _____

11. (Carla) _____

12. (Heather) _____

13. (Kent) _____

D. Using the same family tree as in the previous exercise, complete the statements about how the various people are related to one another.

EXAMPLE: ギルバートさんはメアリーさんの<u>むす子</u>さんです。

1. テリーさんはニコラスさんの _____ です。

2. シャーリーさんとトムさんはサマンサさんの _____ です。

3. サマンサさんはギルバートさんの _____ です。

4. マイクさんとニコラスさんとロバートさんはカーラさんの _____ です。

5. スーザンさんはヘザーさんの _____ です。

6. キムさんはマイクさんの _____ です。

7. マイクさんはキムさんの _____ です。

8. カーラさんやテリーさんはバーバラさんとウェインさんの _____ です。

9. ギルバートさんはロバートさんやニコラスさんの _____ です。

10. スーザンさんはジェイムスさんの _____ です。

11. バーバラさんとウェインさんは _____ です。

E. Draw a family tree for your own family. Include at least six family members (You may have to go back a generation or two if your family is small.) Then write a brief paragraph about each person, telling his or her name, age, relation to you, and at least one interesting fact about him or her. If you do not know how to write the person's name in カタカナ, ask your instructor.

1. _____

_____

_____

2. _____

_____

_____

3. _____

_____

_____

4. _____

_____

_____

5. _____

_____

_____

6. _____

_____

_____

F. Complete the dialogues.

1. お姉_{ねえ}さんのしゅみは何ですか。

_____ のしゅみは、りょうりをすることです。

2. お父_{とう}さんのしゅみは何ですか。

_____ のしゅみは、スキーを _____ ことです。

3. _____ のしゅみは…。

母_{はは}のしゅみは、音楽_{おんがく}を _____ ことです。

4. _____ のしゅみは何ですか。

弟_{おとうと}のしゅみは、スポーツを見_みる _____。

5. おばあさんのしゅみは何ですか。

_____ のしゅみは、生_いけばなです。

6. 妹_{いもうと}さんのしゅみは何ですか。

_____ のしゅみは、しゃしんを _____ です。

7. むす子_こさんのしゅみは何ですか。

_____ のしゅみは、つりです。

8. _____ のしゅみは何ですか。

つまのしゅみは、テレビを _____ です。

9. ごしゅ人のしゅみは何ですか。

　　　＿＿＿＿＿＿＿＿のしゅみは、ゴルフです。

10. おじいさんのしゅみは何ですか。

　　　＿＿＿＿＿＿＿＿のしゅみは、読書(どくしょ)です。

G. These two pictures are similar, but there are five major differences between them. Write statements comparing the pictures, describing the points of difference.

A	B

 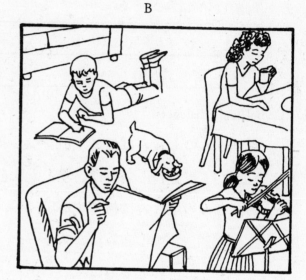

EXAMPLE:　Aの男(おとこ)の人は本を読(よ)んでいますが、Bの男(おとこ)の人はしん聞を読(よ)んでいます。

1. _____

2. _____

3. _____

4. _____

H. Remember our murder mystery? The time of the murder has been determined, and the detective wants to know what each person's alibi is for that time. Help him out.

1. Ms. Smith was watching a TV drama. She remembers the story.
2. Mr. Li was taking a bath. His wife heard him singing in the bath.
3. Mr. Young was talking with a nextdoor neighbor in his room.
4. Ms. Kim was playing cards with three friends.
5. You ???

　　EXAMPLE:　Mr. Green was drinking at a bar with a friend.

　　　グリーンさんはバーでともだちと飲(の)んでいました。

1. _____
2. _____
3. _____
4. _____
5. _____

I. This week is a university vacation, but John Kawamura has nothing to do and is bored. He would like to do something with one of his classmates, but when he tries to get in touch with them, he discovers that they all have other plans. Write down what each person is doing.

1. Heather Gibson: gone mountain climbing to Nagano Prefecture
2. Toshiko Yokoi: gone home to Kyoto
3. Masao Hayashi: in bed with a bad cold (to have a cold = かぜをひく)
4. Henry Curtis: parents are visiting from Atlanta
5. Hitomi Machida: working at a departments store every day

   EXAMPLE: Linda Brown: on a trip to Kyushu with Mei Lin Chin
   　ブラウンさんはチンさんと九しゅうへりょ行に行っています。

1. _____
2. _____
3. _____
4. _____
5. _____

J. What were you doing at the following time yesterday? Give the details: place, with whom, how, how many, etc.

   EXAMPLE:　午後11時→一人でうちでねていました。

1. 午前6時 _____
2. 午前8時 _____
3. 午前10時半_____
4. 午後12時 _____
5. 午後3時 _____
6. 午後7時半_____
7. 午後9時 _____
8. 午前12時 _____

K. Make up sentences using the words given. Be sure to pay attention to the time words so that you use the past, present, and ている form correctly.

EXAMPLE: 空手（からて）／できる／人／田中さん

空手（からて）ができる人は、田中さんです。

1. 昨日（きのう）／およぐ／学生／カワムラさん

_____

2. ゴルフができる／学生／何人／いる／か

_____

3. 一番（いちばん）／人気（にんき）がある (popular) ／しゅみ／読書（どくしょ）

_____

4. ブラウンさん／食（た）べている／もの／何／か

_____

5. カーティスさん／先週（せんしゅう）／書（か）いている／もの／何／か

_____

6. アメリカ人／よくする／スポーツ／何／か

_____

7. お金（かね）(money) ／かかる (cost) ／しゅみ／サーフィン

_____

L. You are at a party with a Japanese acquaintance. He has met a lot of the people at this party but cannot remember their names. Tell him which person is which, following the example.

Coronado (the man playing the piano)
Yu (the woman talking with Smith)
Kraus (the man eating potato chips)
Kim (the woman drinking beer)
Scott (the man watching TV)

EXAMPLE: Smith (the man drinking coffee)

スミスさんはコーヒーを飲（の）んでいる男（おとこ）の人です。

1. _____

2. _____

3. _____

4. _____

5. _____

M. We are back to our murder mystery. The detective has to report to the chief of detectives about how the case is going, but the chief has trouble remembering which witness is which. Pretend that you are the detective, and refresh the chief's memory by describing each person. Use the structure "Mr./Ms. X is the person who…"

1. Ms. Smith was watching a TV drama. She remembers the story.
2. Mr. Li was taking a bath. His wife heard him singing in the bath.
3. Mr. Young was talking with a nextdoor neighbor in his room.
4. Ms. Kim was playing cards with three friends.
5. You ???

   EXAMPLE: Mr. Green is the person who was drinking at a bar with a friend.

   グリーンさんはバーでともだちと飲んでいた人です。

1. _____

2. _____

3. _____

4. _____

5. _____

N. Fill in the blanks with either に or the く form of the adjective, whichever is appropriate.

   EXAMPLE: えい語の先生_____ なりました。

   えい語の先生になりました。

1. むすめは、今年、大学生_____ なりました。

2. むす子は、えい語が上手_____ なりました。

3. ギブソンさんは、きれい_____ なりました。

4. 日本語は、だんだん (gradually) むずかし_____ なっています。

5. ゴルフが好き_____ なりました。

6. おさけがきらい_____ なりました。

7. フランス語がにが手_____ なるかもしれません。

8. 日本のえんは、やす_____ なるでしょう。

9. 夏は、ひま_____ なるかもしれません。

10. 12月になって、とても寒_____ なりました。

O. A Japanese friend would like to know how long it takes to become good at the following skills. Of course it depends upon the individual, but give him/her your opinion, stating your guess in days, weeks, months, or years.

EXAMPLE: （えい語）

えい語は5年ぐらいで (in about five years) 上手 (じょうず) になるでしょう。

1. （スキー）_____

2. （りょうり）_____

3. （すいえい）_____

4. （ギター）_____

P. The first drawing shows Kazuo's family as they looked five years ago, and the second one shows them as they look now. Compare the two drawings and write statements about how the people have changed. (Kazuo is the boy on the left, and the girl next to him is his sister, Kyoko.)

Useful Vocabulary: かみ *hair,* め *eye*

EXAMPLE: きょう子さんはせ(height)が高くなりました。

1. _____
2. _____
3. _____
4. _____
5. _____

Chapter 5 Review

A. You are an executive at a company and want to hire an assistant. Think of six things you want your assistant to be able to do, and prepare questions to ask during the employment interview. (Write the questions in both the ことができます and potential forms.)

EXAMPLE: タイプをうつ(to hit/type)ことができますか。

タイプがうてますか。

1. _____
2. _____
3. _____
4. _____

5. _____

6. _____

B. Your Japanese acquaintance would like to know what you can and can't do in Japanese. Using both the potential form and ことができる structures, tell him/her about your Japanese ability. Some things to consider are your listening ability (what you understand), reading ability (what kinds of things you can read), writing ability (what you can write, using what characters), and speaking ability (what you can talk about). Write at least five sentences.

1. _____

2. _____

3. _____

4. _____

5. _____

C. You are a North American student studying in Japan, and you get a phone call from a public opinion pollster conducting a survey on the lives and habits of foreign students. These are some of the pollster's questions. Answer them truthfully.

1. あなたは今何をする時間が一番ほしいですか。

   _____

2. あなたが今まで読んだ本の中でどれが一番おもしろかったですか。

   _____

3. あなたのりそうの (ideal) ごしゅ人／おくさんは何ができる人ですか。

   _____

4. あなたが今これを書いているところはどこですか。そこは、ほかに (other than that) 何ができるところですか。

   _____

5. あなたはどこから来た先生に日本語をならって (learn) いますか。

   _____

CHAPTER **6**

FOOD

食べ物

Listening Comprehension Activities

Vocabulary and Grammar 6A: Foods and Beverages

A. Listen to the names of food items, and write them down in katakana. The name of each item will be pronounced only once.

1. _____   3. _____   5. _____

2. _____   4. _____

B. Professor Yokoi has asked her students to talk about their eating habits, and Henry Curtis and Linda Brown are conversation partners. Listen to their conversation, and then choose the option that best completes the following sentences.

Useful Vocabulary: たいてい *mostly,* だから *that's why,* スマート *slim*

Brown:

1. eats meals _____ times a day.
   a. two   b. three   c. four

2. _____ eats breakfast.
   a. always   b. sometimes   c. never

3. usually has a _____ lunch.
   a. vegetarian   b. Japanese style   c. heavy

4. sometimes eats _____ for dinner.
   a. beef   b. pork   c. chicken

5. is slim because of her _____.
   a. job   b. diet   c. exercise

C. Henry Curtis and Hitomi Machida are wondering what to make for dinner. Listen to their conversation, and then list the main ingredient(s) for each of the following dishes.

今ばんのメニュー

1. てりやきチキン：＿＿＿＿＿＿＿＿

2. サラダ：＿＿＿＿＿＿ ＿＿＿＿＿＿ ＿＿＿＿＿＿

3. メキシカン・ライス：＿＿＿＿＿＿ ＿＿＿＿＿＿ ＿＿＿＿＿

D. You will hear a description of four common foods or beverages. Listen to the descriptions and write the names of the items in Japanese in the blanks.

1. ＿＿＿＿＿＿   2. ＿＿＿＿＿＿   3. ＿＿＿＿＿＿   4. ＿＿＿＿＿＿

Vocabulary and Grammar 6B: Flavors and Tastes

A. Listen as John Kawamura tells Hitomi Machida about a new restaurant. Then mark each of the following statements either true (T) or false (F).

Useful Vocabulary: できた *was built*

1. ＿＿＿＿＿ The new restaurant that opened last week is in front of the university.

2. ＿＿＿＿＿ Both Kawamura and Machida have heard about the restaurant but have never been there.

3. ＿＿＿＿＿ A Spanish omelet is made of eggs and potatoes.

4. ＿＿＿＿＿ Machida knew about paella because she has tried it.

5. ＿＿＿＿＿ There are no rice dishes in that restaurant.

6. ＿＿＿＿＿ Machida likes to drink wine.

B. Listen as Masaru Honda continues interviewing Himiko. Then complete each of the following sentences by writing the initial of the person it best describes. (H: Himiko, M: Masaru Honda, B: both)

1. ＿＿＿＿＿ is/are on a diet.

2. ＿＿＿＿＿ know(s) that tofu is good for you.

3. ＿＿＿＿＿ think(s) tofu has no taste.

4. ＿＿＿＿＿ like(s) tofu flavored with soy sauce.

5. ＿＿＿＿＿ love(s) sweet tofu.

6. ＿＿＿＿＿ prefer(s) spicy tofu.

C. Listen as a reporter introduces two women on a television talk show and asks them about their lives and desires. Then complete the following sentences by writing in Y if the statement is true of the company employee, Yoshiko Yamada, and S if the statement is true of the actress, Kirara Shimizu.

Useful Vocabulary: こい人 girl/boy friend, じょゆう actress, ゆっくり leisurely

1. _____ wants her own apartment.

2. _____ wants time to sleep.

3. _____ wants to go on drives in her new car.

4. _____ wants quiet time to read.

5. _____ wants to eat out with her boyfriend.

6. _____ wants to stay single.

7. _____ wants to chat with friends.

8. _____ wants to have a family.

9. _____ does not want children.

10. _____ wants to cook at home.

D. Listen as Masao Hayashi and Mei Lin Chin talk about Hitomi Machida's birthday present. Fill in the blanks, choosing the correct option from a–c.

1. Machida's birthday is February _____.
   a. 1st   b. 2nd   c. 3rd

2. They will have _____ for Machida.
   a. a party   b. a gift   c. both a and b

3. Mchida _____ a camera.
   a. wants   b. has   c. will buy

4. A camera may _____ for a birthday gift.
   a. not be exciting   b. be too expensive   c. be cheap

5. Machida wants a calendar, but Hayashi and Chin think it is _____.
   a. not interesting   b. too inexpensive   c. hard to find a good one

6. Hayashi and Chin think Machida will enjoy _____ using tickets they will give her.
   a. a movie   b. a concert   c. an opera

Vocabulary and Grammar 6C: Cooking

A. Kawamura gets his information on good restaurants in Tokyo from Machida. Listen to Kawamura talk about some restaurants that Machida recommended. Then circle all the choices from a-d that describe the three restaurants mentioned.

1. Ashoka:
   a. located in Shinjuku
   b. serves Indian food
   c. rather expensive
   d. a good place for spicy food

2. La Vie:
   a. located near Tokyo Station
   b. located in Ginza
   c. elegant atmosphere
   d. a good place to try snails

3. Fuji:
   a. old and big
   b. rather expensive
   c. is frequented by students
   d. a good place for fish dishes

B. Listen to the composition Linda Brown wrote about her plans for the winter. Then read the following list and circle the things she plans to do during the holidays.

Useful Vocabulary: すごす *to spend (time)*

1. Work   4. See her family

2. Go skiing   5. Spend Christmas in the mountains

3. Sightsee in New York   6. Study Japanese

C. Listen to the conversation between John Kawamura and Hitomi Machida. Then fill in the blanks to complete the summary of their conversation.

Machida was going _____ when she saw Kawamura. Kawamura asked if Machida

wanted to go to _____ with _____ and him. Machida was thinking

of _____ the house. Kawamura thinks Machida's house is always

_____. So Machida decides to go with them. Before that, Kawamura wants to call

_____ to ask _____. So Machida and Kawamura will go to a nearby

phone and call.

D. Mei Lin Chin and Linda Brown are talking about their plans for dinner as they head home. Listen to their conversation, and complete the sentences by circling the right word.

1. Chin thought there was leftover (a. rice b. stew c. curry) from yesterday.

2. Brown ate the dish today for (a. breakfast b. lunch c. dinner).

3. Chin asked about the tempura that they cooked (a. yesterday b. two days ago c. three days ago).

4. Brown ate the tempura with (a. rice b. udon c. soba).

5. Chin suggests that they eat (a. ramen b. gyoza c. fried rice) at Tenshin.

6. Brown (a. has b. has not) been to Tenshin, but she also suggests (a. sukiyaki b. shabushabu c. tonkatsu) at Ebisu Garden.

7. Chin (a. has b. has not) been to Ebisu Garden, and she wants to go there.

8. They find out that they have (a. little b. some c. a lot of) money.

9. They end up going to a convenience store to buy (a. a TV dinner b. a cooked meal c. instant ramen).

E. John Kawamura is in the food section of a department store in Tokyo. He is asked to sample several things by a saleswoman. Fill in the blanks to complete the summary of their conversation.

Useful Vocabulary: でん子レンジ *microwave oven*

The saleswoman is selling _____ and _____. She says both items can

be cooked in a _____. Kawamura first tries _____, and it tastes very

good. The second item he tries has _____ taste. The saleswoman suggests putting some

_____ on it. Kawamura decides to buy _____ with

_____. In the end, he finds himself buying _____ as well, because it

is on sale today.

F. Listen to Heather Gibson complaining about her roommate. What does her roommate do simultaneously? Complete each pair, choosing two actions from the list.

She _____ while she _____.

She _____ while she _____.

She _____ while she _____.

She _____ while she _____.

eats her meals	takes a shower	studies
takes notes	drinks cola	sings with music
watches TV	eats snacks	drives

G. Kawamura has a black eye, and Machida has a bandage on her finger. Listen to them talk about how it happened. Then fill in the blanks to complete the summary in English.

Kawamura was injured when he was _____ to his friends while playing

_____. Machida cut her finger when she was _____ while

_____. They decided to go to a restaurant to _____ something good

while _____.

Kanji Practice and Exercises

1	思 思	シ、おも-う think				
	思う：おもう (to think) 高いと思います：たかいとおもいます (I think that it is expensive.)		悪	思		
2	終 終	シュウ、お-わる、お-える come/bring to an end おわり end, conclusion つい-に finally, in the end				
	終わる：おわる (to come to an end) クラスが終わりました：くらすがおわりました (The class ended.)		終	終		
3	始 始	シ、はじ-まる、はじ-める start, begin				
	クラスが始まる：くらすがはじまる (The class starts.) クラスを始める：くらすをはじめる (to begin class)		始	始		
4	物 物	ブツ、モツ、もの thing, object				
	食べ物：たべもの (food) 飲み物：のみもの (beverage) くだ物：くだもの (fruit)		物	物		

5	肉 肉	ニク meat, flesh			
	肉：にく (meat) 牛肉：ぎゅうにく (beef) 鳥肉：とりにく (chicken) ぶた肉：ぶたにく (pork)		肉	肉	
6	事 事	ジ、ズ、こと、-ごと thing, matter			
	食事：しょくじ (meal) 食事をする：しょくじをする (have a meal)		事	事	
7	茶 茶	チャ、サ tea; light brown			
	（お）茶：（お）ちゃ (tea) 茶わん：ちゃわん (rice bowl / tea cup) 茶道：さどう (tea ceremony)		茶	茶	
8	酒 酒	シュ、さけ、さか- sake, rice wine; alcoholic drink, liquor			
	（お）酒：（お）さけ (sake, liquor) お酒を飲みますか：おさけをのみますか (Do you drink sake?) 日本酒：にほんしゅ (Japanese sake)		酒	酒	
9	牛 牛	ギュウ、ゴ、うし cow, bull, ox, cattle			
	牛肉：ぎゅうにく (beef) 牛にゅう：ぎゅうにゅう (cow's milk)		牛	牛	
10	鳥 鳥	チョウ、とり bird			
	鳥肉：とりにく (chicken [meat])		鳥	鳥	

11	湯 湯	トウ、ゆ hot water			
	（お）湯：（お）ゆ （hot water） お湯はありますか：おゆはありますか （Do you have hot water?)		湯	湯	
12	野 野	ヤ field; the opposition (parties); rustic; wild の field			
	野さい：やさい （vegetables） 野きゅう：やきゅう （baseball） 中野：なかの （Nakano）		野	野	
13	魚 魚	ギョ、さかな、うお fish			
	魚：さかな （fish） 魚と肉とどちらの方が好きですか：さかなとにく とどちらのほうがすきですか （Which do you like better, fish or meat?)		魚	魚	
14	味 味	ミ、あじ taste, flavor あじ-わう taste; relish, appreciate			
	味：あじ （taste） 味見する：あじみする （to taste a sample） 味わう：あじわう （to taste, to appreciate） 味そ：みそ （fermented soybean paste）		味	味	
15	悪 悪	アク evil, vice オ、あ-し、わる-い bad			
	味が悪い：あじがわるい （tastes bad） 今日は天気が悪いです：きょうはてんきがわるい です （Today, the weather is bad.） 悪い天気：わるいてんき （bad weather）		悪	悪	
16	料 料	リョウ materials; fee, charge			
	ちょう味料：ちょうみりょう （seasoning） じゅぎょう料：じゅぎょうりょう （tuition） 料理：りょうり （cuisine, cooking）		料	料	

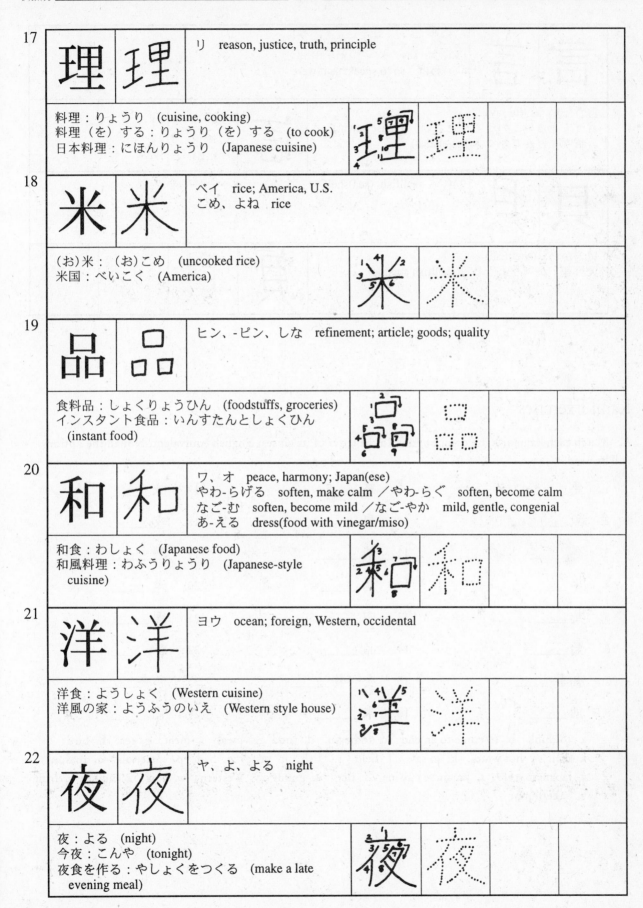

17 理 理   リ   reason, justice, truth, principle

料理：りょうり　(cuisine, cooking)
料理（を）する：りょうり（を）する　(to cook)
日本料理：にほんりょうり　(Japanese cuisine)

18 米 米   ベイ　rice; America, U.S.
　　　　　　こめ、よね　rice

（お）米：（お）こめ　(uncooked rice)
米国：べいこく　(America)

19 品 品   ヒン、-ピン、しな　refinement; article; goods; quality

食料品：しょくりょうひん　(foodstuffs, groceries)
インスタント食品：いんすたんとしょくひん
　(instant food)

20 和 和   ワ、オ　peace, harmony; Japan(ese)
　　　　　　やわ-らげる　soften, make calm／やわ-らぐ　soften, become calm
　　　　　　なご-む　soften, become mild／なご-やか　mild, gentle, congenial
　　　　　　あ-える　dress(food with vinegar/miso)

和食：わしょく　(Japanese food)
和風料理：わふうりょうり　(Japanese-style
　cuisine)

21 洋 洋   ヨウ　ocean; foreign, Western, occidental

洋食：ようしょく　(Western cuisine)
洋風の家：ようふうのいえ　(Western style house)

22 夜 夜   ヤ、よ、よる　night

夜：よる　(night)
今夜：こんや　(tonight)
夜食を作る：やしょくをつくる　(make a late
　evening meal)

23	言	言	ゲン、ゴン、こと　word い-う　say い-わば　so to speak, as it were				
	言う：いう　(to say) 言って下さい：いってください　(Please say it.) 言語学：げんごがく　(linguistics)				言		
24	貝	貝	かい　shellfish, (sea)shell				
	貝：かい　(shellfish) 貝料理：かいりょうり　(shellfish cuisine)				貝		

Kanji Exercises

A. Match each kanji or kanji compound with the letter of its closest English equivalent. Not all the options will be used.

1. 悪 _____
2. 魚 _____
3. 思 _____
4. 牛 _____
5. 鳥 _____
6. 始 _____
7. 食事 _____
8. 酒 _____
9. 終 _____
10. 貝 _____
11. 茶 _____
12. 湯 _____
13. 肉 _____
14. 品 _____
15. 食べ物 _____
16. 米 _____
17. 味 _____
18. 夜 _____
19. 野 _____
20. 洋 _____
21. 理 _____
22. 料 _____
23. 和食 _____
24. 言 _____

a. to think b. to come to an end c. to begin d. food e. meal f. meat g. tea h. bird
i. shell j. hot water k. to say l. field m. fish n. taste o. bad p. materials q. reason
r. Japanese style s. Japanese cuisine t. rice u. goods v. Western w. cow x. night y. fruit
z. sake/liquor

Name _____ Date _____ Class _____

B. Write hurigana for each kanji or kanji compound.

1. 酒
   _____

2. 日本酒
   _____

3. 味わう
   _____

4. 湯
   _____

5. 茶
   _____

6. 茶道
   _____

7. 終わる
   _____

8. 始める
   _____

9. 米
   _____

10. 野さい
    _____

11. 牛肉
    _____

12. 魚
    _____

13. 料理
    _____

14. 食事
    _____

15. 食べ物
    _____

16. 夜
    _____

17. 今夜
    _____

18. 夜食
    _____

19. 貝
    _____

20. 思う
    _____

21. 言う
    _____

22. 和食
    _____

23. 洋食
    _____

24. 食料品
    _____

25. 鳥肉
    _____

26. 悪い
    _____

C. Write the appropriate kanji for the hiragana written under the blanks.

1. _____ を _____ るのはむずかしいと _____ う。
   にくりょうり   つく   おも

2. _____ のお _____ を _____ んだことがありますか。
   にほん   さけ   の

3. _____ と _____ とどちらが _____ きですか。
   わしょく   ようしょく   す

4. _____ さいを _____ ってサラダを _____ りました。
　　　や　　　　　　　つか　　　　　　　　　　　つく

5. _____ この _____ を _____ み _____ めました。
　　きのう　　　　　ほん　　　　　よ　　　　はじ

6. この _____ べ _____ は _____ が _____ いです。
　　　　た　　　　もの　　　　あじ　　　　わる

7. _____ かお _____ を _____ もうと _____ います。
　　みず　　　　　ちゃ　　　　　の　　　　おも

8. _____ を _____ べましょう。
　　やしょく　　　　た

9. えいがはもう _____ わりました。
　　　　　　　　　お

10. お _____ を _____ し _____ さい。
　　　こめ　　　　すこ　　　くだ

11. インスタント _____ はだれにでも _____ れます。
　　　　　　　しょくひん　　　　　　　　つく

12. ラーメンに _____ うお _____ はありますか。
　　　　　　つか　　　　ゆ

13. _____ は _____ が _____ べたいです。
　　こんや　　　さかな　　　た

14. あのレストランで _____ をしました。
　　　　　　　　　しょくじ

15. もう _____ _____ って _____ さい。
　　　いちど　　　い　　　　くだ

16. _____ より _____ の _____ が _____ がいい。
　　ぎゅうにく　　　とりにく　　　ほう　　　あじ

17. そのみせの _____ は _____ です。
　　　　　　かいりょうり　　ゆうめい

310　　Chapter Six

Kanji in Everyday Life

1. You have been watching a Japanese TV serial drama and like it very much, although you have missed it a couple of times. When you were watching today's show, it previewed some segments of the next show. The word 最終回 also appeared on the screen. Do you want to watch it by all means or would it be all right if you have to miss it? Why?

_____

2. While you are looking at a book in Japanese about 野生動物, you see the word 弱肉強食 on a certain page. What do 野生動物 and 弱肉強食 mean respectively?

野生動物： _____

弱肉強食： _____

3. When you read about a bag-snatching incident in the newspaper, your Japanese friend said, そんなこと、このごろではにちじょうさはんじだよ. You asked him to write にちじょうさはんじ in kanji. What do you think 日常茶飯事（にちじょうさはんじ）means?

_____

4. You are asked to navigate for your Japanese friend who is driving. On the road map you see that 有料道路 leads you to the destination directly. You show your friend the road, but he does not want to take the 有料道路. Why?

_____

5. You are reading the sports column in the newspaper and find a comment from a baseball player 外野手 in yesterday's game. What position does he play?

_____

6. You were walking around in a tourist town and saw the sign 天下一品 at a souvenir shop. What do you think 天下一品 means?

_____

Writing Activities

Vocabulary and Grammar 6A: Foods and Beverages

A. Your Japanese acquaintance would like to know what typical American breakfasts and lunches are like. Answer the following questions.

1. アメリカ人は朝ごはんと昼ごはんを食べますか。

_____

2. 朝ごはんはどんな物を食べますか。二つ、三つおしえて下さい。

_____

3. 朝ごはんは週まつもへい日もおなじですか。

_____

4. 朝の飲み物は何ですか。

_____

5. 朝ごはんを食べない人もいますか。あなたは。

_____

6. アメリカ人がよく食べる昼ごはんにはどんな物がありますか。

_____

7. アメリカ人の学生はたいてい(mostly)どこで昼ごはんを食べますか。

_____

8. 大学のカフェテリアの昼ごはんはたいてい(mostly)いくらぐらいですか。

_____

9. アメリカ人の学生はどんなサンドイッチが好きですか。

_____

10. 昼ごはんを全ぜん食べない学生もたくさんいますか。

_____

B. You have become acquainted with a Japanese student who is intrigued by the fact that you are studying Japanese. This student is very curious about your life in general and your experiences with Japanese culture in particular and wants to know whether you have ever done certain things. Make up the questions that this Japanese student might ask, based on the following cue sentences. Then answer the questions truthfully.

EXAMPLE:　さしみを（食べる）
　　　　　さしみを食べたことがありますか。
　　　　　—ええ、食べたことがあります。

1. お酒を（飲む）

_____

_____

2. 日本語のクラスで（ねる）

_____

_____

3. フランスのえいがを（見る）

_____

_____

4. ロンドンに（行く）

_____

_____

5. ラブレターを（書^かく）

_____

_____

6. クラスを（休む）

_____

_____

7. 中か料理^{りょうり}を（作^{つく}る）

_____

_____

8. 朝5時に学こうに（来る）

_____

_____

9. 有名人^{じん}に（会う）

_____

_____

10. 日本を（りょ行する）

_____

_____

C. Write down whether or not you have ever done each of the following, using こ と が あ る. Then ask three Japanese students or members of your Japanese class whether they have ever done these things. After the interview, write down the name of the person whose experiences most closely match yours.

1. going to Japan   2. meeting the president (大とうりょう) of the U.S. in person   3. working as a waiter/waitress   4. studying Spanish   5. seeing the movie "The Godfather"

Your experiences:

1. _____

2. _____

3. _____

4. _____

5. _____

The name of the person whose experiences are closest to yours and his/her experiences:

Name: _____

1. _____

2. _____

3. _____

4. _____

5. _____

D. What kind of things have you done in Japanese? List three things. (A few hints: Have you written a letter in Japanese? Have you spoken to a Japanese student? Have you ordered a meal in Japanese?)

1. _____

2. _____

3. _____

E. Change each of the following verbs to its -tai form. Then expand the sentence by telling what you want to drink, where you want to go, etc.

EXAMPLE: （食べる）→ てんぷらが食べたいです。

1. 飲む _____

_____

2. 行く _____

_____

3.　聞く _____

_____

4.　ねる _____

_____

5.　作る _____
　　つく

_____

6.　あそぶ _____

_____

7.　かう _____

_____

8.　お風ろに入る _____
　　　ふ

_____

9.　勉強する _____
　　べんきょう

_____

10.　でん話をかける _____

_____

11.　話す _____

_____

12.　およぐ _____

_____

13.　来る _____

_____

14.　書く _____
　　か

_____

15.　なる _____

_____

F. Answer the following questions.

1. 金曜日の夜にと書かんで勉強したいですか。

_____

2. 毎日レストランで食事をしたいですか。

_____

3. かんじをおぼえたいですか。（おぼえる = to remember, memorize）

_____

4. 夏、ラーメンが食べたいですか。

_____

5. 毎朝ワインが飲みたいですか。

_____

6. 毎日お風ろに入りたいですか。

_____

7. 毎ばん肉が食べたいですか。

_____

8. 毎日料理をしたいですか。

_____

G. Answer the questions.

1. 今度のたん生日に何がほしいですか。

_____

2. きょ年のたん生日に何がほしかったですか。

_____

3. 三むらさんのしゅ味はパーティーへ行くことです。
    今年のクリスマスに何をほしがっていると思いますか。

_____

4. ブラウンさんのしゅ味は料理をすることです。
   今年のクリスマスに何をほしがっていると思いますか。

   _____

5. ギブソンさんのしゅ味は、スキーです。
   今度のたん生日に何をほしがっていると思いますか。

   _____

6. カーティスさんのしゅ味は、ぶんげい作品 (literary works) を読むことです。
   今度のたん生日に何をほしがっていると思いますか。

   _____

H. What would you like to eat or drink in the following situations? Read each situation, and then state what food or beverage you would like to have at such a time.

EXAMPLE: 今日はとてもむずかしいテストがありました。やっと (finally)
終わって、ほっとしました (relieved)。
ビールが飲みたいですねえ。
つめたいコーラが飲みたいですねえ。

1. 今日はとても暑かったです。気おんが38度でした。

   _____

2. 今日はとても寒いです。外は雪がふっています。

   _____

3. 今、午後7時です。朝から何も食べていないので、とてもおなかがすいて
   います。

   _____

4. 今週いそがしかったので、毎日ファストフードを食べていました。もう
   ファストフードは見たくありません。

   _____

5. あなたは先月から毎日日本料理を食べています。

   _____

I. Interview a classmate or a Japanese acquaintance in Japanese about things that he or she wants to do. Then report both your questions and your partner's answers in the spaces provided.

> EXAMPLE: Find out what s/he wants to eat now.
>
> QUESTION: 今何が一番<ruby>食<rt>ばん</rt></ruby>べたいですか。
>
> REPORT: スミスさんはすしを一番<ruby>食<rt>ばん</rt></ruby>べたがっています。

The name of the person you interviewed: _____

1. Find out what movie s/he wants to see most.

   QUESTION: _____

   REPORT: _____

2. Find out what s/he wants to do next Saturday evening.

   QUESTION: _____

   REPORT: _____

3. Find out who s/he wants to see (meet) most now.

   QUESTION: _____

   REPORT: _____

4. Find out what s/he wants to buy.

   QUESTION: _____

   REPORT: _____

5. Find out where s/he wants to go most.

   QUESTION: _____

   REPORT: _____

J. What are some of the things you want to do in Japan if you go there in the near future? Write at least four things.

> EXAMPLE: おいしいおすしが食べたいです。

1. _____

2. _____

3. _____

4. _____

K. Ask four of your classmates what they most want to do during their next vacation and write down the things they mentioned.

      EXAMPLE: スミスさんは山のぼりをしたがっています。

1. _____

2. _____

3. _____

4. _____

L. When you were a child, there must have been things you wanted but couldn't (or weren't allowed to) do and things you did not want to do but had to. Write down three of each.

      EXAMPLE: (1) 夜おそく (late) まで起きていたかったです。

              (2) 夜はやくねたくなかったです。

Things you wanted to do:

1. _____

2. _____

3. _____

Things you did not want to do:

1. _____

2. _____

3. _____

Vocabulary and Grammar 6B: Flavors and Tastes

A. Answer each question in the form of a statement of opinion using …と思います.

      EXAMPLE: 明日雨がふりますか。

              ええ、ふると思います。

1. このスープはおいしいですか。

   はい、_____

2. その時けいは高かったですか。

   はい、_____

3. 東きょうはにぎやかですか。

   はい、_____

4. このうたは有名でしたか。

   はい、_____

5. 先生は日本人ですか。

   はい、_____

6. 先生は東きょう大学の学生でしたか。

   はい、_____

7. はやしさんは学こうに行きましたか。

   はい、_____

8. はやしさんは今うちにいますか。

   はい、_____

9. ブラウンさんはぶん学を勉強していますか。

   はい、_____

10. だれが日本に行きたがっているんですか。

    わたしの兄が_____

11. この男の人に会ったことがありますか。

    いいえ、_____

12. チンさんはあまい物が好きでしょうか。

    はい、_____

13. ブラウンさんのお母さんは日本語が話せますか。

    いいえ、_____

14. ニューヨークはしずかですか。

    いいえ、_____

15. しけんはむずかしかったですか。

    いいえ、_____

16. 明日、カワムラさんは学こうに来るでしょうか。

いいえ、_____

17. 日本料理と中か料理とどちらの方が高いですか。

_____

18. 家から大学までくるまで何分ぐらいですか。

_____

B. Here is a list of the hobbies and interests of some of John Kawamura's friends. Then read the following personal statements and guess who said each one.

NAME	HOBBIES
Hitomi Machida	cooking, cycling
Heather Gibson	skiing, skating, hiking
Henry Curtis	poetry, stamp collecting
Mei Lin Chin	reading
Takeshi Mimura	partying
Sayuri Yamamoto	watching TV, music

EXAMPLE: 「わたしは週まつにあたらしい本を読みたいと思っています。」

この人はチンさんだと思います。

1. 「わたしは来週の日曜日に日本アルプスへ行きたいと思っています。」

_____

2. 「わたしは今ばんケーキをやきたい（やく＝bake）と思っています。」

_____

3. 「わたしは土曜日のばんにともだちを30人ぐらい家によびたい（よぶ＝to invite）と思っています。」

_____

4. 「わたしは明日あたらしいCDをかいたいと思っています。」

_____

C. What's your opinion? Write a brief response to each question.

1. あなたの大学をどう思いますか。

_____

2. あなたの大学のじゅぎょう料(tuition)は1年にいくらぐらいですか。やすいと思いますか。

_____

3. あなたの大学の日本語のクラスをどう思いますか。

_____

4. あなたの大学のカフェテリアはどうですか。日本人の学生はカフェテリアで食べると思いますか。

_____

5. あなたの大学で一番きれいなたて物は何だと思いますか。

_____

6. あなたの大学の本やをどう思いますか。

_____

D. Answer the following questions by saying that the item has too much of the quality being asked about or that you have already done too much of what you are being asked to do.

EXAMPLE:　このケーキはあまいですか。
ええ、ちょっとあますぎますね。

もっとかって下さい。
いいえ、もうかいすぎました。

1. この味そしるはしおからいですか。

ええ、ちょっと _____

2. このドレッシングはすっぱいですか。

ええ、ちょっと _____

3. このカレーはからいですか。

ええ、ちょっと _____

4. このビールはにがいですか。

ええ、ちょっと _____

5. このとうふは、味がないですか。(ない→なさすぎる)

ええ、ちょっと _____

6. もう少し食べて下さい。

   いいえ、もう_____

7. もう少し飲んで下さい。

   いいえ、もう_____

8. もっとあそびたいですか。

   いいえ、もう_____

9. このセーターは大きいですか。

   ええ、ちょっと_____

10. このくるまは高いですか。

    ええ、ちょっと_____

11. このへんはしずかですか。

    ええ、ちょっと_____

12. このしけんはかんたん (simple/easy) でしたか。

    ええ、ちょっと_____

E. In each of the following situations, someone has made a critical comment about some food that you and a friend are cooking. What suggestions could you make in response to these comments?

   EXAMPLE: このおすしはあますぎます。
   　　　　じゃあ、もう少しすを入れましょう。

1. このスパゲッティーソースは味がありません。

   _____

2. このチョコレートソースは全ぜんあまくありません。

   _____

3. この味そしるはしおからすぎます。

   _____

4. このすきやきはあますぎます。

   _____

5. このハンバーガーはおかしな (strange) 味がしますよ。ふるいんでしょうか。

   _____

F. What do you think of the following? Use 〜すぎる／〜すぎたと思います whenever appropriate.

EXAMPLE: 大学のじゅぎょう料：高すぎると思います。

1. あなたの大学のりょう：＿＿＿＿＿＿＿＿＿＿＿＿＿＿

2. ウェンディーズのハンバーガー：＿＿＿＿＿＿＿＿＿＿＿

3. このワークブック：＿＿＿＿＿＿＿＿＿＿＿＿＿＿＿＿

4. この前の (previous) 日本語のテスト：＿＿＿＿＿＿＿＿＿

5. きょ年の夏の天気：＿＿＿＿＿＿＿＿＿＿＿＿＿＿＿＿

G. Answer the following questions using という to name people, places, and things.

EXAMPLE: あなたの一番したしい (close) ともだちはだれですか。
田中さんという人です。

1. あなたはどの大学で勉強していますか。

＿＿＿＿＿＿＿＿＿＿＿＿＿＿＿＿＿＿＿＿＿＿＿＿＿＿＿

2. あなたはどんな日本料理が好きですか。

＿＿＿＿＿＿＿＿＿＿＿＿＿＿＿＿＿＿＿＿＿＿＿＿＿＿＿

3. あなたの日本語の先生はだれですか。

＿＿＿＿＿＿＿＿＿＿＿＿＿＿＿＿＿＿＿＿＿＿＿＿＿＿＿

4. あなたの日本語のクラスはどのたて物でありますか。

＿＿＿＿＿＿＿＿＿＿＿＿＿＿＿＿＿＿＿＿＿＿＿＿＿＿＿

5. あなたの生まれた (was born) ところはどこですか。

＿＿＿＿＿＿＿＿＿＿＿＿＿＿＿＿＿＿＿＿＿＿＿＿＿＿＿

H. Complete the sentences, telling what you supposedly said in response to what the first person said.

EXAMPLE: 先生が「おはようございます。」と言ったので、わたしも＿＿＿＿＿＿。

→先生が「おはようございます。」と言ったので、
わたしも「おはようございます。」と言いました。

1. はやしさんが「おげん気ですか。」と言ったので、

わたしは＿＿＿＿＿＿＿＿＿＿＿＿＿＿＿＿＿＿＿＿＿＿

2. みどりさんがわたしの日本語が上手になったと言ったので、

わたしは＿＿＿＿＿＿＿＿＿＿＿＿＿＿＿＿＿＿＿＿＿＿

3. チンさんがさしみを食べたことがないと言ったので、

   わたしは _____

4. ブラウンさんがすしがきらいだと言ったので、

   わたしも _____

5. ギブソンさんが日本語はやさしいと言ったので、

   わたしも _____

6. ともだちが明日は雨がふるかもしれないと言ったので、

   わたしは _____

I. Ask a classmate the following and report his/her answers using …と言いました。

   1. two things s/he did yesterday
   2. two things s/he is planning to do next year
   3. two things s/he is planning to do next weekend (use つもり or the verb volitional form + と思う)

   EXAMPLE: スミスさんは昨日一時間ぐらいジョギングをしたと言いました。

   1. _____

   _____

   2. _____

   _____

   3. _____

Vocabulary and Grammar 6C: Cooking

A. Answer the following questions about your intentions, using the ～(よ)うと思っています form.

   EXAMPLE: 今週の日曜日は何をするつもりですか。
   　　　　　せんたくをしようと思っています。

   1. 今日はどこへ行くつもりですか。

   _____

   2. 何か食べるつもりですか。

   _____

3. 何か作るつもりですか。

_____

4. 今日ははやくかえるつもりですか。

_____

5. 夏休みは何をするつもりですか。

_____

6. 今日はどこかへ出かけるつもりですか。

_____

7. 何になるつもりですか。

_____

8. 何時間ぐらいねるつもりですか。

_____

B. Someone wants to know why you didn't do (or did) certain things. Explain to him/her that your intention was to do (or not to do) them and give a reason why you didn't (or did) do so using the 〜んです structure.

    EXAMPLE: どうして昼ごはんを食べなかったんですか。
                  食べるつもりでしたが、時間がなかったんです。

1. どうしてしゅくだいをしなかったんですか。

_____

2. どうしてパーティーに来なかったんですか。

_____

3. どうしてテストをうけなかったんですか。(うける = to take)

_____

4. どうしてあんな高いくるまをかったんですか。

_____

5. どうしてあんなにたくさんお酒を飲んだんですか。

_____

C. What are you planning to do for your next birthday? Write down four things using つもりです. You may include food items you are planning to eat or serve, the kinds of activities you will do, and the people you will see ("meet").

1. _____

2. _____

3. _____

4. _____

D. What would you make or serve if the following people came over for dinner? Write two or three sentences using the volitional form of such verbs as 作る、出す (to serve), ちゅうもんする (to order), かう, バーベキューをする, ～にする(to decide on), etc. + と思います. If you can, give reasons for your choices.

EXAMPLE:　(your Japanese acquaintance)
アメリカ料理がいいでしょうから、ハンバーガーを作ろうと思います。それから、アイスクリームを出そうと思います。飲み物はビールにしようと思います。

1. (your parents) _____

_____

_____

2. (your Japanese teacher) _____

_____

_____

3. (your best friend) _____

_____

_____

4. (someone you have a romantic interest in) _____

_____

_____

5. (your least favorite relative) _____

_____

_____

E. How would you answer the questions in the following situations? Write your answer using the volitional form of the verb + ⋯と思う.

> EXAMPLE: (You have won a million dollars in the lottery.)
> 百万ドルのお金で何をしますか。
> 大きい家をかおうと思います。

1. (Someone you have a crush on has just asked you out on a date.)
じゃあ、土曜日のばんはデートをするんですか。

_____

2. (You have just realized that your Japanese grade has been going down steadily since the beginning of the year.)
日本語のせいせき (grade) がとても悪いですよ。どうしますか。

_____

3. (You have not paid the rent for your apartment for two months, and the landlord wants you to move out next week if you can't pay immediately.)
いつはらう (pay) つもりですか。

_____

4. (You have noticed that you've been gaining weight recently. You have told your friends that you have decided to go on a diet.)
どんなダイエットをするつもりですか。

_____

F. Make up sentences putting each of the following verbs into its ⋯てみる form. Be creative!

> EXAMPLE: 食べる→ヒミコさんのとうふパイを食べてみました。

1. _____ (飲む)

2. _____ (のる)

3. _____ (きる)

4. _____ (ねる)

5. _____ (使う)

6. _____ (来る)

7. _____ (書く)

8. _____ (読む)

G. What would you say in the following situations? Answer using a form of ～てみる.

1. You just baked a cake with a new recipe, and you ask a friend to taste it.

   _____

2. Your classmate has a question about homework, but you don't know the answer either, so you suggest that s/he try asking the teacher.

   _____

3. Your college's basketball team is playing tonight, and it should be a very good game. Invite a classmate to go see it.

   _____

4. Your friend has just read a very interesting book and would like you to read it, too, so s/he gives it to you. Tell him/her you will try reading it.

   _____

5. A new type of beer is on the market. You have a friend who is a beer lover. Find out if s/he has tried it.

   _____

H. There are many times that people end up doing things they shouldn't. Write down a few of those things using …てしまう according to the directions.

   EXAMPLE: りょうしんのるすに (in my parents' absence) クッキーを全部食べて
   しまいました。

1. Something that you were not supposed to do but ended up doing when you were little.

   _____

2. Something that a friend did to you.

   _____

3. Something you did in class.

   _____

4. Something that your pet did.

   _____

5. Something that you did recently.

   _____

I. Complete the dialogues using て行きましょう.

    EXAMPLE: 今日は寒いですね。
                じゃ、セーターを（もつ）
                じゃ、セーターをもって行きましょう。

1. 今日は雨がふるかもしれませんよ。

   じゃ、かさを _____。（もつ）

2. このレコードはいいですよ。

   じゃ、ちょっと _____。（聞く）

3. このみかんはおいしいですよ。

   じゃ、ちょっと_____。（食べる）

4. お茶はいかがですか。

   じゃ、ちょっと _____。（飲む）

5. まだ時間がありますね。

   じゃ、_____。（あるく）

6. あたらしいきっ茶てんですね。

   じゃ、ちょっと _____。（休む）

7. おもしろいえいががありますよ。

   じゃ、ちょっと _____。（見る）

J. Make up sentences putting each of the following verbs into its …てくる form. Be creative.

    EXAMPLE: 食べる→あまり時間がなかったので、マクドナルドでハンバーガーを
              食べてきました。

1. _____。（行く）
2. _____。（かう）
3. _____。（見る）
4. _____。（する）
5. _____。（勉強する）
6. _____。（し事をする）

K. Make up sentences using the following pairs of verbs to indicate that one person is doing both things at once. Be creative.

EXAMPLE: 食べる＋見る
キャンディーを食べながら、えいがを見ます。

1. 話す＋あるく

   _____

2. 見る＋しゅくだいをする

   _____

3. 飲む＋話す

   _____

4. 食べる＋読む

   _____

5. 飲む＋聞く

   _____

6. 運_{うん}てんする＋おぼえる

   _____

L. What do you do while eating or drinking the following? Answer using ながら. If you do not eat or drink some of these items, talk about what other people do when they eat them.

EXAMPLE: （クッキー）たいてい(mostly) クッキーを食べながら、しゅくだいをします。

1. （ポップコーン）_____

2. （コーヒー）_____

3. （ビール or コーラ）_____

4. （お酒_{さけ}）_____

5. （ポテトチップ）_____

M. What do you drink while you eat the following? Answer following the example.

    EXAMPLE:　（おすし）お酒を飲みながら、おすしを食べます。

  1.　（ポテトチップ）_____

  2.　（フランス料理）_____

  3.　（タコス）_____

  4.　（中か料理）_____

  5.　（ハンバーガー）_____

  6.　（ピザ）_____

N. There is a term ながら族 in Japanese. 族 means a tribe, and the term refers to people who do two or more things at once, which has traditionally been regarded as bad manners or inappropriate behavior. A good example is a student who does homework while watching TV. Are you a member of the ながら族? If you are, what do you do? If you are not, do you know anyone who is? What does s/he do? Write three examples of people who are part of the ながら族.

  1.　_____

  2.　_____

  3.　_____

Chapter 6 Review

A. The following chart shows what some of the people in the Japanese class ate yesterday. After studying the chart, give your opinion of each person's eating habits and at least one reason why you think so.

名前	朝食	昼食	夕食	おやつ
スミス	つめたいピザ	ハンバーガー	ピザ	ハンバーガー
コロナド	トースト	チキンサラダ	スパゲッティ	—
クラウス	コーンフレーク	野さいサンドイッチ	ステーキとサラダ	りんご
キム	—	—	フルーツサラダ	—
スコット	ドーナツ	ケーキ	ホットドッグ	アイスクリーム

    EXAMPLE:　スミス：あまりよくありません。全部の食事がファストフードだからです。

  1.　コロナド_____

  2.　クラウス_____

3. キム _____

4. スコット _____

B. Your Japanese acquaintance who has recently come to your town wants to know about the restaurants there. Answer the questions, using the telephone directory or newspaper ads as necessary. Differentiate facts and your opinions using …と思います and don't hesitate to say 分かりません if you don't know the answer.

1. この町には日本料理のレストランがありますか。(If your answer is yes,) その料理の
   レストランをどう思いますか。

   _____

   _____

   _____

2. この町で一番おいしい中か料理てんはどこですか。そのみせで一番おいしい料理
   は何ですか。そのみせの料理は高いですか。

   _____

   _____

   _____

3. この町にピザやは何けんありますか。一番はやいみせのでん話番ごうをおしえて
   ください。

   _____

   _____

   _____

4. この町にフランス料理のレストランはありますか。味はどうですか。ねだん
   (price) は。

   _____

   _____

   _____

5. この町で一番きれいなハンバーガーやはどこですか。そこにはおいしいチキンバーガーもありますか。

_____

_____

6. この町で一番おいしいメキシコ料理のレストランはどこですか。そのみせは何時から何時までですか。

_____

_____

C. Complete the chart, following the example on the first line.

Verb: Class 1, 2, and 3, plain form

verb class and meaning	plain non-past affirmative (dictionary)	plain non-past negative (―ない)	plain past affirmative (―た)	potential form (―れる／―られる)	volitional form (―う／―よう)
2. to eat	食べる	食べない	食べた	食べられる	食べよう
2. to look					
2. to go to bed					
2. to get up					
2. to be clear	はれる			(N/A)	(N/A)
1. to listen					
1. to write					
1. to go					
1. to swim					
1. to finish					
1. to begin	始まる			(N/A)	(N/A)

1. to make	作る			
1. to return				
1. to rain	ふる		(N/A)	(N/A)
1. to wait				
1. to sing				
1. to wash				
1. to say				
1. to meet	あう			
1. to play	あそぶ			
1. to read				
1. to drink				
1. to rest				
1. to die	しぬ			
1. to talk				
3. to come				
3. to do				

D. There is a custom of gift-giving to show your appreciation for help and kindness. It takes place twice a year, in August and December, and is called お中元（おちゅうげん）and お歳暮（おせいぼ）, respectively. You have been in Japan for several months when お中元（おちゅうげん）approaches. Although Japanese people usually send food items, drinks, or linens prepackaged for such purposes, you would like to send something special to some of the people who have been extremely nice to you. The following are the names of people and the circumstances you'd like to consider. Decide what you would like to give them. (Use あげようと思う.) You can spend up to $200 for all the gifts, but you may want to spend as much as $40 for the person you feel you owe most. If you do not know the name of the thing you want to give that person, either check the dictionary or ask a Japanese friend. If neither helps, write the word in katakana.

1. 山下先生（日本語の先生）：クラシック音楽が好きで、とくにベートーベンが
   大好きです。

   _____

2. わたなべさん（アパートの大家[landlord]さん）：りょ行がしゅ味です。今年はハ
   ワイと中国へ行くつもりだと言っています。

   _____

3. よしむらさん（となりのアパートの人）：5月にはじめての (the first time) あかちゃん (baby) が生まれました。

_____

4. 田なべさん（ともだちのお姉さん）：10月にけっこんして (get married)、ごしゅ人と一しょにイギリスへ行きます。

_____

5. やすうら先生（アドバイザーの先生）：お酒がとても好きです。アメリカに行ったことがあるので、アメリカのワインやビール、ウイスキーをよくしっています。

_____

6. おくむら先生（近じょのいしゃ [medical doctor]）：ほしい物は何でももっています。しゅ味はゴルフとコンピューターゲーム（！！）ですが、いそがしいので、する時間がありません。

_____

7. と田さん（ともだち）：くるまが大好きです。ポルシェを買いたがっているのですが、お金がありません。

_____

8. 山本さん（ともだち）：あたらしい洋ふくやアクセサリーを買うのがしゅ味です。有名なブランドの物が好きです。

_____

E. The company you are working for has decided to transfer you to a new location. There are five possible locations from which you can choose. (If you already live in one of them, you will have to move to a different location.) Write for each location what you think are the pros and cons, using …だろうと思います. Then decide which place you'd like to go to and indicate it using たい. If you decide that you definitely do not want to move to any location, say so and write your reason for not wanting to move. (You will have to prepare to quit the company, though!)

LOCATIONS	PROS	CONS
オーランド (FL)	_____	_____
	_____	_____
	_____	_____

ニューヨーク(NY)　_____　_____

_____　_____

_____　_____

ペオリア(IL)　_____　_____

_____　_____

_____　_____

ミネアポリス(MN)　_____　_____

_____　_____

_____　_____

ホノルル(HI)　_____　_____

_____　_____

_____　_____

シアトル(WA)　_____　_____

_____　_____

_____　_____

CONCLUSION:　_____　_____

_____　_____

CHAPTER 7

SHOPPING

買い物
<small>か　もの</small>

Listening Comprehension Activities

Vocabulary and Grammar 7A: Shops and Stores

A. Where are you when you say this? Choose the most appropriate store based of the statement.

1. _____   2. _____   3. _____   4. _____   5. _____   6. _____   7. _____   8. _____

a. やっきょく
b. めがね屋<small>や</small>
c. 花屋<small>はなや</small>
d. 肉屋<small>にくや</small>

e. 本屋<small>や</small>
f. ＣＤショップ
g. ケーキ屋<small>や</small>
h. 魚屋<small>さかなや</small>

i. くだ物屋<small>ものや</small>
j. ぶんぼうぐ屋<small>や</small>
k. カメラ屋<small>や</small>

B. John Kawamura had been shopping earlier in the day and now Mei Lin Chin is visiting at Kawamura and Henry Curtis' place when Curtis comes home looking exhausted and carrying a lot of shopping bags. Listen to the following conversation. Then list the stores that Kawamura and Curtis went to during the day, and write down in English the items they bought at each store.

	STORES	ITEMS BOUGHT
1.	_____	_____
2.	_____	_____
3.	_____	_____
4.	_____	_____
5.	_____	_____

C. Professor Yokoi is asking John Kawamura what he does at certain times. Listen to their conversation and choose the best option to indicate when he does the following activities.

John Kawamura:

1. goes to the park for a walk _____.

2. listen to his favorite music at home _____.

3. goes to the library _____.

4. takes medicine and goes to bed _____.

a. when it rains
b. when he studies Japanese
c. when it is nice weather
d. when he calls his friends
e. when he is sick

D. Takako Matsui is asking Henry Curtis for some advice on shopping. Listen to their conversation, and then mark each of the following statements either true (T) or false (F).

Useful Vocabulary: えらんで下さい *Please choose.*

1. _____ Matsui wants to know how to get to Central Shopping Center.

2. _____ The shopping center is a good place to shop because it carries a lot of goods.

3. _____ Curtis is quite familiar with the shopping center.

4. _____ "Collection" sells cards, posters and calendars.

5. _____ Curtis rarely shops at "Collection."

6. _____ Matsui and Curtis will go shopping tomorrow.

7. _____ Curtis' birthday present will be a poster.

E. Listen as Heather Gibson asks Hitomi Machida for advice on local shops and services. Then complete each of the following sentences by filling in the blanks.

Useful Vocabulary: 出す *to send, to hand in*

1. The hair salon Camille is convenient because it is _____.

2. Camille is a little expensive but _____.

3. Campus Cleaning is convenient for Machida because it is _____

    _____.

4. Gibson cannot go to Campus Cleaning on weekends because it _____.

5. When Gibson has clothes to send to the cleaners, _____

    _____.

F. Linda Brown is looking for a gift to send to her mother for her birthday. Listen as she shops at a kimono shop in Tokyo. Then complete each sentence below by choosing the best alternative from a, b, and c.

1. Brown wants to find something _____ for her mother.
   a. expensive   b. gorgeous   c. Japanese

2. The green and brown kimono is _____.
   a. made of polyester   b. washable at home   c. both a and b

3. She does not want a green and brown one because it is too _____.
   a. pretty   b. expensive   c. large

4. She does not want a yellow one because it is too _____.
   a. subdued   b. bright   c. cheap

5. She decides to buy a _____ one for 18,000 yen.
   a. light blue and purple   b. black and white   c. red and blue

Vocabulary and Grammar 7B: Shopping

A. Listen to the questions about yourself and answer each question orally. Then stop the tape and write the answers in Japanese.

1. _____

2. _____

3. _____

4. _____

5. _____

B. Listen to Mei Lin Chin and Takako Matsui talk about the new shopping center. Then complete each sentence by writing in the initial of the person it best describes. (C = Chin, M = Matsui, B = Both)

Useful Vocabulary: すてきな *nice, lovely*

1. _____ has been to the new shopping center.

2. _____ went to shopping there last weekend.

3. _____ cannot shop at expensive stores.

4. _____ would like to buy a jacket.

5. _____ will go shopping at the new shopping center next weekend.

6. _____ will try to gave money this week.

Vocabulary and Grammar 7C: Clothes

A. Today is Friday, and everyone in the Japanese class seems to have plans for the afternoon. Listen as Mei Lin Chin observes her classmates, and try to guess what each person is going to do this afternoon.

Useful Vocabulary: おしゃれ *stylish, chic*

1. _____ is going to a job interview.

2. _____ is going to play tennis.

3. _____ is going to the beach.

4. _____ is going to study.

5. _____ is going to a party.

B. Listen as Hitomi Machida and Heather Gibson discuss what to wear to the international students' party. Then complete the summary by filling in the blanks.

Heather Gibson will wear a silk blouse with _____ and a _____. But

if it is _____, she will wear a white dress with _____ and a

_____ as an accessory. Hitomi Machida will wear a kimono if it is

_____, but will wear a _____ if it is _____. She

does not have good _____, so she will wear Gibson's yellow _____

and _____ when she wears a _____.

C. Mei Lin Chin and Takako Matsui are at the new shopping center. Listen to their conversation, and then mark each of the following sentences either true (T) or false (F).

1. _____ Chin and Matsui are at a sale at a clothing store.

2. _____ Chin does not want to buy the pink jacket because it is too expensive.

3. _____ Matsui prefers cotton for summer.

4. _____ Chin does not want the white jacket because of its color.

5. _____ Matsui wants to buy the green jacket because both the size and price are right.

6. _____ Chin is going to shop around while Matsui pays the cashier.

D. Listen to Professor Yokoi and her class talk about their weekend activities, and then complete the following sentences by filling in the blanks.

1. Chin went to the new shopping center to buy _____ and found many

_____ and _____ things. There will be another sale this

weekend, so she will go there again to buy _____.

2. Curtis and Kawamura went to the shopping center to _____. At the Italian

   restaurant they went to, the food was _____ and the price was

   _____ .

3. Hayashi went to the shopping center with Mimura to _____ because it costs only

   _____ this month. Professor Yokoi will go there to _____ ,

   _____ , and _____ .

E. Listen as Heather Gibson asks Takeshi Mimura about his girlfriend. Then fill in the blanks to complete
the following report of what you heard about his girlfriend.

三むらさんのガールフレンドは、あまり _____ けれど、

_____ そうだ。そして、_____ の学生で、

_____ そうだ。だから、三むらさんのしらないこともよく

_____ そうだ。二人は本屋で、はじめて _____ そうだ。

三むらさんのガールフレンドは、その本屋で _____ そうだ。三むらさ

んはかの女をはじめて見た時、かわいいと _____ そうだ。

F. Listen as Professor Yokoi asks John Kawamura and Heather Gibson about their childhood. Then mark O
for what they remember and X for what they do not remember about their childhood.

	YOKOI	KAWAMURA	GIBSON
whether or not they studied hard	——		
whether or not they played with friends			
whether or not they went out with their parents			

G. Listen as John Kawamura and Linda Brown talk about the new shopping center. Then mark each of the
following sentences either true (T) or false (F).

1. _____ Kawamura and Brown went to the new shopping center last weekend.

2. _____ Kawamura did not do any shopping there.

3. _____ Kawamura bought a golf club there at a 40% to 60% discount.

4. _____ Brown will go there this weekend for the sale.

5. _____ Brown needs to buy some clothes.

6. _____ The movie Brown wants to see is now playing at the shopping center movie theater.

7. _____ The movie is said to be dull because it is too long.

8. _____ Neither Kawamura nor Brown knows Gibson's schedule for the weekend.

9. _____ They will call Professor Yokoi to ask if she would like to go to the shopping center with them this weekend.

H. Listen as Masaru Honda interviews Himiko about her clothing. Then mark each of the following sentences either true (T) or false (F).

1. _____ Himiko owns a boutique in Aoyama.

2. _____ Himiko doesn't care what she wears when she is at home.

3. _____ Honda sometimes spends the whole day in pajamas.

4. _____ Himiko wears casual clothes for work.

5. _____ Himiko's boyfriend can design dresses well.

6. _____ Himiko's boyfriend is handsome and smart, but cannot cook or drive.

7. _____ There is nothing that Himiko's boyfriend cannot do.

I. Henry Curtis and Hitomi Machida have accomplished many things this weekend. Listen to their conversation, and write in English what Curtis and Machida did, and did not do.

What Curtis did: _____

What Machida did: _____

What they did not do: _____

Kanji Practice and Exercises

1	同 同	ドウ、おな-じ　the same			
	同じ：おなじ　(the same) 同じサイズ：おなじさいず　(the same size) 同じではありません：おなじではありません　(is not the same)		同	同	
2	長 長	チョウ　long; (especially as suffix) head, chief, director なが-い　long			
	長い：ながい　(long) 長そでのシャツ：ながそでのしゃつ　(long-sleeved shirt)		長	長	

3	市 市	シ　city, town; market いち　market; fair				
	市：し　(city) ロサンゼルス市：ろさんぜるすし　(city of Los Angeles) 市場：いちば　(market)	市	市		
4	場 場	ジョウ、ば　place				
	市場：いちば　(market) ゴルフ場：ごるふじょう　(golf course)	場	場		
5	主 主	シュ、ス　master, Lord, the main thing ぬし　owner; master あるじ　master おも　main, principal				
	主人：しゅじん　(master, owner, my husband)	主	主		
6	電 電	デン　electricity				
	電気：でんき　(electricity) 電話：でんわ　(telephone) 電子メール：でんしめえる　(e-mail)	電	電		
7	売 売	バイ、う-る　sell う-れる　sell, can sell, be in demand				
	売る：うる　(to sell) 売り出し：うりだし　(sale)	売	売		
8	買 買	バイ、か-う　buy				
	買う：かう　(to buy) 買い物：かいもの　(shopping)	買	買		

9	着 着	チャク、ジャク　arrive at; put on, wear; (counter for suits) き-る、つ-ける　put on, wear -ぎ　…clothes き-せる　clothe, dress, put on ／つ-く　arrive at				
	着る：きる　(to wear)　着物：きもの　(kimono) 下着：したぎ　(underwear) 水着：みずぎ　(swimwear) 上着：うわぎ　(coat)		着	着		
10	切 切	セツ、サイ、き-る、-ぎ-る　cut -き-る　finish, do completely, be able to き-れる　can cut, cut well, be sharp き-れ　piece, cut, slice, scrap　き-らす　run out of, be short of				
	切る：きる　(to cut) ね切る：ねぎる　(to bargain) 切手：きって　(stamp) しん切な人：しんせつなひと　(kind person)		切	切		
11	円 円	エン　circle; yen まる-い　round (like a disk) まろ-やか　round; mellow まど-か　round; tranquil				
	三百円です：さんびゃくえんです　(It's 300 yen.) 一万円：いちまんえん　(10,000 yen)		円	円		
12	引 引	イン　ひ-く　pull; attract; retreat, recede, withdraw; reduce, discount -び-き　…discount ひ-ける　close, be over				
	引く：ひく　(to pull) 40% 引き：40 ぱーせんとびき　(40% off) 百円引き：ひゃくえんびき　(100 yen off)		引	引		
13	安 安	アン　peacefulness やす-い　cheap, inexpensive やす-らか　peaceful, tranquil				
	安い：やすい　(inexpensive)		安	安		
14	店 店	テン、みせ　shop, store				
	店：みせ　(shop) 食料品店：しょくりょうひんてん　(grocery store) 洋品店：ようひんてん　([western] clothing store)		店	店		

15	員 員	イン member
	店員：てんいん　(clerk) デパートの店員：でぱあとのてんいん　(clerk of a 　department store)	員 員

16	色 色	ショク、シキ、いろ　color
	色：いろ　(color)　何色ですか：なにいろですか 　(What color is it?)　何色ですか：なんしょくです 　か　(How many colors?)　色々な物：いろいろな 　もの　(various things)	色 色

17	黒 黒	コク、くろ、くろ-い　black くろ-ばむ, くろ-ずむ, くろ-まる　become black/dark
	黒：くろ　(black)　黒い：くろい　(black) 黒いかばん：くろいかばん　(black bag) 黒ばん：こくばん　(blackboard)	黒 黒

18	白 白	ハク、ビャク、しろ、しろ-い、しら-　white しら-む　grow light しら　feigned ignorance
	白：しろ　(white) 白い：しろい　(white) 白いドレス：しろいどれす　(white dress)	白 白

19	青 青	セイ、ショウ、あお、あお-い　blue
	青：あお　(blue) 青い：あおい　(blue) 青い空：あおいそら　(blue sky)	青 青

20	赤 赤	セキ、シャク、あか、あか-い　red あか-らむ　become red, blush あか-らめる　make red, blush
	赤：あか　(red) 赤い：あかい　(red) 赤いセーター：あかいせえたあ　(red sweater)	赤 赤

21	黄 黄	コウ、オウ、き、こ　yellow き-ばむ　turn yellowish			
	黄色：きいろ　(yellow) 黄色い：きいろい　(yellow) 黄色いくつ：きいろいくつ　(yellow shoes)	黄	黄		
22	服 服	フク　clothes, dress; dose; obey, serve; admit to			
	服：ふく　(clothes) 洋服：ようふく　(western-type clothes) 和服：わふく　(Japanese clothes)	服	服		
23	返 返	ヘン、かえ-す、かえ-る　return			
	返す：かえす　(to return) 返品：へんぴん　(returned goods) 店にくつを返しました：みせにくつをかえしました　(I returned the shoes to the store.)	返	返		
24	花 花	カ、ケ、はな、-ばな　flower			
	花：はな　(flower) 花屋：はなや　(flower shop) 生け花：いけばな　(flower arranging)	花	花		
25	屋 屋	オク、や　roof, house; shop, dealer			
	肉屋：にくや　(butcher shop)　魚屋：さかなや (fish store)　本屋：ほんや　(bookstore) 部屋：へや　(room) 酒屋：さかや　(liquor store)	屋	屋		
26	暗 暗	アン、くら-い　dark くら-がり　darkness くら-む　grow dark; be dazzled/blinded くら-ます　hide, slip away			
	暗い：くらい　(dark) 暗い色：くらいいろ　(dark color) 部屋が暗いです：へやがくらいです　(The room is dark.)	暗	暗		

Kanji Exercises

A. Match each kanji or kanji compound with the letter of its closest English equivalent.

1. 暗 _____	10. 場 _____	19. 同 _____
2. 員 _____	11. 色 _____	20. 買 _____
3. 引 _____	12. 青 _____	21. 売 _____
4. 黄 _____	13. 赤 _____	22. 白 _____
5. 部屋 _____	14. 切 _____	23. 服 _____
6. 花 _____	15. 着 _____	24. 返 _____
7. 黒 _____	16. 長 _____	25. 円 _____
8. 市 _____	17. 店 _____	26. 魚屋 _____
9. 主 _____	18. 電 _____	

a. same b. long c. place d. city e. master f. electricity g. to sell h. to wear i. to cut
j. shop k. discount l. white m. fish store n. black o. color p. to buy q. blue r. room
s. red t. clothes u. to return v. flower w. yen x. yellow y. member z. dark

B. Write the hurigana for each kanji or kanji compound.

1. 同じ	7. 着る	13. 黄色い
_____	_____	_____
2. 長い	8. 下着	14. 買う
_____	_____	_____
3. 市場	9. 白い	15. 暗い
_____	_____	_____
4. 主人	10. 黒い	16. 切る
_____	_____	_____
5. 電気	11. 赤い	17. 切手
_____	_____	_____
6. 売り出し	12. 青い	18. 服
_____	_____	_____

19. 店

　　_____

20. 店員

　　_____

21. 返す

　　_____

22. 引く

　　_____

23. 30%引き

　　_____

24. 部屋

　　_____

25. 八百屋

　　_____

26. 八百円

　　_____

27. 花

　　_____

28. 生け花

　　_____

29. ロサンゼルス市

　　_____

C. Fill in the blanks with the kanji for the words or phrases that are spelled out in hiragana below the lines.

1. _____、_____ に _____ ったら、_____ さんに
　　きのう　　　　はなや　　　　い　　　　　　やまだ

　　_____ いました。
　　あ

2. この _____ と _____ じ _____ のくつを _____
　　　　　ふく　　　　おな　　　　いろ　　　　　　か

　　おうと _____ っています。
　　　　　おも

3. この _____ で _____ っているかどうか _____ に
　　　　みせ　　　　う　　　　　　　　　　　てんいん

　　_____ いてみましょう。
　　き

4. かみが _____ くなったので、みじかく _____ りました。
　　　　　なが　　　　　　　　　　　　　　　　き

5. _____ の _____ を _____ たことがありますか。
　　にほん　　　　きもの　　　　き

6. _____ は _____ へ _____ や _____ を _____
　　はは　　　　いちば　　　　にく　　　　さかな　　　　か

　　いに _____ きました。
　　　　い

7. _____ いセーターを _____ ている _____ の _____
    くろ   き   おとこ   ひと

はだれですか。

8. _____ が _____ し _____ くなりました。
    へや   すこ   くら

9. _____ いのも _____ いのもどちらも _____ きです。
    あか   あお   す

10. _____ い _____ わったら _____ して _____ さい。
    つか   お   かえ   くだ

11. パーティーの _____ 、 _____ いドレスを _____ ようと
        とき   しろ   き

_____ います。
  おも

12. _____ のご _____ が、 _____ は _____ 15%
    でんきや   しゅじん   きょう   ぜんぶ

_____ きだと _____ いました。
  び   い

13. この _____ い _____ は _____ _____ です。
    きいろ   はな   いっぽん ごじゅうえん

14. _____ いので _____ おうと _____ ったら、もう
    やす   か   おも

_____ り _____ れでした。
  う   き

Kanji in Everyday Life

1. When walking by the park near your Japanese host family's house, you notice there are a lot of stands selling fruits and vegetables in the park. The entrance says いらっしゃいませ、青空市場へ and 入場無料. What do 青空市場 and 入場無料 mean?

_____

2. You are in the department store and a clerk gives you a small box which contains some goodies. You think they will be good souvenirs for your friends at home. You want to buy some of them, so you ask the clerk how much they are, but he points to the back of the box which says 非売品. What does it mean?

_____

3. You are in front of an electric appliance store, whose door does not open automatically. When you see the kanji 引, what will you do?

_____

4. Going into the electric appliance store mentioned above, you see an electric cord with a switch, which says 入 on one side and 切 on the other. When you want to turn it on, which side should you use?

_____

5. There is a phrase 十人十色 in Japanese. What do you think is the English equivalent of this proverb?

_____

6. You see an article about a new movie in the Japanese newspaper and notice the word 日米共同製作 in the article. How many countries were involved in the making of this movie? Name them.

_____

Writing Activities

Vocabulary and Grammar 7A: Shops and Stores

A. Make up sentences using the following elements and ⋯時.

EXAMPLE: （子ども）（日本に行きました）
→ 子どもの時、日本に行きました。
（お金がありません）（じてんしゃで行きます）
→ お金がない時、じてんしゃで行きます。

1. （オリンピック）（長野に行きました）

_____

2. （学生）（ドイツ語を勉強しましたか）

_____

3. （寒いです）（どんなセーターを着ますか）

_____

4. （いそがしくありません）（来て下さい）

_____

5. (あたらしい野さいがほしいです)（どの八百屋へ行きますか)

_____

6. (切手が買いたいです)（ゆうびんきょくへ行きます)

_____

7. (あたまがいたいです)（うちでねます)

_____

8. (げん気です)（ジョギングをします)

_____

9. (ひまです)（ゆっくり本を読みます)

_____

10. (日本に行きます)（カメラ屋でカメラを買います)

_____

11. (日本に行きました)（東きょうで着物を買いました)

_____

12. (ねます)（何を着ますか)

_____

13. (テレビを見ていました)（先生が来ました)

_____

B. Complete each dialogue by filling in the blanks with appropriate words or phrases. Be creative, especially for the last line of each dialogue.

1. A: 昨日、くだ物屋に行った時、カワムラさんに会いました。

   B: そうですか。

   A: _____ を買っていましたよ。

   B: _____

2. A: 昨日、_____ に行った時、チンさんに会いました。

   B: そうですか。

   A: ビールをたくさん買っていましたよ。

   B: _____

3. A: 昨日、本屋に行った時、ブラウンさんに会いました。

   B: _____

   A: まんが(comics) を _____

   B: _____

4. A: 昨日、_____に行った時、山口さんに会いました。

   B: そうですか。

   A: 赤いばら (rose) をたくさん_____

   B: _____

5. A: 昨日、デパートに行った時、ギブソンさんに会いました。

   B: _____

   A: _____を買っていましたよ。

   B: _____

C. At what sorts of times do you patronize the following businesses or services? Write one possible occasion for each place, using 時 as in the example:

   EXAMPLE: スーパー：
   いろいろな食べ物を買いたい時に行きます。

1. びょういん：_____

2. ゆうびんきょく：_____

3. ぶんぼうぐ屋：_____

4. 電気屋：_____

5. コンビニエンスストア：_____

D. The following people went shopping and bought the items listed. Write down which stores each person went to using the …と…と…へ行って来たでしょう structure. (Unfortunately the nearby スーパー was closed today.)

1. カワムラ：牛肉、ネギ、とうふ、ビール

   _____

   _____

2. ギブソン：ケーキ、ぶどう、花、クッキー

   _____

   _____

3. はやし：アスピリン、スニーカー、ネクタイ

   _____

   _____

4. よこい：じ書、ストッキング、まくら (pillow) カバー、コールドクリーム

   _____

   _____

5. おおの：せんべい (rice crackers) 、日本酒、電気がま (electric rice cooker)

   _____

   _____

E. The following are what John Kawamura did in preparation for his trip to Japan. Write in Japanese what he did, and when, using 時.

WHAT HE DID	WHEN
1. started studying Japanese	when he decided to go to Japan
2. sent letters to Japanese colleges	when he first got* an A in Japanese
3. applied for** a visa	when it was decided that he would go† to Japan
4. wrote a letter to his relatives in Japan	when he started to look for‡ a place to live.
5. bought airline tickets	when he had money
6. bought gifts for his relatives	when he was to leave town

EXAMPLE: decided to go to Japan, sophomore year in collage

大学二年生の時に、日本へ行くことにきめました。

1. _____

2. _____

3. _____

4. _____

5. _____

6. _____

---

* get = とる

** apply for 〜 = 〜をしんせいする

† decided that he would go = 行くことができる

‡ start to look for 〜 = 〜をさがし始める

F. Part 1: Do you have your crayons or colored pencils handy? If so, then color the items in the following drawing as directed. (…ぬって下さい means "please paint/color it in.")

1. カーペットをあい色にぬって下さい。
2. しょく物(plant)をみどりに、はち(pot)を茶色にぬって下さい。
3. コンピュータとキーボードとマウスをグレーにぬって下さい。
4. 電話をは手なピンクにぬって下さい。
5. えんぴつを青くぬって下さい。
6. つくえをどちらも茶色にぬって下さい。

Part 2: Please color the following in your favorite colors, and then report below how you colored them.

EXAMPLE:　かべ(wall)：かべをグレーにぬりました。

1. ファイルキャビネット：＿＿＿＿＿＿＿＿＿＿＿＿＿＿＿＿＿＿＿＿＿

2. がくぶち (picture frame)：＿＿＿＿＿＿＿＿＿＿＿＿＿＿＿＿＿＿＿

3. プリンター：＿＿＿＿＿＿＿＿＿＿＿＿＿＿＿＿＿＿＿＿＿＿＿＿＿＿

4. えんぴつたて (pencil holder)：＿＿＿＿＿＿＿＿＿＿＿＿＿＿＿＿＿

5. カーテン (curtains)：＿＿＿＿＿＿＿＿＿＿＿＿＿＿＿＿＿＿＿＿＿

G. Answer the following questions.

1. 白いくるまと黒いくるまとどちらの方が好きですか。

   _____

2. 金色の時けいとぎん色の時けいとどちらの方が好きですか。

   _____

3. 赤いりんごと青いりんご (green apple) とどちらの方がおいしいと思いますか。

   _____

4. むらさき色の花には何がありますか。

   _____

5. 黄色は暗い色ですか。

   _____

6. ピンクは明るい色ですか。

   _____

7. とうめいな物は何ですか。

   _____

8. はい色は、は手ですか、じ味ですか。

   _____

9. あなたのめ (eyes) は何色ですか。

   _____

10. あなたのかみ (hair) は何色ですか。

    _____

H. Rewrite the following sentences using pronominal …の to replace the nouns.

　　EXAMPLE:　もっと安いセーターはありますか。

　　　　→ もっと安いのはありますか。

1. もっとおいしいコーヒーはありますか。

   _____

2. もっと赤いトマトはありますか。

   _____

3. もっとは手なドレスを買いたいんですが。

_____

4. もっと明るい色が好きです。

_____

5. もっとやさしいかんじをおしえて下さい。

_____

I. You would like to buy the following items. The clerk asks, どんなのがよろしいですか。(What kind would you like?) so tell her/him the type you like, using の as in the example. Use such expressions as 見せて下さい、さがしているんですが、買いたいんです, and ありますか to start the dialogue.

EXAMPLE: （トースター）
YOU: トースターを見せて下さい。
CLERK: はい、どんなのがよろしいですか。
YOU: 小さくて安いのをおねがいします。

1. （かばん）

YOU: _____

CLERK: はい、どんなのがよろしいですか。

YOU: _____

2. （スラックス）

YOU: _____

CLERK: はい、どんなのがよろしいですか。

YOU: _____

3. （うで時けい： watch）

YOU: _____

CLERK: はい、どんなのがよろしいですか。

YOU: _____

4. （くるま）

YOU: _____

CLERK: はい、どんなのがよろしいですか。

YOU: _____

5. （まんがの本： comic book）

YOU: _____

CLERK: はい、どんなのがよろしいですか。

YOU: _____

J. What kind do you like? Answer the questions using the indefinite pronoun の.

EXAMPLE: あなたはどんなケーキが好きですか。
あまりあまくないのが好きです。それから、チョコレートの入ってい
ないのが好きです。

1. あなたはどんなスポーツが好きですか。(hint: individual/team? fast? using a ball?)

_____

2. あなたはどんなくるまが買いたいですか。

_____

3. あなたはどんなステレオがほしいですか。

_____

4. あなたがすむ (to live) のにはどんなアパートがいいですか。

_____

K. It's late at night now, and you can see the silhouettes of some people in their rooms through the curtained windows. By using the list of hobbies, figure out and write down who is doing what, as in the example.

NAME	HOBBY
Yooichi Takada	work
Sayuri Yamamoto	watching TV, music
Yoshiko Sano	sewing
Daisuke Yamaguchi	classical music
Masao Hayashi	eating
Henry Curtis	poetry, literature

EXAMPLE:　本を読んでいるのはカーティスさんでしょう。

1. _____

2. _____

3. _____

4. _____

5. _____

Vocabulary and Grammar 7B: Shopping

A. Choose words from the list at the end of the exercise to complete these sentences. Each word will be used once.

1. _____ が高すぎる時^{とき}は、だれも買^かいません。

2. 3,000 円^{えん}のセーターを買^かって、5,000 えんはらうと、_____ は 1,500 円^{えん}です。

3. デパートで「いらっしゃいませ」と言^いうのは、_____ です。

4. このコンピュータは30%_____ です。たくさんのきゃくが買^かいました。

5. 今^{いま}、_____ がありません。クレジットカードではらいます。

6. ピザ屋^やは、30分^{ふん}でうちまでピザを_____ します。

7. 昨日このブラウスを買いましたが、少し大きすぎます。_____ したいん
ですが。

8. 店でお金をはらうのは、_____ です。

a. おつり	d. げん金	g. 店員
b. はいたつ	e. ねだん	h. きゃく
c. 返品	f. わり引き	

B. What do you call the following in Japanese? Write the name of the item or job defined by the following phrases.

      EXAMPLE: 店でお金をはらうところ：
               レジといいます。

1. とくに (especially) 安く売っているセール：_____

2. お金をはらいすぎた時に返してくれる (give back) お金：_____

3. お金をはらったら店員が書くかみ：_____

4. 店ではたらいている人：_____

5. 店をもっている人：_____

6. げん金がなくても使えるプラスチックのカード：_____

7. 一度にお金をはらわないで (without paying) 毎月少しずつはらうこと：_____

8. 「安くして下さい。」とたのむ (ask) こと：_____

9. 家までもって来てもらうこと：_____

10. 一度買った物を返すこと：_____

C. Complete each sentence with the 〜たら form of the verb or adjective given in parentheses. Then write the English equivalent of the sentence.

1. ふるいコンピュータ _____、だれも買わないでしょう。(だ)

   _____

2. あの女の人 _____、日本語をしっているかもしれません。(だ)

   _____

3. 子どもの時、もっと _____、よかったんですが。(まじめだ)

   _____

4. もっとピアノが＿＿＿＿＿＿＿＿＿、ピアニストになりたいです。(上手だ)

＿＿＿＿＿＿＿＿＿＿＿＿＿＿＿＿＿＿＿＿＿＿＿＿＿＿＿＿＿＿＿＿

5. メロンが＿＿＿＿＿＿＿＿＿、買って来て下さい。(安い)

＿＿＿＿＿＿＿＿＿＿＿＿＿＿＿＿＿＿＿＿＿＿＿＿＿＿＿＿＿＿＿＿

6. このえいがが＿＿＿＿＿＿＿＿＿、どうしますか。(おもしろくない)

＿＿＿＿＿＿＿＿＿＿＿＿＿＿＿＿＿＿＿＿＿＿＿＿＿＿＿＿＿＿＿＿

7. もっと勉強＿＿＿＿＿＿＿＿＿、日本語が上手になりますか。(する)

＿＿＿＿＿＿＿＿＿＿＿＿＿＿＿＿＿＿＿＿＿＿＿＿＿＿＿＿＿＿＿＿

8. 日曜日にと書かんに＿＿＿＿＿＿＿＿＿、カワムラさんが本を読んでいました。
(行く)

＿＿＿＿＿＿＿＿＿＿＿＿＿＿＿＿＿＿＿＿＿＿＿＿＿＿＿＿＿＿＿＿

9. 日本から＿＿＿＿＿＿＿＿＿、電話します。(かえる)

＿＿＿＿＿＿＿＿＿＿＿＿＿＿＿＿＿＿＿＿＿＿＿＿＿＿＿＿＿＿＿＿

10. もっとお金が＿＿＿＿＿＿＿＿＿、大きくてきれいな家を買いたいです。(ある)

＿＿＿＿＿＿＿＿＿＿＿＿＿＿＿＿＿＿＿＿＿＿＿＿＿＿＿＿＿＿＿＿

11. もし明日テストが＿＿＿＿＿＿＿＿＿、今日はポテトチップスを食べながら、テ
レビを見ます。(ない)

＿＿＿＿＿＿＿＿＿＿＿＿＿＿＿＿＿＿＿＿＿＿＿＿＿＿＿＿＿＿＿＿

D. Under what conditions would you buy the following? The conditions may be related to your preferences or to price. You may decide that you would buy it as is, or that you would not buy it under any circumstances.

EXAMPLE: 1) name-brand running shoes, size 3, $65.

もっと大きかったら買います。

2) tickets to a mud-wrestling tournament, $50 each.

ぜったいに (no matter what) 買いません。

3) a T-shirt in your size, in your favorite color, with the name of your favorite vacation spot written on it, $12.

買います。

1. excellent quality name-brand jeans, size 36, $50

＿＿＿＿＿＿＿＿＿＿＿＿＿＿＿＿＿＿＿＿＿＿＿＿＿＿＿＿＿＿＿＿

2. a CD player, made in Japan, loaded with fancy features, $580

    _____

3. 1990 BMW, a few dents, some engine problem, $18,000

    _____

4. . fashionable sunglasses, made in France, purplish in color, $200

    _____

5. a Japanese word processor, uses non-standard diskettes, very easy to use, many useful features, $700

    _____

6. a backpack, 30 liters, inner frame, famous brand, 5-year warranty, $100 (liquidation sale!)

    _____

E. What would you do if the following happened to you? Write as much as you can.

1. もし日本語のクラスでFをとったら (receive) どうしますか。

    _____

    _____

    _____

2. もしあなたのボーイフレンド／ガールフレンドがほかの (other) 人とデートしているのを見たらどうしますか。

    _____

    _____

3. もしだれかが、いつでも行きたい時に日本へ行ってもいいと言ったら、いつ行きますか。

    _____

    _____

    _____

4. もしあなたの大学のじゅぎょう料が3ばい (three times the amount) になったらどうしますか。

_____

_____

_____

5. もしやくそく (promise; appointment) の時間にともだちが来なかったら、何分ぐらいまちますか。それでも (even so) 来なかったらどうしますか。

_____

_____

_____

Vocabulary and Grammar 7C: Clothes

A. After each verb for wearing or putting on clothes and accessories, choose the items from the list that are used with the verb.

EXAMPLE: はきます： a (You find the others.)

1. 着ます： _____

2. かぶります： _____

3. しめます： _____

4. かけます： _____

5. します： _____

6. はきます： _____

a. ズボン	e. ぼう子	j. ブーツ
b. ブラウス	f. ベルト	k. ストッキング
c. スカート	g. コート	l. ネクタイ
d. 時けい	h. ブラジャー	m. めがね
	i. ショートパンツ	

B. The following is the description of clothing that John Kawamura and Linda Brown are wearing. Please draw the clothes on John and Linda, using colors if you can.

1. カワムラさんはこんのジーンズをはいて、青と赤のチェックの半そでのシャツを着ています。ベルトはこげ茶 (dark brown) です。手に茶色の上着をもっています。白いくつ下と白いスニーカーをはいていますが、スニーカーはちょっとよごれて (dirty) います。くび (neck) にみじかい金のネックレスをして、左のみみに小さくてまるい金のピアスをしています。

2. ブラウンさんはみどりのむじのフレアースカートをはいて、みどりとピンクと黄色と白の花のプリントのブラウスを着ています。スカートはひざ (knee) 下 10 センチぐらいで、ブラウスは長そでです。上着も白です。白いストッキングとみどりのハイヒールをはいています。手にはベージュのロングコートとみどりのハンドバッグをもっています。小さいエメラルドのイヤリングをしています。

C. What would you wear on the days like these? Choose your clothes.

EXAMPLE: 雪の日

オーバーを着て、マフラーをします。ぼう子もかぶります。あつい
(thick) くつ下とブーツをはきます。

1. あたたかい日 _____

2. 寒い日 _____

3. 暑い日 _____

4. 雨の日 _____

D. Write a brief paragraph about what you are wearing today. If you can remember, tell when and/or where you bought or received each item.

_____

_____

_____

_____

_____

_____

E. A Japanese student, who is planning to study for a year at your university/college, would like to know what s/he should bring for clothing. Please advise him/her by answering the questions. (You can decide the sex of the student: you may find it easier to advise someone who is the same sex as you are.)

EXAMPLE: ふつう (usually) 大学のクラスへはどんな服を着て行きますか。

Tシャツを着て、ジーンズをはいて行きます。

1. 夏もTシャツを着て、ジーンズをはいて行きますか。

_____

2. 冬もTシャツを着て行きますか。

_____

3. どんなくつをはいて行きますか。夏も冬も同じですか。

_____

4. 冬にはコートを着ますか。どんなコートがいります (is needed) か。

_____

5. 家ではどんな服を着ていますか。

_____

6. カジュアルなパーティーには何を着て行きますか。フォーマルなパーティーの時には。

_____

7. 雨の日にはどんな服を着ますか。

_____

8. ほかに (besides) どんな物をもって行ったらいいでしょうか。

_____

F. Fill in the blanks with a suitable purpose for going, coming, or returning to each place.

EXAMPLE: 毎日と書かんへ日本のしん聞を読みに行きます。

1. 今日はレストランへ _____ に来ました。
2. 電気屋へ _____ に行きましょう。
3. えいがかんへ _____ に行きたいです。
4. ゆうびんきょくへ _____ に行って下さい。
5. うちへ _____ にかえりたいです。
6. デパートへ _____ に行くつもりです。
7. 日本へ _____ に行けたらいいです。

G. Have you been to the following recently (in the last couple of weeks)? If you have, write the purpose for going there. If you haven't been, write how long it has been since your last visit.

EXAMPLE: 肉屋：昨日ステーキを買いに行きました。
わたしはさい食主ぎしゃ（ベジタリアン）ですから、肉屋へは三年ぐらい行っていません。

1. スーパー _____
2. ぎん行 _____
3. ゆうびんきょく _____
4. ぶんぼうぐ屋 _____
5. パン屋 _____
6. デパート _____

H. Change the following sentences so that they become something you have heard indirectly rather than something you know for a fact.

EXAMPLE: 先生のお母さんはびょう気(sick)です。
→先生のお母さんはびょう気だそうです。

1. ギブソンさんはカワムラさんのガールフレンドではありません。

   ギブソンさんはカワムラさんの＿＿＿＿＿＿＿＿＿＿＿＿＿＿＿＿＿

2. ブラウンさんが着ているブラウスは、フランスのです。

   ブラウンさんが着ているブラウスは＿＿＿＿＿＿＿＿＿＿＿＿＿＿＿

3. 山口さんはきょ年この大学の学生でした。

   山口さんはきょ年＿＿＿＿＿＿＿＿＿＿＿＿＿＿＿＿＿＿＿＿＿＿

4. チンさんが昨日買ったのは、青いジーンズではありませんでした。

   チンさんが昨日買ったのは、＿＿＿＿＿＿＿＿＿＿＿＿＿＿＿＿＿

5. この店の店員は、あまりしん切ではありません。

   この店の店員は＿＿＿＿＿＿＿＿＿＿＿＿＿＿＿＿＿＿＿＿＿＿＿

6. 山本さんのお父さんは有名です。

   山本さんのお父さんは＿＿＿＿＿＿＿＿＿＿＿＿＿＿＿＿＿＿＿＿

7. カーティスさんはギブソンさんが好きでした。

   カーティスさんは＿＿＿＿＿＿＿＿＿＿＿＿＿＿＿＿＿＿＿＿＿＿

8. 昨日見たアパートは、あまりきれいではありませんでした。

   昨日見たアパートは、＿＿＿＿＿＿＿＿＿＿＿＿＿＿＿＿＿＿＿＿

9. 日本の夏は暑いです。

   日本の夏は＿＿＿＿＿＿＿＿＿＿＿＿＿＿＿＿＿＿＿＿＿＿＿＿＿

10. そのネクタイの色はよくありません。

    そのネクタイの色は＿＿＿＿＿＿＿＿＿＿＿＿＿＿＿＿＿＿＿＿＿

11. はやしさんのお兄さんは、学生の時、かみ(hair)が長かったです。

    はやしさんのお兄さんは、＿＿＿＿＿＿＿＿＿＿＿＿＿＿＿＿＿＿

12. 昨日のえいがはあまりおもしろくありませんでした。

    昨日のえいがは＿＿＿＿＿＿＿＿＿＿＿＿＿＿＿＿＿＿＿＿＿＿

13. 町田さんはゆうびんきょくへ切手を買いに行きました。

町田さんは_____

14. チンさんは明日中国へかえります。

チンさんは_____

15. さ野さんは、今はえい語を勉強していません。

さ野さんは、_____

16. 1830年には日本にくるまがありませんでした。

1830年には _____

I. Your Japanese acquaintance would like to know the following things about a grocery store in your town. If you think you know the answers, please write them down using …と思います. If you are not sure, ask friends or call the store and report the answers using …そうです. Or, if that's not possible, give your best guess using …かもしれません.

1. この町で一番安いスーパーはどこですか。

_____

2. そのスーパーで今日一番安いくだ物は何ですか。

_____

3. そのスーパーではクレジットカードが使えますか。トラベラーズチェックは。

_____

4. そのスーパーにはデリカテッセンがありますか。そこのアメリカンチーズは1ポンドいくらですか。

_____

5. そのスーパーにはやっきょくがありますか。

_____

6. そのスーパーでは魚を売っていますか。しんせんな (fresh) 魚ですか。れいとうの (frozen) だけですか。

_____

J. Find a person who is from a town you have never been to. (It could be a town in the U.S., Japan, or any other country.) Ask him/her the following questions about the town and report the answers using 〜さんの 話では／〜さんによると…そうです.

place you are reporting on: ＿＿＿＿＿＿＿＿＿＿＿＿＿＿＿＿＿＿＿＿＿＿＿

1. 人口はどのぐらいですか。＿＿＿＿＿＿＿＿＿＿＿＿＿＿＿＿
   ＿＿＿＿＿＿＿＿＿＿＿＿＿＿＿＿＿＿＿＿＿＿＿＿＿＿＿＿＿

2. 気こうはどうですか。 ＿＿＿＿＿＿＿＿＿＿＿＿＿＿＿＿＿
   ＿＿＿＿＿＿＿＿＿＿＿＿＿＿＿＿＿＿＿＿＿＿＿＿＿＿＿＿＿

3. ここからそこまで何で行けますか。どのぐらいかかりますか。 ＿＿＿＿＿＿＿
   ＿＿＿＿＿＿＿＿＿＿＿＿＿＿＿＿＿＿＿＿＿＿＿＿＿＿＿＿＿

4. どんなこうきょうこうつうきかん (public transportation system) がありますか。
   ＿＿＿＿＿＿＿＿＿＿＿＿＿＿＿＿＿＿＿＿＿＿＿＿＿＿＿＿＿

5. 大きなしょう店がいやデパートがあって、買い物にべんりですか。
   ＿＿＿＿＿＿＿＿＿＿＿＿＿＿＿＿＿＿＿＿＿＿＿＿＿＿＿＿＿

6. そこのとくさん物 (special product; speciality) は何ですか。＿＿＿＿＿＿＿＿
   ＿＿＿＿＿＿＿＿＿＿＿＿＿＿＿＿＿＿＿＿＿＿＿＿＿＿＿＿＿

K. Answer the following questions using the "whether or not" construction.

EXAMPLE: 日本語はむずかしいですか。
→ むずかしいかどうかわかりません。

1. カワムラさんは、いつもコンタクトレンズをしていますか。
   ＿＿＿＿＿＿＿＿＿＿＿＿＿＿＿ しりません。

2. 赤いシャツを着ている人は先生ですか。
   ＿＿＿＿＿＿＿＿＿＿＿＿＿＿＿ 聞きましょうか。

3. 明日は雨がふりますか。
   ＿＿＿＿＿＿＿＿＿＿＿＿＿＿＿ わかりません。

4. 今、日本は暑いですか。
   ＿＿＿＿＿＿＿＿＿＿＿＿＿＿＿ しりません。

5. 山口さんは、おげん気ですか。

   _____ わかりません。

6. 昨日、日本語のテストがありましたか。

   _____ しりません。

7. 大学からえきまでは遠かったですか。

   _____ わすれました。

8. 高田さんは、黒のジーンズをはいていましたか。

   _____ おぼえていません。

L. Answer the following questions concerning your Japanese class. If you do not know an answer, state that you don't know, that you forgot, that you will find out, that you will ask someone, etc., using the ⋯かどうか structure.

EXAMPLE: 明日、小テスト (quiz) がありますか。
はい、あります。／いいえ、ありません。or
あるかどうかわかりません。／あるかどうか先生に聞いてみます。

1. 今学き (this term/semester) は長いオーラルテストがありますか。 _____

   _____

2. このきょうか書は今学きで全部終わりますか。 _____

   _____

3. 来年も同じ先生が日本語をおしえますか。 _____

   _____

4. あなたのこのクラスの今学きのせいせき (grade) はAですか。 _____

   _____

5. 今学きのきまつしけん (final exam) はむずかしいですか。 _____

   _____

M. Put the adjectives or phrases into the ⋯し、⋯し construction, and then write your own conclusion.

EXAMPLE: 安いです／おいしいです
→ このハンバーガーは安いし、おいしいし、いいですね。

1. 高いです／大きすぎます

   そのシャツは_____ し、_____ し、_____。

2. きれいです／やさしいです

   ギブソンさんは、＿＿＿＿＿＿＿＿ し、＿＿＿＿＿＿＿＿ し、

   ＿＿＿＿＿＿＿＿。

3. テストがあります／デートがあります

   明日は＿＿＿＿＿＿＿＿ し、＿＿＿＿＿＿＿＿ し、＿＿＿＿＿＿＿＿。

4. 雨がふりました／寒かったです

   昨日は、＿＿＿＿＿＿＿＿ し、＿＿＿＿＿＿＿＿ し、＿＿＿＿＿＿＿＿。

5. 日曜日です／天気もいいです

   今日は＿＿＿＿＿＿＿＿ し、＿＿＿＿＿＿＿＿ し、＿＿＿＿＿＿＿＿。

6. ポップコーンはできました／ソーダもあります

   ＿＿＿＿＿＿＿＿ し、＿＿＿＿＿＿＿＿ し、＿＿＿＿＿＿＿＿。

N. If you were to buy the following, what brand/make would you choose? Write at least two reasons using …し, following the example.

> EXAMPLE: *frozen apple pie*
>
> わたしはウェートウォッチャーのを買います。カロリーが少ないし、おいしいし、かんたん (simple/easy) ですから。

1. pizza ＿＿＿＿＿＿＿＿＿＿＿＿＿＿＿＿＿＿＿＿＿＿＿＿＿＿

   ＿＿＿＿＿＿＿＿＿＿＿＿＿＿＿＿＿＿＿＿＿＿＿＿＿＿＿＿＿＿

2. jeans ＿＿＿＿＿＿＿＿＿＿＿＿＿＿＿＿＿＿＿＿＿＿＿＿＿＿

3. car ＿＿＿＿＿＿＿＿＿＿＿＿＿＿＿＿＿＿＿＿＿＿＿＿＿＿＿

   ＿＿＿＿＿＿＿＿＿＿＿＿＿＿＿＿＿＿＿＿＿＿＿＿＿＿＿＿＿＿

4. watch ＿＿＿＿＿＿＿＿＿＿＿＿＿＿＿＿＿＿＿＿＿＿＿＿＿＿

   ＿＿＿＿＿＿＿＿＿＿＿＿＿＿＿＿＿＿＿＿＿＿＿＿＿＿＿＿＿＿

5. pain medicine ＿＿＿＿＿＿＿＿＿＿＿＿＿＿＿＿＿＿＿＿＿＿

   ＿＿＿＿＿＿＿＿＿＿＿＿＿＿＿＿＿＿＿＿＿＿＿＿＿＿＿＿＿＿

6. beverage ＿＿＿＿＿＿＿＿＿＿＿＿＿＿＿＿＿＿＿＿＿＿＿＿

   ＿＿＿＿＿＿＿＿＿＿＿＿＿＿＿＿＿＿＿＿＿＿＿＿＿＿＿＿＿＿

O. For each of the following verbs, write a statement about something that is either easy or hard to do, using the 〜やすい or 〜にくい form.

EXAMPLE: （食べる）
すしは食べにくいです。

1. （する）_____

2. （着る）_____

3. （ねる）_____

4. （使う）_____

5. （勉強する）_____

6. （ふる）_____

7. （料理する）_____

8. （分かる）_____

9. （わすれる）_____

10. （ぬぐ）_____

Chapter 7 Review

A. Match each numbered expression with the letter of the appropriate response. Each response will be used once.

1. _____ 何をおさがしでしょうか。

2. _____ 食べてみてもいいですか。

3. _____ もう少し明るい色のはありますか。

4. _____ じゃ、これを下さい。

5. _____ 下着売り場はどこですか。

6. _____ かさはありますか。

7. _____ これ、おいくらですか。

a. 3かいでございます。
b. はい、ございます。
c. 一つ370円です。
d. この白いのはいかがですか。
e. どうぞ。食べてみて下さい。
f. はい、ありがとうございます。
g. ワイシャツがほしいんですが。

B. Look around the room where you are now. Write down a couple of things that you can see that have the following colors. If there isn't anything of that color in the room, say so.

EXAMPLE: (red) 赤い物はわたしのジャケットとカーネーションです。

(gold) 金色の物はありません。

1. (blue) _____

2. (green) _____

3. (yellow) _____

4. (brown) _____

5. (purple) _____

6. (silver) _____

C. A Japanese student has some questions concerning young people's life in the U.S. Please answer them. If you do not know the answers, ask someone and then answer with そうです.

1. アメリカではいつもカジュアルな服を着ますか。フォーマルな服を着ることもありますか。どん時に着ますか。

   _____

   _____

2. アメリカではどんな時にボーイフレンドやガールフレンドにプレゼントをしますか。

   _____

   _____

3. アメリカ人はあまりいしゃ (medical doctor) へ行かないと聞きましたが、本とうですか。かぜをひいた時にはどうしますか。

   _____

   _____

4. アメリカの学生は、夜勉強していておなかがすいた時にはどうしますか。どんな物を食べますか。

   _____

   _____

5. アメリカ人は "thank-you card" というカードをよく書くと聞きましたが、どんな時に書くんですか。

_____

_____

6. アメリカでは冬に雪がたくさんふるところが多いと聞きましたが、そういうところの人は雪の時どうするんですか。いつも家の中でテレビを見ているんでしょうか。

_____

_____

D. What do you think of the following? Why? Write down your feelings about them using …し、…し or …し…から….

EXAMPLE: あなたのお母さんはどんな人ですか。
とてもやさしいし、しん切だし、とてもいい人です。or
とてもやさしいし、しん切だから、大好きです。

1. あなたの日本語の先生はどうですか。

_____

2. あなたの大学はいいですか。

_____

3. あなたの今すんでいるところ（アパート、家、りょうの部屋）をどう思いますか。

_____

4. あなたの町にある、一番大きいデパートはべんりですか。

_____

5. あなたの今学き (this semester/term) のスケジュールはどうですか。

_____

6. 先週の週まつは楽しかったですか。先々週(two weeks ago) は。